CHRISTIAN COMMUNITY
IN HISTORY

CHRISTIAN COMMUNITY
IN HISTORY

VOLUME 3

Ecclesial Existence

ROGER HAIGHT, S.J.

continuum

NEW YORK • LONDON

2008

The Continuum International Publishing Group Inc
80 Maiden Lane, New York, NY 10038

The Continuum International Publishing Group Ltd
The Tower Building, 11 York Road, London SE1 7NX

www.continuumbooks.com

Continuum is a member of Green Press Initiative, a nonprofit program dedicated to supporting publishers in their efforts to reduce their use of fiber obtained from endangered forests. We have elected to print this title on 50% postconsumer waste recycled paper. For more information, go to www.greenpressinitiative.org.

Printed in the United States of America

Library of Congress Cataloging-in-Publication Data
Haight, Roger.
    Christian community in history / Roger Haight.
      p. cm.
    Includes bibliographical references and index.
    ISBN 978-0-8264-1630-8 (v. 1 : hardcover : alk. paper)
    ISBN 978-0-8264-1631-5 (v. 2 : hardcover : alk. paper)
    ISBN 978-0-8264-2947-6 (v. 3 : hardcover : alk. paper)
  BV600.3.H35 2004
  262'.009 – dc22   2004004006

Grateful acknowledgment is made to the World Council of Churches for permission to quote from the following documents:

World Council of Churches, *Baptism, Eucharist and Ministry*, Faith and Order Paper 111. Geneva: WCC Publications, 1982.

World Council of Churches, *The Nature and Mission of the Church: A Stage on the Way to a Common Statement*, Faith and Order Paper 198. Geneva: WCC Publications, 2005.

Max Thurian, ed., *Churches Respond to BEM, I–VI*, Faith and Order Papers 129, 132, 135, 237, 143–44. Geneva: WCC Publications, 1986–88.

Contents

Preface

When I began work on *Christian Community in History*[1] in January 2000, I conceived the project as a historical ecclesiology propaedeutic to writing a constructive, systematic Roman Catholic ecclesiology. Such a systematic ecclesiology would have to be attentive to the history of the church's journey to this point in time. In order to generate a receptive historical consciousness, I sought to consider the extensive changes that the church and its self-understanding underwent in the course of that long temporal and cultural span. Only against such a background would the remarkable consistency of the church as a movement of faith and an institution appear in its substantive depths. The postmodern intellectual culture in which we live only yields an appreciation of truth when truth stands out by contrast within and rising above the aggregate of human experiences that dazzle present-day awareness. The goal, then, was to integrate this historical consciousness into the method and content of systematic reflection on the self-understanding of the Roman Catholic Church.

But the methodology that guided the research, the actual writing of the first two volumes of CCH, and a significant number of principles that were learned in the writing led to an appreciation of other needs in the church at the beginning of the twenty-first century. I will try to characterize those needs and a strategy for addressing them presently. But I want to insist at the start that the new direction that this systematics has taken in no way invalidates or competes with the task of developing denominational ecclesiologies. In fact denominational ecclesiology must be done continuously and seriously, with a pointed concern for the identity of the various churches. This work is an essay in transdenominational ecclesiology. That infelicitous name is

---

1. Roger Haight, *Christian Community in History*, vols. 1 and 2 (New York: Continuum, 2004–5). This work is referred to as CCH.

tentative and awaits a more generative and genial alternative. In this it reflects the project itself, which is always tentative because it is always moving. But I reject at the outset the idea that the pursuit of a transdenominational ecclesiology in any way undermines the need for denominational ecclesiologies.

These autobiographical notes, however, raise questions about the reasons that impelled a shift in the nature of the project. This preface will briefly allude to the new exigencies that this ecclesiological essay seeks to address. These can be simply named because all are familiar with them. Against the backdrop of these experiences I will try to formulate the insight that governs the strategy of the work in terms of a distinction between pluralism and relativism. I add to this an indication of the logic by which I try to accomplish the strategy. This will set the stage for the first part of the book, which gives a fuller account of the nature of the project.

Since the Christian community exists in history, there is no time when it is not entering a new period where it encounters new challenges. Each period feels that it is distinctive in this regard, because each set of problems is different. In our hyperreflective age all seem to be aware of the distinctive exigencies of our time. But three elements of our newly globalized world and postmodern intellectual culture unsettle things and provide an occasion for new initiatives in ecclesiology.

The first set of experiences arises out of the new presence of different cultures and traditions to each other. Instant communication around the world and worldwide commercial interconnectedness force recognition of the "other." Both the migration of peoples and close personal and familial interactions make these differences real and give them substance. The prevalence and acknowledged imperative for intercultural study and understanding, and not least interreligious dialogue, show that everyone at his or her own level is aware that major transitions in human life in our world are actually occurring during our lifetime.

Looking now within Christianity, I find in another current development an important fact that should have an influence on the way the church is understood. Christianity extends beyond the borders of Western culture, and the non-Western churches inevitably and rightfully are gaining new influence by their numerical strength. Ironically, this major historic development runs parallel to a certain decline of Christianity or the churches in the West with special reference to Europe and North America. This generalization needs a good deal of qualification; as stated, it may be misleading. But it correlates with a general consciousness that the center of gravity of Christianity is shifting and that the Christian message is losing some of its impact, or at least its enthusiasm, among whole groups of people in the developed world.

A third area of concern for the church today revolves around a tension between the inculturation of the church outside the West and a fragmentation of the churches that seems to accompany it. The churches in Asia and Africa, and to some extent Latin America, which trace their history back to the missionary movements from Western churches, have become self-consciously aware that they need to become incarnate in their indigenous culture. I use the term "inculturation" positively. Inculturation represents the antithesis of surrendering authentic Christianity to an idolatrous cultural form. It represents an authentic appropriation of genuine Christianity by a culture as its own. Yet the subtlety of the dialectic of inculturation does not allow easy judgments of success. What appears to be successful inculturation to some appears to others as fragmentation, or syncretism, or heresy. Certainly the diversification among the churches is increasing in a manner and a rate that is unparalleled in Christian history, given the size and range of the Christian church today. The question is whether Christian identity itself is going to dissolve into a million indigenous pieces.

These three elements of our contemporary situation form a background against which a so-called transdenominational ecclesiology makes sense as an ongoing project running parallel to denominational ecclesiologies. The insight that grounds this judgment lies in a recognition that the antithesis between uniformity and relativism has lost its diagnostic power; it does not illumine the situation, because uniformity is neither possible nor an ideal. The realistic antithesis to relativism is better formulated as pluralism. The word "pluralism" is used constantly throughout this work, and

its positive meaning in contrast to plurality and relativism needs
some justification.[2]

By pluralism I mean differences within a common framework, a
definition that is repeated in the course of the work. Pluralism refers
to a situation in which differences are held together within a unifying
field; it points to unity amid differences. By contrast, it does not refer
to pure diversity, or the existence of differences that, because they are
unrelated, require no mediation or negotiation. It seems plain enough
that many different cultural interpretations of human existence have
lived peaceably at the same time because they were isolated or did not
mutually engage each other. Relative to that situation, globalization is
genuinely new. And it raises the question of whether and how human
beings can find a common and shared level of experience across their
obvious diversity. Pluralism affirms that human existence, and by
extension Christian ecclesial existence, shares a common structure
and truth across its many differences.

The idea of pluralism just described goes against the grain. Many
seem so struck by the differences among cultures, religions, nations,
classes, and individuals that the idea of some ground of unity that can
bind them together has lost traction. The movement from a classical-
universalist consciousness to a historical-empiricist consciousness
is so complete that people suspect totalitarian or imperialist tendencies in all transcendental thinking. From this perspective of historical
consciousness, the task of arguing for some form of pluralism in ecclesiology requires a specific strategy. That strategy can no longer
consist in moving from a monistic concept of the church to various
instances of an established essential nature. It must move in the opposite direction, from the history of the church and its ecclesiology to
a formulation of the common life that is shared by all the churches.
The full scope of the common nature of the Christian church cannot
be found in the transcendental ecclesiological consciousness of the
Western church, the Eastern church, or any individual church, but
must be found through a historical phenomenological method that

---

2. Relativism, as a negative term, needs no close definition. Generally, it stands for
the position that, whether or not transcultural or ultimate truths exist, they cannot be
known as such or agreed upon. All knowledge is particular and culturally determined
without remainder.

tries to embrace the whole Christian movement. The search for the one must be found in the many and not in any a priori conception of unity projected on the many. I will point out in chapter 2 how this requires an analogical imagination, which, prior to analogical predication, can penetrate differences more deeply to find among them similarity. I am convinced that the current attraction of "communion" language in ecclesiology comes from a deep acceptance of the plurality of the churches and a desire to find a way through it to some real common bonds between the churches.

Acceptance of this concept of pluralism at some level represents a condition for a positive appreciation of this work. It sets up a strategic premise: everything looks different in the light of a positive appreciation of pluralism. The roots of pluralism and conscious appreciation of it reach down through each congregation to the particularity that constitutes historical existence and the individuality of each person. As it has been defined, a sense of pluralism can be so internalized that it becomes a consistent principle of interpretation or appreciation of diversity. This, in turn, forms a basis for a noncompetitive viewpoint. It allows openness to the other. More strongly, lack of a recognition of pluralism as in some measure something positive tends to generate a spontaneously suspicious or negative reaction to what is other.

This relatively abstract statement of an insight still requires a tactic or a method by which it might become programmatic. How are we to find the apostolicity, the catholicity, and the unity across the plurality of the churches? Roughly speaking, the first two volumes of CCH represent historical diversity in the church across its history and among the churches. By contrast, *Ecclesial Existence,* or CCH, III, represents an essay at describing what the churches possess in common. The transition from the historical to the constructive is negotiated by a historical phenomenology that recognizes and raises up principles and ecclesiological constants that are found to be continuously operative in the church across its many historical incarnations. On the basis of those principles and the phenomenon of historical continuity, an implicit method of comparison allows the possibility of constructing dimensions of the church shared in common. Such is the strategy of this work. Drawing on the history of the church and its ecclesiology developed in the first two volumes of CCH, this present work retrieves ecclesiological constants from history reaching back to scriptural origins in an attempt to construct and portray the common ecclesial existence shared by the churches.[3]

The method and principles of this work will be discussed in more detail in part I. But it will be helpful to bring forward at this point some general theological criteria that underlie the whole trilogy on theology, Jesus Christ, and the church of which this work is a part.[4] The following general principles of theological epistemology and four criteria for theology and specifically ecclesiology are at work in this essay.

A condition for the possibility of positively appreciating the strategy and tactics of this work lies in a distinction between faith and beliefs. Faith refers to the fundamental trust and commitment that is consistent amid the changes in the development of a person's beliefs. Beliefs are discursive statements about the object of faith. The faith of a community is the existential life shared in common despite the fact that individuals in a community may construe the words expressing the common faith differently. Faith is existential, whereas the beliefs that articulate the cognitive aspect of faith are common, social, and objective. Faith and belief are intimately connected and dialectically interact with each other, but they are distinct and neither can be reduced to the other. This distinction is the ground that allows the constructive possibility of pluralism.

An analogous distinction, one that has roots in the difference between faith and belief but with specific reference to the church, posits a difference between the essential elements constituting the church and what sixteenth-century ecclesiology called adiaphora. Adiaphora, or "things indifferent," are recognized in a distinction and contrast

---

3. Although *Ecclesial Existence* is volume 3 of *Christian Community in History*, it can be read on its own independently of the first two volumes, which dealt with the history of ecclesiology. That history would obviously add a historical depth to one's appreciation of the project of volume 3. In chapter 2 I will draw forward some elements of that history in order to situate the constructive chapters of part 2.

4. The reference is to Roger Haight, *Dynamics of Theology* (Mahwah, N.J.: Paulist Press, 1990; Maryknoll, N.Y.: Orbis Books, 2001); *Jesus Symbol of God* (Maryknoll, N.Y.: Orbis Books, 1999); and CCH.

between "the immutable and the mutable, the essential and the ac-
cidental, the necessary and the contingent, the important and the
indifferent."[5] A distinction like this is absolutely necessary for a
project that seeks to differentiate and characterize what churches possess in common. Commonality can only be appreciated as existing
within difference even though it transcends difference.

Besides these basic distinctions, four criteria for evaluating the
truth of theological positions are at work in this essay. These theological criteria are not consistently brought forward and explicitly
applied at each turn of the argument. But they join as a unit to define
a certain mindset. Together they constitute a heuristic framework for
accepting or bypassing elements from the history of the church and
its ecclesiology into a characterization of ecclesial existence. The first
of these criteria is a relationship to scripture. This does not mean
that one can find a description of a twenty-first-century church in
the Bible. But the Christian church should not be at odds with scriptural ideals and should be able to draw positive lines of congruity or
development between scriptural vision and present-day church.

Second, the history of the church and its ecclesiology should in-
form the essential structure of the church today. This may be too
broad a norm to yield a precise application. But it functions negatively to prevent the idea that a contemporary church can be based
solely upon the charismatic faith of its leaders. A church that is utterly spontaneous and without connection with the past remains a
mere shell without Christian substance. Historical continuity is a
dimension of the lifeblood of the church. The Christian community
has historical roots through which it continually draws nourishment.

Third, the ecclesiology of the church must be coherent and intelligible. The content of Christian faith remains transcendent mystery;
as such the object of faith is incomprehensible. But that quality of
the object of faith cannot be used as a form of mystification relative to the basic structures of the church. The implicit comparative
character of the essay that follows, that is, its reliance on many ecclesiologies together representing the whole, is a helpful guard against
too rapid an appeal to mystery.

---

5. CCH, II, 210.

Fourth, a criterion for the viability of theological language is its ability to empower the Christian life. In the comparative and synthetic account of a common ecclesial existence that follows, this quality of empowering combines with the ability of language to awaken a common and shared experience. Churches must seek communion with other churches. Communion requires mutual recognition. An ecclesiology that cuts a specific church off from communion with other churches on all levels cannot be authentic. Ecclesial existence reaches out to and shares experience with other churches. This criterion, therefore, functions both negatively and positively. It discounts closed eccentricity and appreciates language and structures that include.

Finally, the title of this work, "Ecclesial Existence," is a designation of the object of study. Surely the Christian church is a community in history. Moreover, that community cannot continue to exist as a community without an institutional spine. But the institutional structure alone does not provide the deeper object of this study. Within the particular forms of the churches breathes the Christian life of the community of the church members. With the existentialist title I have tried to designate a corporate level of being-a-Christian that is shared by all Christians across their home churches.[6] "Ecclesial existence" thus refers to the mode of Christian life that subsists in the many institutional forms the churches take. This work tries to characterize that ecclesial existence as one that is continuous across history with the churches of the apostolic period. It seeks to represent in today's language the apostolic faith to which all churches appeal and on which they base their authenticity. Ecclesial existence cannot be authentic without a faith that is "apostolic" and alive in

---

6. The phrase "ecclesial existence" as it is being characterized here has a peculiar logical status. It cannot be understood as objectified without remainder in any single set of historical forms, because it would then be reduced to the confines of a particular church. "Ecclesial existence" is thus an abstraction from particular churches but points to the most actual or lived experience within, and not apart from, these organizational structures and institutional forms. This is the positive insight that guided the quest for the essence of Christianity. A simple example illustrates the point. Let us assume that baptism by total immersion and baptism by poured water are both authentic ordinances. They generate relatively different sensible experiences. But one can characterize the common features of the experiences they represent or mediate and point to a common spiritual effect.

the Spirit, or "holy." If it is apostolic and alive in the Spirit, it will be "catholic" and, as such, "one," and shared with members of other churches. The measure of the authenticity of the individual churches ultimately lies in the degree to which they institutionalize and protect the four marks of true ecclesial existence: apostolic, catholic, one, and holy.

I have been encouraged and helped along the way toward completion of this lengthy study in ecclesiology by more people than I can name. Some have read whole manuscripts in the early drafts; others have offered sound editorial advice. My thanks to Cheryl Waschenko and to Patrick Amer, who carefully read the manuscript of *Ecclesial Existence* and offered sound advice. T. Howland Sanks, S.J., has accompanied me along the whole way of these three volumes. His theological expertise and knowledge of ecclesiology have been invaluable and helped me reshape the work at crucial junctures. Thank you to Michael Fahey, S.J., who also read this text and encouraged the work. I want to thank Gerard Mannion especially for promoting this work and giving me several opportunities to move it forward in discussion and collaboration with other ecclesiologists. Paul Avis too offered me sound advice relative to the conclusion of the work and a helpful stimulus toward its completion.

I reserve a special word of thanks for Frank Oveis, recently retired senior editor at Continuum, who has shepherded all three volumes of this work to their completion. His sheer love of a good book translated his interest in my work in ecclesiology into the deepest form of support. His river of knowledge and expertise have even overflowed the dam of retirement and carried this book downstream to the open seas of publication. Many will miss his presence in the world of religious publishing. But I am particularly grateful.

Abbreviations

BEM
World Council of Churches, *Baptism, Eucharist and Ministry*, Faith and Order Paper 111. Geneva: WCC Publications, 1982.

BEMresponses
Max Thurian, ed., *Churches Respond to BEM, I-VI*, Faith and Order Papers 129, 132, 135, 237, 143–44. Geneva: World Council of Churches, 1986–88.

BEMreport
World Council of Churches, *Baptism, Eucharist and Ministry 1982–1990: Report on the Process and Responses*, Faith and Order Paper 149. Geneva: WCC Publications, 1990.

CCH, I-II
Roger Haight, *Christian Community in History, I-II*. New York: Continuum International, 2004–5.

CF
Friedrich Schleiermacher, *The Christian Faith*, ed. H. R. Mackintosh and J. S. Stewart. New York: Harper & Row, 1963.

Institutes
John Calvin, *Calvin: Institutes of the Christian Religion, I-II*, ed. John T. McNeill. Philadelphia: Westminster Press, 1955.

JSG
Roger Haight, *Jesus Symbol of God*. Maryknoll, N.Y.: Orbis Books, 1999.

NMC
World Council of Churches, *The Nature and Mission of the Church: A Stage on the Way to a Common Statement*, Faith and Order Paper 198. Geneva: WCC Publications, 2005.

NPC
The World Council of Churches, *The Nature and Purpose of the Church: A Stage on the Way to a Common Statement*, Faith and Order Paper 181, 1998. *http://wccoe.org/wcc/what/faith/nature1.html*.

Part I

THE NOTION
OF A CONSTRUCTIVE
TRANSDENOMINATIONAL
ECCLESIOLOGY

Chapter 1

Where We Dwell in Common

The great surge of Christian missionary activity during the course of the nineteenth century elicited a new concern for church unity. Was this missionary activity, after all, spreading division? In 1910 representatives of Protestant churches came together to respond to that question in Edinburgh at the World Missionary Conference. The conference in its turn channeled the concern to the sending churches. Although somewhat slowed down by World War I, the ecumenical movement gathered momentum at this time, and its growth was punctuated by landmark events in the Universal Christian Conference on Life and Work (Stockholm, 1925) and the World Conference of Faith and Order (Lausanne, 1927). The report of this second conference included a description of what the churches assembled in their representatives shared in common and the many things that distinguished and sometimes divided them. When the World Council of Churches came into existence in August of 1948, the Faith and Order movement was integrated into it as a distinct agency whose concern was the doctrinal unity of the churches. Its signal achievement thus far has been the document entitled *Baptism, Eucharist and Ministry*, frequently referred to as the Lima document, which sketches a proposal for a common understanding of these three aspects of the church across the churches. After BEM the Faith and Order Commission followed up with *The Nature and Mission of the Church: A Stage on the Way to a Common Statement.*[1] These two

---

1. World Council of Churches, *Baptism, Eucharist and Ministry*, Faith and Order Paper 111 (Geneva: WCC Publications, 1982) (referred to as BEM); idem, *The Nature and Mission of the Church: A Stage on the Way to a Common Statement*, Faith and Order Paper 198 (Geneva: WCC Publications, 2005) (referred to as NMC). In the course of this work I will occasionally make reference to *The Nature and Purpose of the Church*, which is the prior draft of NMC published in 1998 at *http://wcc-coe.org/wcc/what/faith/nature1.html*. This work is cited as NPC.

3

texts are the best examples of what I will call "transdenominational ecclesiology." The fact that BEM has received so much attention from the churches indicates that it plays some important role in the whole church.[2]

The quest for unity in the whole church struggles uphill against the gravitational pull toward a fragmentation of Christianity into churches. The break between the churches of the East and the West brought little scandal because they had gone separate ways since the patristic period and lived in separate worlds. But the Reformation so irreparably shattered the unity of the Western church that in time Christians accommodated themselves to the divisions. Ecclesiology became a discipline proper to each church and polemical in its self-definition over against other churches. Today distinctive identities are taken for granted, nurtured, and cherished. At the height of the enthusiasm of the ecumenical movement, H. Richard Niebuhr showed how deeply denominationalism finds its roots in the whole everyday life of the community and cannot be reduced to matters of doctrine.[3] Historical consciousness has explained diversity and made it acceptable. The idealism of the ecumenical movement and the achievement of the World Council of Churches appear against this background of dispersion and fragmentation. But whereas many theological disciplines have become eclectic across confessional boundaries, ecclesiology has remained a more or less tribal discipline.

The title for this chapter could be "The Case for Transdenominational Ecclesiology." The name points to the effort to cut across denominational ecclesiologies and characterize a common Christian ecclesial life. Modeled on the efforts of Faith and Order, it seeks to formulate a characterization of the church that is common to the

---

2. In the course of the 1980s the Christian churches of the world reacted to BEM and these reactions filled six volumes: Max Thurian, ed., *Churches Respond to BEM, I-VI*, Faith and Order Paper 129, 132, 135, 237, 143–44 (Geneva: World Council of Churches, 1986–88). (Cited hereafter as BEMresponses by volume and page number.)

A summary response of the Faith and Order committee of the WCC is *Baptism, Eucharist and Ministry 1982–1990: Report on the Process and Responses*, Faith and Order Paper 149 (Geneva: WCC Publications, 1990). This work is cited as BEMreport.

3. H. Richard Niebuhr, *The Social Sources of Denominationalism* (New York: Meridian, 1957, orig. 1929).

Christian churches or denominations.[4] It is a form of comparative ecclesiology that explicitly deals with pluralism by integrating into its method of understanding church sources that transcend the boundaries of a single church. It operates by comparison and contrast, by assimilation and distinction, and seeks to achieve a unified understanding of the church that all churches could recognize and in some measure claim as their own. Although not an attainable goal, it is still useful as a project and in its limited results.

The point of this chapter and ultimately this book is to argue for broader participation in this kind of work. This requires that such an effort be "situated" in the sense of responding to certain needs in the church at large and at the present time. It would entail a careful definition of such a subdiscipline and a fuller account of its sources and method. Making the case for transdenominational ecclesiology would also have to argue the goals and merits of such an enterprise as well as respond to some obvious objections to it.

With these goals in mind, this chapter has been divided into four parts. The first part raises up some historical considerations that help situate this ecclesiological project and define some of the premises that in effect make up its presuppositions. The second part then responds to the main objection to such a project, namely, that the object of this ecclesiology does not exist because no one belongs to a common church but only to particular churches. The third part deepens the response to the objection by further clarifying the method and goals of a transdenominational ecclesiology, and the fourth proposes a broad structure for building such an ecclesiology.

PREMISES OF A
TRANSDENOMINATIONAL ECCLESIOLOGY

I begin by situating the quest for a transdenominational ecclesiology. What allowed the Christian ecumenical movement to occur in the late modern period? The centripetal force of the ideal of Christian unity was never lost and polemic itself bears witness both to a

---

4. The terms "denominations" and "churches" are not used technically in this book but loosely and almost synonymously.

sense that truth is one and to a desire for unity. But why did the value of unity become so forceful in the twentieth century that it could challenge the ingrained division among the churches? To situate transdenominational ecclesiology I appeal to history and two seminal ideas or forms of consciousness that serve as its premises: historical consciousness and a positive appreciation of pluralism.

The most dramatic shift in the history of ecclesiology after the period of the Reformation was mediated by the rise of historical consciousness. Historical consciousness allowed the latent ideal of unity to take on a new importance in thinking about the church. This can be illustrated most clearly in the ecclesiology of Friedrich Schleiermacher.[5]

Schleiermacher manifested the historical consciousness that characterized his thinking in his systematics when he defined dogmatic theology as "the science which systematizes the doctrine prevalent in a Christian church at a given time" (CF, #19). He recognized the fact that human consciousness and ideas are always tied to the particular world in which they are thought (CF, #5, #30). The development of doctrine is a natural consequence. "No definition of doctrine, then, even when arrived at with the most perfect community of feeling, can be regarded as irreformable and valid for all time" (CF, #154).

Schleiermacher's theology was itself ecumenical and sought to bridge the Lutheran and Reformed traditions in a common doctrine.[6] The church for him was the community of the followers of Jesus Christ who shared in the God-consciousness mediated by the Redeemer and were animated by the Spirit. This community was structured, on the one hand, by essential and invariable elements given through Christ and the Spirit at its origins, and, on the other, by mutable elements in virtue of its constant interaction with the world. This gave his ecclesiology the flexibility to encompass many of the variations to which history gives rise. His sense of history allowed

---

5. The ecclesiology of Schleiermacher is contained in his systematics, *The Christian Faith*, ed. H. R. Mackintosh and J. S. Stewart (New York: Harper Torchbooks, 1963), 525–695. (Cited in the text as CF by paragraph.) An interpretation of Schleiermacher's ecclesiology is found in CCH, II, 311–36.

6. "Author's Preface to the Second Edition," CF, xxiv.

him to develop several principles that helped orchestrate or manage the diversity that existed in the churches beyond the essential structures. In other words, diversity in Schleiermacher did not automatically translate into division but should be able to be contained by communion. Some of these principles are the following: "Whensoever separations actually occur in the Christian church, there can never be lacking an endeavor to unite the separated" (CF, #150). "The complete suspension of fellowship between different parts of the visible church is unchristian" (CF, #151). "All separations in the church are merely temporary" (CF, #152). Christian loyalty to a specific denomination is conditional: "The essential thing is that each should love the special form of Christianity to which he adheres only as a transient form of the one abiding church, though a form that involves a temporary being of its own" (CF, #152).

The historical consciousness that is reflected in Schleiermacher and increasingly after him has a dialectical character, in the sense that it contains two dimensions that are in tension and pull against each other. On the one hand, historical consciousness legitimizes diversity; it explains difference through the mediation of culture and society; it deabsolutizes aspects of the church that are not essential. It thus retrieves the distinction developed in the Reformation and contained in the term *adiaphora:* there are elements in the constitution of any given church that are indifferent, that do not make a difference, and where differences may be tolerated in an essential unity. It also looks forward to such ideas as the hierarchy of truths (Vatican II). In matters of doctrine it recognizes that transcendent reality cannot ultimately be circumscribed and contained by human formulas. But, on the other hand, historical consciousness proffers recognition of certain essential elements of the church. History displays constants that always appear wherever the church exists because they define its essential being even as they relativize the differences. These are fundamental insights and lessons without which there could not have been an ecumenical movement.

The second experience and set of ideas that form a premise for a transdenominational ecclesiology can be summarized as a positive appreciation of pluralism. Pluralism here does not mean sheer diversity, but difference that subsists in a larger common matrix of shared ideas, values, and living space. Pluralism is unity amid difference. A positive construction of pluralism means that differences are not merely tolerated as a necessary evil, but recognized as a value. While such a recognition may be implicit in historical consciousness itself, and therefore is implicit in the ecumenical movement, still a positive experience of difference has to be continually learned and the ecumenical movement itself deepened this conviction even as it in turn sustained the ecumenical movement.

An analysis of the origins of the ecumenical movement reveals that it was driven by a fundamental corporate experience that took the shape of a negative experience of contrast.[7] Negatively, missionaries came to the awareness that the divisions generated in the West or sending countries were inappropriately imposed on new Christians. Missionaries were literally spreading Christian dissension wherever individual missionaries or mission churches competed with each other. Positively, the way forward in this situation obviously had to entail some form of cooperation, and this was modeled by nondenominational missionary societies formed by people of multiple denominations who came together not on the basis of their own denominations but on principles that were shared by but transcended all the denominations. When this energy was pooled, as in the World Missionary Conference (1910) and subsequent ecumenical gatherings, it mediated the experience and the insight of how pluralism can work constructively. This became the positive energy that drove the ecumenical movement forward. Unity can sublate or draw up into itself and not negate plurality and difference.[8] One has to add here that such a notion of pluralism is indeed a "beautiful idea," but one that is often impracticable and frequently fails. Pluralism is existential and has to be negotiated anew at every turn; the World Council of Churches is itself a constant manifestation of that.

---

7. I follow Edward Schillebeeckx's schematization of this elementary human reaction as having three simultaneous and interacting dimensions: the first is a negative experience that something is fundamentally wrong; second, a positive background of an ideal allows the negative to appear as such; and, third, a spontaneous impulse seeks to resist or negate the negation. Edward Schillebeeckx, *The Church: The Human Story of God* (New York: Crossroad, 1990), 5–6.

8. CCH, II, 370–71.

The practical demands of ecumenical association and common participation forced certain ecclesiological principles onto the table. Early on the World Council of Churches made it clear that it was not a church, yet it had to face ecclesiological questions. The WCC could only exist on the basis of certain ecclesiological principles that it had to formulate in a way that would satisfy its constituents. Three such principles help to clarify its status and shed light on the whole church. First, all the churches that make up the WCC share a unity on the basis of their common faith in Christ and participation in the Spirit. This is foundational. Second, recognition of this profound, substantial, and transcendently grounded unity among the churches weakens the boundaries that divide the churches. The distinctive provisions that define churches over against each other bear less import than their common life in Christ and the Spirit. This is a dialectical conviction: these provisions give each church its identity, but they are in fact also restrictions which are transcended by the real unity that is shared and experienced in common. Third, this dialectical tension gives rise to the impulse and movement to try to capture that common existence that was begun by Faith and Order at Lausanne, is reflected in BEM, and continues today.

These two forms of consciousness, a sense of historicity or historical consciousness and a positive appreciation of pluralism, respond to the present situation of the church. That situation can be characterized as one of increased tension between the impulse toward unity and the forces of dispersion and fragmentation. Perhaps at no time in the history of the church has the whole Christian movement witnessed more diversification than today as the church becomes ever more deeply contextualized outside of Western cultures. This is especially visible in the breathtaking spread of pentecostal Christianity and a corresponding constriction or proportional shrinking of the mainline churches of the West.[9] The fragmentation among the churches in the West, generally from the Reformation up to the present but especially in North America, pales in comparison with the multiplication of churches that is presently going on especially in

---

9. See, for example, the analysis of world Christianity as proffered by Philip Jenkins, *The New Christendom* (Oxford: University Press, 2002) and "The Next Christianity," *The Atlantic Monthly* 290 (October 2002): 53–68.

former missionary countries. The forces of fragmentation are felt as well within worldwide churches and communions of churches. We witness a confusion between the bonds that should hold a church or a communion together and what ordinarily would be called *adiaphora*, things that should not be allowed to break or prevent unity. Instead of an expansive and free existence in Christ, more and more churches are seeking a narrow sectarian or culture-based and excluding identity. The tension between unity and difference has grown palpable across the world church today and the deep insights that were internalized in the ecumenical movement need constant relearning and radicalization.

Finally, a definition of the situation of the church today has to be set in one further all-encompassing context, namely, the consciousness and the recognition of the world religions with which Christianity coexists today. The situation of the church is one in which churches, church, and world religions all live together in an increasingly smaller, globalized world. Members of these religions are gradually becoming more familiar with each other in an interconnected world of business and migration. The force of this new interaction between the religions is overt and profound. Christians share a newly homogenized identity in the bigger picture defined by their relationship with the other religions. This new common identity appears both in the eyes of others and in our own self-definition in dialogue with other faiths. Together, as Christians who make up one Christian church, we have a feeling that we must dialogue with other religions and apply the same principles of historicity and pluralism to understand them as we did to understand each other, lest religion and our relationship to the God of all become another reason for conflict rather than an antidote to it in a world ripe for massive violence.

THE REFERENT OF A TRANSDENOMINATIONAL ECCLESIOLOGY

The question implicit in this subheading is whether or not a transdenominational church exists. The main reservation relative to the project of constructing a transdenominational ecclesiology lies in the realization that no such church actually exists, nor can it. No one belongs to a transdenominational church because all churches are specific historical organizations with a particular identity. Even the theological construct of a universal, invisible church is not really a church but precisely a dimension of the churches taken abstractly. So, too, a transdenominational church and an ecclesiology that represents it are fictive constructions, assemblies of abstract notions, which do not refer to anything real, and one cannot pledge loyalty to an abstraction. So goes the typical objection.

Much of what is said in this observation is true, and it raises the question of the logical status of a transdenominational ecclesiology. What is referred to by a transdenominational ecclesiology? It is clearly not the same kind of reality as a particular church; a transdenominational ecclesiology will not share the same logical status as a Lutheran or an Orthodox ecclesiology, for example. An examination of the relationship between a transdenominational ecclesiology and the ecclesiology of a particular denomination will help to clarify the object of study. What follows provides a first appreciation of a transdenominational ecclesiology, and the next section on method will indicate more fully its logical status.

While from one point of view no one belongs to a transdenominational church, from another perspective everyone belongs to this church because it consists in that ecclesial existence that all Christians share in common. By definition, then, a transdenominational ecclesiology refers to an abstraction, but a kind of abstraction that need not be regarded pejoratively. This "church" is not a particular church, but the foundational elements of every church or what all ecclesial existence shares in common. In fact this common ecclesial existence may take different forms. So, for example, one baptism may be administered in different ways; one function of oversight and regulation of community life may take different political forms; one *ministerium* may be organized differently in different churches and ecclesiologies. This common church and its corresponding ecclesiology is indeed an abstraction, because it only subsists in actual concrete churches with their proper self-definitions and understandings based on their particular historical existences, practices, and beliefs. But it is nonetheless real as the fundamental core of the actual churches.[10]

The reality of the referent of a transdenominational ecclesiology is ultimately proven by the spontaneous demand for it that arose with the ecumenical movement and the continued striving for a statement of what the member churches of the World Council of Churches share in common. The reactions of the churches to BEM in the 1980s prove that that document had traction, that it came close enough to a description of the churches which engaged in the process of designing and criticizing it that they entered into dialogue with it. Any attempt to put into formulas what members of the many churches share in common will by definition aim at being the property of all the churches. But, at the same time, in its reduced and abstract or generalized form, the description of this ecclesiology will only approach this goal asymptotically. Not only is this common existence historical and thus always shifting, as an ideal theological reality it will take as many different concrete forms as there are particular churches.

A transdenominational ecclesiology is not a substitute for or a rival of any denominational ecclesiology. Logically, it must not be lined up on the same plane as the ecclesiologies of the churches. It has to be read alongside, not instead of, the ecclesiology of any given church. Transdenominational ecclesiology is not postdenominational; it does not compete with actual ecclesiologies or aim at replacing them. Rather, it relates to each one of them ideally as a description of that which is shared in common among all ecclesiologies.

To sum up: this is not the ecclesiology of a single or particular church, but aims at being a common possession of all the churches.

---

10. Edward Farley describes "ecclesial existence," which is a foundational form of what is intended here, as related to the nineteenth-century quest for the essence of Christianity. But it is no mere abstraction or unchanging kernel in the husk. Rather, it is defined both historically and theologically. In its historicity, common ecclesial existence is always changing; because it is theological, it cannot be reduced to any of its particular historical manifestations or to a particular abstract, static construction. Ecclesial existence has the quality of an ideal, but one that is always being readjusted to historical conditions. Edward Farley, *Ecclesial Reflection: An Anatomy of Theological Method* (Philadelphia: Fortress Press, 1982), 198–205.

It does not replace or rival any denominational ecclesiology. This ecclesiology provides no plan for a merger or federation of churches and takes no position, positive or negative, on the desirability of forming such union churches. This ecclesiology is an attempt to represent an understanding of the church that, in the measure in which it is accepted and shared among the churches, points to bonds of unity across differences. Therefore the status and function of this ecclesiology are dialectical, and it can only be appreciated dialectically. This means that it entails an intrinsic tension between the elements or dimensions that define it. The most prominent tension within this ecclesiology is the quality by which it simultaneously reflects unity and encourages differences within that unity. This ecclesiology has an ideological function of expressing common identity amid real diversity. The success of this ecclesiology has to be measured in degrees by the various parties to which it appeals: the highest degree will be found in its ability to express with relative adequacy a real common understanding of the church that can also acknowledge real differences without allowing them to undermine the unity constituted by shared reality and meaning. Individual churches will have more to say about their own particular identities and their own understandings of the elements that make up this common ecclesiology. But that "more" will not transcend, in the sense of "leave behind," what the author of Ephesians was referring to when he spoke of "one faith, one baptism, one Lord, and one Spirit."[11] This ecclesiology will consistently reach for the historical and qualitative substance that binds the churches together as church.

METHODOLOGICAL CONSIDERATIONS

Discussion of a method for developing a transdenominational ecclesiology will also define more precisely the logical status of the results. I take up the following considerations relative to this ecclesiology: its

---

11. I use the phrase in quotation marks as a short form of this Pauline text: "Spare no effort to make fast with bonds of peace the unity which the Spirit gives. There is one body and one Spirit, as there is also one hope held out in God's call to you; one Lord, one faith, one baptism; one God and Father of all, who is over all and through all and in all" (Eph 4:3–6).

sources, audience, method, aim, characteristics, and the example of such an ecclesiology provided by the documents of the Faith and Order Commission of the World Council of Churches.

1. The sources for a transdenominational ecclesiology are no different than those for ecclesiology generally, but it is useful to make these explicit. These sources may be divided into historical and theological sources, but materially speaking these two types of data are sometimes contained in the same documents. It is more helpful to divide the sources into historical and contemporary documents.

The first group of sources, then, is historical in the sense of being contained in texts representing the past. These include, first of all, documents that help understand the historical origins or genesis of the church. In fact the main source for this would be the New Testament, even though that history does not lie on the surface of the text, but requires critical exegesis. A whole host of other historical sources other than canonical literature can also be brought to bear to help understand the genesis of the church.

A second historical source is the New Testament precisely as a witness to revelation to which the whole church appeals as the theological norm for its understanding of itself. History alone cannot provide an adequate conception of the church because its members have always understood the church in its relation to God. God is at work in the foundations and ongoing life of the Christian community. The criterion for all Christian theological understandings of the church ultimately refers back in some way to the New Testament witness.

A third historical source consists in the history of the church and the history of ecclesiology within that history. The church is a historical organization with concrete histories in various times and places. The only way to gain a concrete understanding of the actual church is to trace its existence from its origins to the present.

The second group of sources is more or less contemporaneous with the present. They are twofold: the one category of contemporary sources contains all the official documents that define, regulate, and give normative expression to the constitution of the various churches. The church as a whole consists in churches that are public social organizations, and the self-understanding of each one is contained in the public life of the community and the documents that represent it. The other category of contemporary sources consists in the writings of theologians who interpret for the world the many churches to which they belong and which they explicitly or implicitly represent in their writings. Both of these sources usually combine social, historical, and legal material with theological construal. Other disciplines, such as sociology, provide other vehicles and means for access to the life of the church, but one might presume that these will be included in the evidence presented by the theologians.[12]

The Faith and Order texts *Baptism, Eucharist and Ministry* and *The Nature and Mission of the Church* constitute special sources for a transdenominational ecclesiology at this particular time in history. The authors of these documents, their content, and the responses they have provoked all point to a certain authority that they currently possess.

First, the Faith and Order Commission's team that produced these documents consisted, in the case of BEM, in about a hundred theologians representative of a wide variety of different churches. Being thus a work accomplished by a committee plays to the advantage of these texts because they informally embody through representative authors a multilateral dialogue between the churches. Second, these documents are constructed ultimately on the basis of scripture. The results of the commission's work are not the product of a comparison and dialogue geared to negotiating contemporary differences by compromise. The logic consists rather in constructive proposals on the basis of scripture primarily and the traditions of ecclesiology secondarily. Third, this generated extraordinarily positive responses from a wide variety of churches all over the world. Typically, churches wrote as follows: BEM "is a document of a remarkable convergence. It shows how in spite of much diversity in theological expression

---

12. In CCH, I, I showed how ecclesiology from below begins with a historical account of the genesis of the church and consistently compares the meaning of theological witness with the actual historical behavior of the church at any given time. In a given situation in the present, ecclesiology from below would thus include congregational studies and attention to the actual dynamic interactions of congregations and local churches with society and culture.

the churches are coming together in a common understanding of es-sential elements of the Christian Tradition" (BEMresponses, I.31). By distinguishing between dividing and nondividing differences BEM shows "the absence of many previously supposed impediments to unity" (BEMresponses, I.89). Not all responses were so enthusiastic, but few were not appreciative.

These three factors give BEM and perhaps NMC a certain author-ity that is unique. This is not doctrinal authority, nor the authority of any given church, nor the authority of consensus, for these are not statements of consensus, nor an external authority at all. The-ology never commands such direct authority. Rather, the authority of these statements is persuasive; it derives from the use of scrip-tural language, the implied imperative of God's will that division be overcome and the church be one, and the convergences among so many churches.[13] This authority is exhibited in one of two kinds of responses to BEM: the one judges the text on the basis of the doctrine and practice of the given church; the other allows BEM as representative of a wider ecclesial reality to challenge and pose ques-tions to this particular church. For example, instead of complaining that BEM does not represent its ecclesial ethos, a church confesses that "we seek with other churches to reclaim the eucharist as central to the church's life and witness" (BEMresponses, I.117).[14]

2. Before turning to a consideration of the methods used to in-terpret these sources, it will be helpful to consider the audience of such an ecclesiology, since the audience addressed has a good deal of bearing on the methods employed. The effort to characterize the common, transdenominational nature of the church is addressed simultaneously to people inside and outside the church.

The audience for any ecclesiology, in the first place, is made up of the body of fellow Christians. Ecclesiology like Christian theology generally consists in reflection on reality in the light of the symbols of

---

13. Appreciation of this authority correlates with a recognition of the intention of BEM and by extension NMC. This is seen in a response such as this: "Nevertheless, we are also aware that BEM calls us to go beyond simply comparing our beliefs and practices with those of others. It calls each church to 'recognize in this text the faith of the Church through the ages'" (BEMresponses, V.180).

14. These responses to BEM are also valuable sources for this ecclesiology, and I will appeal to them in chapters 3 through 7.

faith by members who share that faith; it addresses, in short, others within the Christian fold. In this respect, ecclesiology uses insider language and appeals to insider experience to express coherently what Christians share in common.

But the church is also a public institution or organization with an existence and, in most conceptions, a function in society. This relationship has been and still is subject to the widest variations among the churches in different times, places, cultures, and societies. In each case such a relationship should be the object of reflection, and it merits attention in a transdenominational ecclesiology as well. The church as a whole needs to make itself known and in some measure intelligible to the differentiated world in which it exists. This outward orientation, whether missionary or simply functional within a secular society, will have a significant effect on the method of interpretation.

3. I turn now to a more focused examination of the method for interpreting or constructing the transdenominational character of the church. Three distinct dimensions of that method stand out as distinct logical processes in dealing with the sources. These procedures are comparative, normative, and apologetic. I take them up in that order.

Comparative. The quest for a formulation of the nature and character of the Christian church in transdenominational terms is an explicitly comparative effort. It takes the form of a comparative ecclesiology that deals with pluralism in constructing an interpretation of the church. This means that to arrive at its conclusion this ecclesiology must weigh a considerable amount of diverse evidence arising from the various churches. It must then, by comparison, contrast, and synthesis, seek a broad understanding that both represents the various ecclesiologies and is identical with none of them. Quite simply, the whole of the evidence for such an ecclesiology comes from historical instances of the church, in the past and in the present, so that every representation of a transdenominational ecclesiology must implicitly appeal to the whole range of historical data which it sifts and measures by comparison.[15]

---

15. I have stated this process in a literal way that makes it an impossible task. Obviously, there are many disciplined short cuts to the consideration of the whole range of the history of the church and its ecclesiologies. BEM, for example, was constructed

Normative. Comparative theology, however, entails a theological imagination, and theology as a normative discipline cannot consist merely in the comparison of historical data. To put this in graphic terms, a transdenominational ecclesiology cannot be reduced to a negotiation of a committee representing actual churches. Theology is not only a historical but also a normative discipline that does not necessarily characterize the way things are, as would a descriptive social science, but the way things should be. In other words, there must be some criteria for judging between the alternatives offered by a mere comparison. And if the result is to be a truly common understanding of the church on which the many churches agree, the criteria by which such understandings and judgments are made must be commonly accepted and consistently applied. For example, the New Testament is the most common and basic authority in the church, and it has to be brought to bear on the process by which comparison and dialectic elicit judgment and decision.[16]

Apologetic. Apology means self-explanation. An apologetic dimension of method means that exposition contains reasons that make plain the positions taken. But explanation may be slightly different for insider and outsider, although the methods approach each other. Reasons for an outsider require a correlation with things familiar or apparent to experience. A method of correlation places in conjunction the propositions of faith and the conditions of the everyday world. This correlation does not generate proof, but a dialogue that in a variety of ways according to different axes of correlation clarifies the path that faith takes. This dialogue with the world corresponds with the impulse of universally relevant truth to be shared and with the missionary character of the church. The apologetic dimension of comparative ecclesiology will appear most clearly when the audience includes those of other religions. For example, when Christian ecclesiology is compared with accounts of the community

---

by a group of theologians, representing many traditions and churches, who entered into critical conversation.

16. There are other places where one can find authoritative interpretations besides the New Testament. For example, a near universal testimony to something in the church across its history in a variety of regions offers a strong testimony to authenticity. Still other criteria can be formulated as well as candidates for loci for a commonly accepted authoritative witness.

life of other religions, its apologetic character becomes more sharply defined.[17] Moreover, given the way in which the secular scientific world has formed a culture that affects everyone, in many cases an apologetic dimension is also needed for insiders.

Together these three qualities of ecclesiological method, its being comparative, normative, and apologetic, describe a way of dealing with the sources in the effort to delineate the common ecclesiology latent in the many ecclesiologies that subdivide the great church into its many churches.

4. Before commenting on the characteristics of a transdenominational ecclesiology, I want simply to reiterate the goal of this project which was already described in the previous section. The aim of this ecclesiology quite thoroughly determines its chief characteristics. The point of transdenominational ecclesiology is to characterize the common nature and characteristics shared by all Christian churches in the welter of different churches which are spread all over the world. The more churches can identify with and appropriate its formulations, given ordinary theological criteria for evaluating conclusions or proposals, the more successful such an ecclesiology will be. This represents an ongoing and never-ending project that can be achieved only by degrees.

5. The ongoing, dynamic method and process of this ecclesiological task, and the difficult and delicate nature of its goal in a world of churches that distinguish themselves from each other in sometimes uncompromising ways, dictate a special kind of style. Two characteristic qualities help define its language.

First of all, this ecclesiology will consist in broad, inclusive, and deliberately nonspecific referential language in its description of church institutions. A remarkably similar set of theological symbols, frequently drawn directly from the New Testament or derived from New Testament tropes, are used to characterize the church in all of its denominations. Differences begin to occur when specific churches are organized in different ways and take up particular sets of ceremonies and devotional and ethical practices, so that the theological language

---

17. See, for example, the comparative ecclesiology of Keith Ward in his *Religion and Community* (Oxford: Clarendon Press, 2000).

takes different concrete shape. As a consequence, an ecclesiology that attempts to characterize what is common to ecclesial life across the churches will have to use language that draws back from the concrete specificity that fills the corporate imagination of the churches and states things in a deliberately generalized way.

Take, for example, the case of baptism. Important and, for some, church-dividing alternative practices of baptism are found in infant baptism and the baptism of believers. These are, moreover, differences that make a difference in the life and style of a community. Implicit imaginative reference to the one or other practice in the context of specific churches, therefore, will completely color the understanding and appreciation of this particular feature of ecclesial life and add up to really different understandings of baptism. But, in fact, one can find coherent and convincing rationales for both of these practices in the history of ecclesiology. Moreover, prescinding from the specific practices, both the churches that baptize infants and the churches that baptize only adults baptize with a baptism that shares many of the same elements. There is also much in common in the two understandings of what is going on in this rite. The general theological grounding of baptism in both cases, that is, as distinct from the specific prescriptions, is based on an appeal to the New Testament. It may even be said at a certain theological and ecclesial level to be the same baptism. It possesses in both cases the same theological and ecclesiological "nature."

Second, this transdenominational ecclesiology will have frequent recourse to the principle of functionality relative to church institution and ministry.

The principle of functionality in ecclesiology refers to the way ministries were adopted in the church to meet the needs of the community. The institutionalization of the church proceeded according to sociological patterns of routinizing the charismatic ministry that addressed the needs of the community as they arose. The goal is always the well-being of the community and the exercise of its mission to continue the ministry of Jesus Christ in history. Whatever is needed to accomplish its mission, wherever there is a need to be met by a certain ministry, that ministry is provided spontaneously by the community in its self-constitution in and through God as Spirit.[18]

Given this genetic structure of ministry and institution, a transdenominational ecclesiology can focus attention on the service that the institutional forms of particular churches provide in order to find continuity and thus bridge the differences with a functional consistency or sameness. This strategy of finding analogies of function can give transdenominational ecclesiology leverage for reading a common substance across denominational boundaries.

Take, for example, the question of the fundamental unit of the church. The issue contained in this question governs an ecclesiological imagination at a fairly fundamental level and can be a thoroughly dividing issue. Is the fundamental unit of the church the congregation, as in many different denominations of "congregational" churches, or is it the diocese, an understanding institutionalized in the Eastern Orthodox, Roman Catholic, and Anglican churches? The question of the nature of episcopacy and its place in the church is closely bound up with a conception of the fundamental organizational structure of the church. This question was faced in the Lutheran–Roman Catholic dialogue and handled functionally.[19] In Lutheran ecclesiology the basic unit of the church is the parish or congregation; in Catholic ecclesiology it is the diocese with the bishop at the center. Through a functional imagination one can cut through the formal, juridical or canonical understandings of the matter to find existential meeting points. So it was in this comparative dialogue. "With respect to Roman Catholics, the international Roman Catholic–Lutheran Joint Commission has noted that, despite the definition of the local church as the diocese, 'in actual fact it is the parish, even more than the diocese, which is familiar to Christians as the place where the church is to be experienced' " (LCD-X,

---

18. CCH, I, 63–64. "By functionality I mean something that gains its value from something else on which it is dependent. The dynamics of functionality are analogous to the interrelationship between means and ends: measures taken lead to certain results; and goals or projected results determine the means to be employed." Ibid., 63.

19. Randall Lee and Jeffrey Gros, eds., *The Church as Koinonia of Salvation: Its Structures and Ministries: Lutherans and Catholics in Dialogue*, X (Washington, D.C.: United States Conference of Catholic Bishops, 2005). This work is cited as LCD-X by page number.

84). This statement is balanced by another statement expressing the regional side of ecclesial existence: " 'The local church is not a free-standing, self-sufficient reality. As part of a network of communion, the local church maintains its reality as church by relating to other local churches' " (LCD-X, 90, citing the "Joint Working Group of the World Council of Churches and the Roman Catholic Church," #13). One sees a frequent appeal to functional equivalence between different formal institutions or different names of offices and operations. Juridicism or fixation on historical institutions as absolute sets up a permanent blockage to elementary religious and theological perception (LCD-X, 121).

In the end, these two characteristics of deliberate vagueness of object-reference and a stress on the existential function of various institutions characterize this form of ecclesiology for a reason. They should not be conceived as weaknesses, but rather as ways of protecting legitimate diversity within unity.

6. The process connected with the development of the document *Baptism, Eucharist and Ministry* by the Faith and Order Commission of the World Council of Churches and the continuing process of reflection after it provide the best examples of a transdenominational ecclesiology. The goal of this effort is "to give expression to what the churches can now say together about the nature and mission of the Church and, within that agreement, to explore the extent to which the remaining church-dividing issues may be overcome" (NMC, 5). More particularly, it attempts to develop specific documents that can be recognized by the churches as the "faith of the church through the ages" (BEMreport, 8). The subject matter is not any church's ecclesiology but "our" Christian ecclesiology. It looks toward a common recognition of a formulation of something that can be agreed upon and held in common as authentically Christian by all parties. The phrase "convergence document" is used to describe "the fruit of what all of [the churches], after a long period of dialogue, [are] now able to affirm together beyond their different theological perceptions" (BEMreport, 9).

These documents are built on a foundational tension between general statement and implicit detail that reflects the tension between unity and diversity. Herein lies the very challenge of such an enterprise. "There is a rich diversity of Christian life and witness born out of the diversity of cultural and historical context" (NMC, 61). Not only unity but also this diversity is a gift of God to the church because the parts enrich the whole (NMC, 60). Faith and Order explicitly addresses the tensive character of these two dimensions. "Each local church must be the place where two things are simultaneously guaranteed: the safeguarding of unity and the flourishing of a legitimate diversity. There are limits within which diversity is an enrichment but outside of which diversity is not only unacceptable, but destructive of the gift of unity. Similarly, unity, particularly when it tends to be identified with uniformity, can be destructive of authentic diversity and thus can become unacceptable" (NMC, 62). To preserve this tension the conceptualization of this ecclesiology must be such that it captures the unity among the churches by implicitly recognizing legitimate differences in particular churches. It reaches for the deepest sources of unity with God and among the churches. It thus challenges the churches to assume critical responsibility for what they consider obstacles to various levels of communion.

Let me close this section: transdenominational ecclesiology uses the same sources as other forms of Christian theology but is attentive to the existence and tradition of the whole church, to the extent this is possible, and not exclusively to the tradition of one denomination. It addresses both insiders and outsiders, but with a particular consciousness that it represents the whole church in the context of other world religions. In other words, the field or horizon for understanding is expanded. The method is simultaneously comparative, normative, and apologetic; it involves a consistent comparison between churches and perhaps religions, a quest for a normative theological understanding allowed by Christian sources of revelation, and a critical correlation with the contemporary world of human experience. The goal is a common Christian understanding of the church. The characteristics of the content of this ecclesiology will be tensive and dialectical. Its broad and generalized formulas will always give rise to the differentiations that exist in all the particular churches. But where it succeeds it will be a common bond between Christians that different churches can embrace. It will form a passageway that will allow easier communication between the churches and perhaps a basis for communion among them.

STRUCTURE FOR UNDERSTANDING
THE CHURCH

How should the elements that constitute the church be organized in a rational way? Is there a way of relating the various dimensions of the church to each other that is descriptive of all churches without being the sole or distinctive property of a particular church? What plan represents a common or neutral ground for laying out the foundation and framework of a transdenominational ecclesiology?

To address these issues I turn to the sociology of organizations to find a schema for understanding organizations as such. The church is much more than a human institution, but it is also a historical community that falls within the scope of the sociology of organizations. The discipline of sociology thus provides a kind of neutral ground, which in turn yields a heuristic structure that can be used to present the elements that make up the church. The reasons for turning to the sociology of organizations for a model for describing a transdenominational ecclesiology can be summarized by shorthand: it offers a pattern for understanding all organizations and thus a shared, nondenominational superstructure containing the elements of a "transdenominational church." Such a broad heuristic structure correlates neatly with the goal of finding a formulation of the church that abstracts from particular churches in order to find what is common among them all. Because it is sociological, it will have to leave room for the question of the distinctive nature and purpose of the Christian church. A sociological understanding cannot be allowed to become reductive and divert the self-understanding of the church from something that exists on the basis of the initiative and support of God to an institution of merely human construction. In other words, the sociology of organizations will have to be adjusted to the reality of the church which it simultaneously interprets so that it not distort the church's own convictions about the kind of organization it is.

I propose the following schema of five elements or dimensions of the church which are drawn from the sociology of organizations and adapted to the study of the Christian church.[20] The manner in which they are laid out here gives the impression that they are objective dimensions of any particular organization. But I employ these five elements as purely formal ideas without specific content. They are heuristic categories, which in turn represent sets of relevant questions that may be asked of any given organization and which will generate responses that help clarify its nature. In fact, these questions are usually answered in the ecclesiology of any given church or denomination; they correspond with and run parallel to actual ecclesiologies. A comparison among various ecclesiologies will show that the more integral an ecclesiology of any particular church is, the more the questions proposed in this schema will be answered.[21]

First, what is the nature and the purpose of the church? How does it understand itself on this basic ontological level? This question has a specifically theological character: what are the common theological symbols, meanings, and values that characterize the church as a whole and hold it together as a body?

Second, what is the institutional or organizational form of the church? Its polity? Its structure of ministry? The lines of its authority?

Third, who are the members of the church? What does it take to become a member? And how do the various roles within the church define how the members relate to each other?

Fourth, what are the activities of the church? What are the actions by which the church fulfills its purpose, goal, or mission? What are the church's patterns of assembly, prayer, worship, and liturgical life? What are its views of the sacraments? What is the ethic of the Christian community? How is Christian behavior or the Christian life or Christian spirituality understood? The last two questions, however, cannot be answered apart from consideration of the next area of attention.

---

20. These five elements of organizations are inspired by W. Richard Scott, *Organizations: Rational, Natural, and Open Systems* (Englewood Cliffs, N.J.: Prentice-Hall, 1981), 13–19 and *passim*.

21. Such is the finding of my study of the history of ecclesiology in CCH, especially in volume 2, which treats comparatively ecclesiologies from the sixteenth century forward.

Fifth, what is the relation between the church and the world? How does the church view the society beyond its boundaries, and how does it draw or define those boundaries? How does the church view itself vis-à-vis the wider world of history and the immediate future? The question of its conception of the absolute future brings the interrogation around full circle and back to the ontological conception of its nature and purpose.

Taken together these questions do not represent the genesis of the church; this is a descriptive and not a developmental model. But the diversity of the sources shows readily enough that the church is no static institution or organization. Moreover, the original genesis of the church can be displayed within the context of this scheme. The New Testament and the noncanonical literature of the first and second centuries show traces of all of these facets of the church as an organization in the process of being formed, that is, in various embryonic and developmental stages of the genesis of the more fully developed institutions that constituted the church. The normative developmental considerations of the church, which are crucial for a transdenominational ecclesiology, are thus not left behind in this interpretive organization of the data but are integrated into it. In sum, this set of categories brings together in dialogue the many churches that exist today all of which share different forms of these elements of common ecclesial existence. It also provides a set of questions addressed to the New Testament and the original genesis or development of the church that opens up a universal authority for a normative understanding.

This chapter has outlined the ongoing task of constructing a transdenominational ecclesiology, not as the exclusive task of ecclesiology, but as a distinct enterprise of constructive comparative ecclesiology alongside denominational ecclesiology. It has discussed in order the premises, nature, method, and structure that such an ecclesiological effort might assume. I conclude with a statement of the role that such an ecclesiology might play. This is not the ecclesiology of any specific church, and thus its relevance cannot be judged by its adequacy in representing a particular church. Constructive transdenominational ecclesiology has to be measured by its service to the whole church, including its relationship to the other religions and the whole world in which we live; it has to attend to the relationship between all the churches and their ecclesiologies.

As a transdenominational ecclesiology becomes more and more accurate in representing what Christian churches share in common, it will accomplish three things. It will, first of all, deepen the understanding of the church shared by all Christians. When such an ecclesiology approaches a formulation of what all churches share in common, it drives theological understanding to the deeper level of the concentrated substance of ecclesial faith. It tends to eliminate widespread confusions between what is substantial in the Christian church and what is changeable and changing. This seems to be quite urgent in the church today as a defense against new impulses toward fragmentation.

Second, such an ecclesiology increases the breadth of our understanding of the church. Transdenominational ecclesiology breaks open the limitations of individual denominational ecclesiologies in its consideration of the broad variety of aspects the whole church has assumed across the varieties of its denominations. This cannot but expand an ecclesiological imagination to conceive new creative possibilities for any particular church and tradition. In this respect pluralism within the great church becomes a sign of richness and fullness of Christian life and not a defect in the church.

Third, transdenominational ecclesiology shows the possibilities for a mutual recognition of the churches of one another. It forms a common bridge, which may allow such mutual recognition to cross over to a more formal communion. This should not be regarded as a simple crossing; it has been and is a difficult corporate mental transition filled with real obstacles. But the process of reflecting on transdenominational ecclesiology is itself a significant movement in this direction.

Chapter 2

From Historical to Constructive Ecclesiology

This chapter constructs a bridge between the historical ecclesiology of *Christian Community in History* and a synthetic, constructive ecclesiology. It is intended not only to respond to the methodological question of how to move from historical to constructive ecclesiology, but also in a certain manner to navigate that route. The chapter also aims at supplying many of the presuppositions upon which the constructive ecclesiology of the following chapters is built. Chapter 1 defined the method and character of a transdenominational or common Christian ecclesiology. The present discussion begins that project by laying out some of the largely formal premises that are drawn from the history of ecclesiology.

It will be helpful to reflect further on the comparative and constructive dimensions of this work. A clue to what is going on here can be gathered by a methodological shift in the process used to generate *Baptism, Eucharist and Ministry*. The first efforts toward making a statement of what Christian churches agreed upon at the Faith and Order Conference in Lausanne in 1927 had a decidedly comparative character. The document laid out the many things that churches shared in common; it listed the areas marked by difference, especially those considered church dividing. In the course of ecumenical work especially after formation of the World Council of Churches, Faith and Order recognized that a method that consisted exclusively in a comparison of the doctrines and practices of the churches at the present time could not generate results that bore normative authority. The effort had to become more intentionally constructive on a Christian theological level; it had to include an appeal to the apostolic teaching of the New Testament. BEM aimed not merely at developing practical formulas that the churches could passively accept. It sought to give witness in the present time to the apostolic faith that all churches take as normative for their community existence. The apostolic faith to which the New Testament bears normative witness serves as both the real premise of transdenominational ecclesiology and its ongoing and always elusive goal. In the logic of BEM, churches may enter into communion with each other not because they are the same in all respects, but because of what they share in common. The churches are not the same, but precisely different. Yet across their differences each church can recognize in the other the apostolic faith.

Analogously, the transdenominational ecclesiology represented in this work is not drawn directly from a comparison between the various ecclesiologies that are found strewn across the history of the church and presently across the cultures of our newly globalized world. Rather it employs the constructive method outlined in the last chapter, one that finds its sources in the New Testament and the earliest church depicted in it and in the history of ecclesiology as it has developed over the centuries. More specifically, I am attempting to move from this historical theological data to a more constructive statement. That transition involves two steps.

In order to move from those normative beginnings and the concrete development of the church across history, I first of all try to isolate various consistent principles that, on a strictly formal level, characterize the material or historical development of the church. Each chapter of *Christian Community in History* contained a summary in terms of these formal, heuristic, and interpretive principles. Their force was derived not from an a priori theory; these are not principles deduced from a system of premises.[1] Rather they are historically generated; they convince according to the degree they reflect insights into the data that the data continually suggest. These principles represent ecclesiological constants across the history of a developing church. But they can also be revised. Second, in this

---

1. In some cases the principles put forward are drawn from sociological theory or the discipline of history. But such principles themselves are empirically derived. These principles function in historical ecclesiology as heuristic categories whose truth comes from the data.

present work and most pointedly in this chapter, I attempt to gather together these principles in a summary form so that they may become the working premises of the constructive ecclesiology of the chapters that follow. This process links this work in systematic constructive ecclesiology to the history of ecclesiology in a way that transcends the mere fact that one follows the other. This work tries not to leave the former work behind. Drawing these principles into the constructive effort makes the history of the church and the historical imagination of the ecclesiologist intrinsic to the process of formulating an ecclesiology for the present-day church.

Finally, I should note that I have arranged these principles according to the structure for an ecclesiology that was suggested in the first chapter. This yields a division of this chapter into six parts. The first is called principles of orientation because of their broad and all-encompassing character. The next five sections correspond with the loci for a systematic ecclesiology: the nature and mission of the church, its polity or organizational structure, its members, the internal activities of the church, and its relationship with its environment or "world." The correlation of the principles with these topics is far from rigid.

PRINCIPLES OF ORIENTATION

As was just noted, principles of orientation are so designated because of their general character. In some cases these principles may appear to be clichés; they are either developed more fully in the first chapter of *Christian Community in History*, I, or they implicitly lie within the development of the whole of those two volumes. I have reduced the number of these principles to four. In the presentation that follows I give these principles a name and then try to provide a formulation in italics.[2] This is followed by a brief explanation.

---

2. This use of italics is ambivalent. On the one hand, it serves the function of defining the principle in a way that gives it clarity and status. One can refer back to each principle, and the sum total of principles defines fairly thoroughly the perspective of this work. On the other hand, the use of italics gives more importance than is warranted to the specific formulation of these principles. They require more adequate analysis than the blunt statement of them may seem to imply. Since these principles for the most part are drawn directly from CCH, they are repetitious. But they also serve

One Church in Two Mutually Influencing Languages

The church is constituted in a two-fold relationship, to God and to the world. These two relationships in their turn require two distinct languages to describe the church, the one theological and the other historical and sociological. These two languages exercise a reciprocal influence on each other. The church's distinctive relationship to the world is determined by its relationship to God; and theological language about the church can only be realistic and credible when the historical referent is in view.

In many respects this principle defines a method of ecclesiology from below, one that begins with history and keeps theological assertions about the church tied to the concrete church of history. Because of its fundamental character, the principle can be discovered at work in various writers on the church in the course of the church's history. It is certainly not the case that theologians writing on the church before the modern period lacked reference to the church of history. But Friedrich Schleiermacher stated the principle in almost the same terms as it is expressed here with explicit reference to its methodological implications.[3] A theological understanding of the church would be purely dogmatic and uncritical without reference to the church of history; and a description of the historical church without any reference to its theological self-understanding would not correspond to the actual, true church.

This dual belonging of the church to God and to the world pervades all language about the church. For example, the scriptural root metaphors for the church overtly display its twofold relationship: "people of God," "the body of Christ," "the temple of God as Spirit."

The Sacramental Principle

God deals with human beings through the church.

This so-called sacramental principle requires some explanation lest it be misunderstood from two different sides at once. The principle

---

as a summary of that work in formal terms and draw out its relevance for constructive ecclesiology.

    3. CF, #126. See also CCH, II, 358.

makes a positive statement without any exclusive intent. That is, it does not necessarily restrict God's dealing with humankind to an ecclesial context.[4] Neither does the principle require conceiving the church as a sacrament. Some evangelical ecclesiology harbors certain reservations about placing sacraments at the center of the church. In order to diffuse these suspicions, I have chosen to formulate this principle in the language of John Calvin, who stated it forcefully and unequivocally from a decisively evangelical perspective.

Calvin conceived the sacramental principle from above; it is not formulated as an anthropological principle. Nor does he refer to it as the sacramental principle, but to the principle of incarnation or accommodation. Nevertheless, it functions in a manner appropriate to an ecclesiology from below. This appears best by contrast. God addresses us in a manner in which we can understand. God could have dealt with humankind individually and privately; God could have dealt with persons exclusively through their subjectivity, through human reason or a particular enlightenment. But God chose to deal with human beings publicly through the historically organized church. The church thus becomes the historical vehicle or means by which the effects of the life, death, and resurrection of Jesus Christ reach human beings in the course of history. This sacramental principle gives the church an intrinsic role in the economy of Christian salvation, and it provides a basis for the responsibility and authority of the ministers of the church to cooperate in the divine mission.[5] This does not exclude God working in human subjectivity; Calvin in fact had a developed theology of the Holy Spirit. But the church as organization assumes considerable importance in this theological vision.

---

4. The question of revelation outside the church, of the availability of salvation beyond the boundaries of the church and outside of the historical influence of Jesus Christ, is better dealt with in christology, and it is not treated deeply in this work.

5. Thus Calvin entitled Book IV of the *Institutes* that contains his ecclesiology in this way: "The External Means or Aims by Which God Invites Us into the Society of Christ and Holds Us Therein." John Calvin, *Calvin: Institutes of the Christian Religion*, I-II, ed. John T. McNeill, trans. Ford Lewis Battles (Philadelphia: Westminster Press, 1955), Bk IV, title. See CCH, II, 104–5, 142–43. Cited hereafter as *Institutes* by book, chapter, and paragraph number.

The Mystagogical Principle

Human existence responds to God through the church.

The mystagogical principle correlates with the sacramental principle when the latter is proposed from above. The mystagogical principle formulates tersely the manner in which the church channels human response through itself and its agencies to God. The principle may be considered a presupposition at work in the whole history of ecclesiology. It has a most effective proponent in John Zizioulas's iconic imagination and Orthodox ecclesiology.

Mystagogy refers to the mind and heart being drawn into transcendent mystery by and through some object or formula that symbolizes the transcendent and appeals to religious experience. The Platonic and Neo-Platonic traditions have given rise to classic formulations of this religious response in Eastern thinkers such as John of Damascus and Pseudo Dionysius, and in Western theologians such as Augustine and Bonaventure. Sacramentality has its correlative in an iconic imagination and response. From this perspective the church appears as the place where the Jesus tradition lives on. The church, in the sense of an actual community and tradition, strives to keep alive the incarnational reality of Jesus Christ in the iconic gestures of its whole life together.

Conceiving the response to God through Jesus Christ in the church in terms of an iconic imagination carries considerable advantages. Some of these are the ways in which it overcomes deleterious alternatives that often unnecessarily divide loyalties. For example, an iconic approach to the church corresponds neatly with an understanding of the church that respects its twofold relationship to God and history, and it readily integrates the historical and theological understanding of the church. Its dialectical character of transcendence mediated by the creaturely reconciles a false dichotomy between functional and ontological presuppositions in approaching the church. An iconic imagination allows no reductionism; the iconic signifies history that opens up the human spirit to the *eschata.* An iconic approach to the church also mediates between false antagonisms between religious authority and freedom. The icon has authority because and insofar as it appeals to human freedom and, in Christian language, releases the power of the Spirit that draws freedom into self-transcendence.[6]

John Zizioulas provides a good example of the mystagogical principle in his interpretation of the meaning of Ignatius of Antioch's assertion that the bishop stands "in the place of God" (Letter to the Magnesians, 6.1; 3.1–2). He explains this "place" iconically or mystagogically. Although place is assigned by ordination, it becomes meaningful when, in the context of presiding at the liturgy, the bishop draws the imagination to the mediation of God that occurs in the eucharistic celebration.[7]

The Structure of a Social Organization

Insofar as the church is a historical community, it has an organizational structure that is influenced by and in various aspects correlates with the historical dynamics of other social organizations.

This commonsensical principle, which is operative in the study of historical, comparative, and constructive-systematic ecclesiology, can give rise to heated debate. Many come to reflection upon the church with ideas fixed by their own tradition and see in this principle a relativism that undermines the normativity of what is familiar and has been doctrinally reinforced. From the right, a sociological approach to the church appears to be merely descriptive and may undermine a divinely warranted church polity. From the left, a postulate about the necessity of structure may seem to restrict the vitality of community life that is generated by contact with the power of Word and Spirit. In every case one needs to be explicit about the relation between the disciplines of history and sociology, on one hand, and theology, on the other, in the discussion of church organization.

Two reflections may help to clarify how this principle operates in this work. The first point goes to the logical status of the principle. This formal and methodological principle does not describe any particular church but governs the approach to understanding

---

6. An account of how Zizioulas's iconic imagination is played out in his understanding of the church is summarized in CCH, II, 440–52. See also 487–88.

7. CCH, II, 447, n. 21.

any given church and the church at large. It follows as a corollary of the simultaneously historical and religious character of the church and does not aim at minimizing either quality. This principle does not subordinate or minimize in either direction the theological and the sociological dimensions of the church. It is not a principle that subtracts from a theological understanding of the church but adds another set of categories for characterizing the church. It does not undermine differences or identities among the churches but helps account for them and thus promotes mutual understanding. This principle raises up something more or less self-evident; nothing really opposes it. Is there a church community in history that is not affected by history?

But this obvious historical principle does have importance precisely because it corrects some vague, deep-seated premises that do not correspond with reality. These positions are reflected in the extremes just mentioned: a vague idea that historical change is bad, or a sign of untruth, or destructive of authority; a vague impression that structure and institution do nothing but restrict and inhibit freedom and creativity. Religion, theology, and ecclesiology tend to generate absolute patterns of thought that resist critical reflection. The framework of social consciousness and the social construction of reality, when applied to the church and ecclesiology, introduce a level of critical reflection that challenges transcendental contentment.

The history of ecclesiology provides many examples of how the church is shaped by the social organizations that surround it and behaves according to the patterns and dynamics of other social entities. In different respects the earliest church resembled other social organizations in the first- and second-century Roman Empire: the household, the synagogue, trade associations, the school. The theological transition from Cyprian's to Augustine's ecclesiology correlates with demographic, sociological, and political shifts in the empire.[8] I have modeled the loci of the ecclesiology of this book on a sociological template for the study of organizations because it correlates neatly with standard theological issues in ecclesiology.

---

8. See CCH, I, 219–34, 258–59.

With this principle in the background, the structure governing the five systematic and constructive chapters of the work are drawn from the sociology of organizations.

NATURE AND MISSION OF THE CHURCH

Study of the history of the church and its ecclesiology reveals a shocking degree of change to someone who presupposes that the church is an unchanging institution whose structure was set up in the beginning. But to another person schooled in history and sociology, the church might provide an example of remarkable historical continuity. In either case, the history of ecclesiology has an impact on the way one understands the church. This chapter will harvest some broadly accepted principles from a historical perspective on the church that might help provide a common ground for a theological understanding of the church that is also historically critical. Each of the five topics that organize an understanding of the church will be treated at greater length in the chapters that follow this one. The task here is limited and focused by this question: can we formulate some general or common principles about the church that are confirmed by the history of the church and its ecclesiology, that together define a perspective that is open to change and difference, and at the same time point to a constant or continuous ecclesial substance? A discussion of the nature and mission of the church provides a good place to begin.

Working Definition of the Nature and Mission of the Church

The church is the institutionalization of the community of people who, animated by the Spirit of God, live in the faith that Jesus is the Christ of God. The mission of the church is to continue and expand Jesus' message in history.[9]

As a working definition this formula needs little comment. It will be the topic of chapter 3. As an initial approach, the statement carefully balances the historical and the theological, the dimension of

---

9. CCH, I, 134.

transcendent faith in God's presence and operation in the church and the human, historical, and social character of the community.

Theological Grounding of the Church in Jesus and the Spirit

The church has its transcendental source and continual grounding in God. Its immediate origin and foundation was Jesus of Nazareth, whose disciples experienced him as the mediator of God's salvation. The church flourished in the eschatological experience of the Spirit of God at work within the movement and nascent community. From the New Testament onward an integral ecclesiology provided a priority of place to the roles of Jesus Christ and the Holy Spirit in its existence.

While the transcendent theological dimension of the church suffuses all of the aspects of the community, it directly controls the nature and mission of the church. The church is a religious organization whose members experience the presence and power of God within it. The two dominant symbols that express exactly where and how God was experienced within the community are Jesus Christ and the Holy Spirit. The community began as the group of disciples who experienced in Jesus' ministry, death, and resurrection salvation from God. Jesus did not found a Christian church, but Jesus interpreted as Messiah constituted the Jesus movement that became the church. The Spirit is the other theological symbol that represents God's immanent presence and activity in the church in an actual, ongoing way. The image of the church as temple of the Holy Spirit summarizes a wide range of testimony to the effective role of God's Spirit within the community.

Patristic authors wrote of the Word of God incarnate in Jesus and the Spirit of God as the two hands of God supporting the Christian movement in history. The two symbols complement each other: Jesus Christ is at the origin of the church and as risen is its head; the Spirit is the interior animating principle of life. Each symbol protects against a distortion of the church that could result from an exclusive or extreme emphasis on the other. An exaggeration of the role of Christ the ruler might lead to a rigidly controlled church; an undue stress on the Spirit within the church could lead to a church that lacks discipline or reflective reason. The complementarity of these two aspects of the influence of the one God in the church reflects the fact that integral ecclesiologies across the history of the church balance the roles of Christ and the Spirit. The ecclesiology of John Calvin illustrates this particularly well.

> Calvin's theology of the complementary roles of Word and Spirit develops [the theological foundation of the church] with considerable nuance. Calvin reinforces his christocentric theology of the Word with a developed theology of the Spirit as divine illuminator and internal witness to the Word of God, the principle of the appropriation of God's revelation, and the sanctifier who leads to holiness. This three-fold construction provides the church with more intrinsic theological support from another perspective. The church cannot be reduced to the organization of Christian people in community. Calvin supplies ecclesiology with profound theological warrant in the trinitarian summary of God's dealing with humankind in history.[10]

One Church with Shifting Ecclesiological Referents

Historical and comparative ecclesiology reveals that the one church is made up of many churches whose ecclesiologies have different churches as their referents. Study of the one church therefore requires an analogical imagination.

Using the history of ecclesiology along with other sources of the discipline, a transdenominational ecclesiology approaches the ever-retreating goal of trying to formulate dimensions of the church that are apostolic and shared across differences. The task is complicated by the plurality of the churches that make up the larger tradition. The same words and phrases and identical abstract conceptions of the church take on different meanings when the references are quite particular and different from each other. This can be seen in a comparison between the ecclesiologies of John Smyth and *The Catechism of the Council of Trent*.[11] The one ecclesiology refers to Smyth's congregation and by extension to others like it; the other refers to a vast

---

10. CCH, II, 143.
11. CCH, II, 245–60, 266–75, 276–88.

united institutional network of local diocesan churches that are subdivided into parish congregations. In the first case the imagination
could fully encompass the whole church including all its individual
members; in the other the imagination reached only as far as offices
and positions within the church. The material church referred to
has a direct bearing on the meaning of the language that is used to
designate these two churches.[12]

An ecclesiology that attempts to reach across the boundaries of different churches must have recourse to an analogical imagination.[13]
While an adequate account of what this entails is not appropriate
here, something should be said about such an essential precondition
for a transdenominational ecclesiology. An analogical imagination,
as distinct from a theory of predication, defines an approach to the
subject matter. It presupposes difference among ecclesiological referents and looks for similarities within and across those differences. A
good example of how the analogical imagination works can be seen by
analyzing human conversation. Each person understands the words
and proposals of the other within the framework of his or her own
experience. We understand by an implicit comparative reference to
personally appropriated individual and social experience. The back
and forth of the conversation shows that analogy describes an intrinsic quality of the way one understands the other as other. But
this in turn forms the basis of a positive strategy for understanding and appreciating, in the sense of hermeneutically appropriating,
the meaning and truth of the other by analogy. Such a strategy will
expand the range of meaning for terms that were formerly more narrowly defined. Imagine John Smyth and Robert Bellarmine having a
serious conversation about the meaning of "church."

---

12. Another example, at random, because the principle extends broadly, attaches to
the meaning of the "one, holy, catholic church" in which those who recited the creed,
including the Reformers, believed. For those who participated in the Reformation it did
not refer to the institutional Roman Catholic Church, but with deliberate ambiguity
to the vast collection of individual true churches where the word of God was preached
and the sacraments authentically administered. See CCH, II, 80.

13. See David Tracy, *The Analogical Imagination: Christian Theology and the Culture of Pluralism* (New York: Crossroad, 1981), 446–56, on how pluralism demands an
analogical imagination. See also David Tracy, "The Analogical Imagination in Catholic Theology," Tracy and John B. Cobb Jr., *Talking about God: Doing Theology in the
Context of Modern Pluralism* (New York: Seabury, 1983), 25–28.

Tension between Ideals and Actuality

The church always contains a gap and a tension between its ideals and its actuality. A transdenominational ecclesiology demands a mixture of realism and the utopianism of the kingdom of God.

The announcement of a gap and a tensive relation between the church's ideals and its actual performance should not surprise anyone; such would be the case in all social organizations. In fact, a certain utopianism characterizes all ecclesiologies. They tend to apply the logic of the eschatological kingdom of God to the church. Ecclesiology as a discipline usually characterizes the church as it should be and not as it actually is.

The question is whether this truism can be put to use in a transdenominational apostolic ecclesiology. At the very least, it suggests that ecclesiology in its comparative phase should not measure the actuality of one tradition by the ideality of another. All ecclesiologies have their limitations, even in their ideal forms, and both dimensions have always to be taken into account. Beyond that, an internalized recognition of this gap and tension should elicit a delicate balance of different a priori attitudes in the project of a transdenominational ecclesiology. On the one hand, ecclesiologists should be realistic in comparing the churches that make up the great church. The characterization of what ought to be has to be recognized as eschatological language as distinct from descriptive and legal language. On the other hand, one should be open to the motivation that utopian, idealistic language is meant to summon forth. Transdenominational ecclesiology cannot confuse hortatory and prescriptive propositions, and it cannot do without them either. Deliberately building this tension into ecclesiological self-understanding itself offers the only chance of success in this project. More positively, this intentional use of language transforms this gap between the actual and the ideal from a source of regret and guilt into a positive asset.

Two examples show how this distinction between realistic and idealistic expectations has a bearing on ecclesiology. Augustine conceived the church as a highly differentiated social body. The Donatist churches were not true churches because, by breaking with the whole international movement, they lacked charity, the effect and sign of God's sanctifying Spirit. Within the true church, most members were not united with God in love and thus not saved. Only the inner core of saints made up the ideal church of the saved. Menno Simons's ecclesiology moved in another direction. He expected that a whole church, that is, congregation, would approach an ideal moral witness to God's grace. Menno could not imagine a true church without the ban to protect its corporate moral fiber.[14] In this particular case, Augustine, within his Catholic framework, leaned toward moral realism. Menno, within his congregational framework, leaned toward idealism.

Unity and Plurality

Pluralism means the coexistence of unity and plurality. In a time when consciousness of diversity is so deep, it is important to emphasize the degree to which the original and early church incorporated pluralism into its self-constitution.

Unity attaches to the very nature of the church. We will return to the theme of unity and diversity with respect to church organization in the section that follows. At this point, however, I raise up and highlight three aspects of the tension between unity and plurality in the self-constitution of the church in its origins and early formation because of the authority that is attached to it.[15]

The first important consideration refers to the diversity that characterized the church in the first century. The church during this period, as it is reflected in and can be reconstructed from the New Testament, was no uniform entity. Unity within the churches and among the churches was a very high value and was continually being urged because it was continually threatened. Any number of images and metaphors for the church stressed its unity. But there were large differences among the churches as well; they did not, for example, share the same organizational structure. The nascent first-century church resembled more a collection of different churches than a single church.

---

14. CCH, I, 226–28; II, 241–43.
15. These reflections are drawn from CCH, I, 132–33, 192–93.

This fact of diversity makes even more important the way the emerging church handled this diversity. The single most important strategy by which the original church managed its plurality was by adopting the canon of scripture that contained a plurality of different witness to and theologies of the church. "This made the very norm for the unity of the church a pluralistic constitution."[16] No document holds more authority for the church and the churches than the New Testament. But the New Testament itself authorizes a variety of different ecclesiologies. No one single ecclesiology within it can be designated apostolic to the exclusion of others; different ecclesiologies can be equally apostolic.

A third subprinciple can be learned from the ecclesiology of Cyprian of Carthage, who enjoyed enormous authority from the third century onward. The principle derives specifically from his reaction to a controversy over sacramental practice with the bishop of Rome. The polity of the whole church at that time could be called episcopalism; the unity of the whole church was maintained by the communion of bishops. The bishops of Carthage and Rome, however, disagreed over the rite of baptism, something that could have been considered important and church-dividing since it involved initiation and membership in the church. Cyprian, however, laid down the principle that maintaining communion was more important than identical practices regarding baptism. This principle, from such an authority, sets a definite tone for a constructive apostolic ecclesiology. Ecclesiology has to think twice about what and to what extent issues should be church-dividing.

Holiness as Objective and Existential

The holiness of the church applies both to its objective institution and to the quality of its corporate life. Holiness cannot be reduced to either one without the other.

The history of the church and its ecclesiology shows that, like unity, holiness names an important quality of the church whose meaning

---

16. CCH, I, 133. See Gerd Theissen, *The Religion of the Earliest Churches: Creating a Symbolic World* (Minneapolis: Fortress Press, 1999), 249–74.

has constantly shifted. At one end of a spectrum, holiness some-times refers chiefly to the character of various objective elements of the church, such as scripture, doctrine, office, sacraments, and other rites. At other times and in many churches, holiness principally qual-ifies the kind of life expected of members of the church. Ordinarily God alone is the Holy One. The ways in which the church has ap-propriated the quality of holiness has varied considerably across the tradition. For example, by the time of Augustine, the moral upright-ness that Tertullian had expected of most members of the church was transferred to the church itself, especially in its sacraments where Christ acted.[17] Calvin thought the consistory was an essential ele-ment of a church's life because it helped maintain the holiness of the Christian life. The Roman Church, by contrast, considered the sacra-ment of penance together with the eucharist as a way of restoring and preserving the moral integrity of the church.[18]

The unsettled and multidimensional character of the holiness of the church should warn ecclesiologists against assigning too much weight to one aspect of the church's holiness to the neglect of other aspects. Actual church life requires a balance between emphasis on the subjective and the objective qualities of the church.

Two other qualities, catholicity and apostolicity, together with unity and holiness make up the four classical marks of the church. I will consider principles from the history of ecclesiology that pertain to catholicity under the heading of church organization with reflec-tions on how the distinction between whole and part applies to the church. Apostolicity will be discussed in chapter 4 with reference to succession.

ORGANIZATION OF THE CHURCH

If the topic of the nature and purpose of the church represents an area where the churches share a great deal of common language,

---

17. Robert Evans, in *One and Holy* (London: SPCK, 1972), traces this development. This is not a complete reduction, however, because, as we just saw, Augustine believed in an inner core of elect and Spirit-filled people within the larger empirical community.
18. The efficacy of the sacraments of penance and eucharist should not, of course, be reduced to these functions. The point is not to slight other mystical considerations.

the organization of the church signals diversity and fragmentation. Chapter 4 will require a nimble analogical imagination to identify the threads of similitude among the institutions by which the churches are organized. But on this initial level of the principles and correlative attitudes generated by a historical ecclesiology, one can be quite straightforward in naming four themes that are directly relevant to the retrieval of what we share in common. These relate to the historicity of church development, the manner in which transcendent and historical dimensions are intertwined, a whole-part distinction that releases inclusive energy in the church, and the salutary tensions that result from organizational structures that unify churches but allow for differences. In what follows I consider each one of these in turn by commentary on a theoretical proposal drawn from the history of ecclesiology.

The Historical-Social Development of the Church

The church as an organization developed and continues to develop historically and sociologically. This development entails several tensions that can be approached through conceptual distinctions such as institutional objectification, tensions between community and institution, between charism and office, between progressive and conservative forces, and between continuity and change. Finally, church development can be looked upon as an ongoing process of inculturation.

The principle of historical development ranks with the four initial principles of orientation in its importance and comprehensive influence. The principle rests on historical data and consists in the conviction that the organizational forms or structures of the church were the products of historical development. In ecclesiology this principle includes an appreciation of God as Spirit at work in these developments. This framework for approaching the organizational structures of the church deabsolutizes the products of development and opens the imagination to the positive character of changes that are negotiated over time and through different situations. Historical development provides the grounds for a positive appreciation of pluralism.

The history of the church provides examples of what are sometimes quite dramatic developments of new structures of the community. But it is most instructive to consider analytically how certain enduring institutions arose during the first two centuries. Episcopal ministry, the organization of the church around a bishop, and the communion of churches through the bishop make up a principal case in point.[19] Historians reckon that by the end of the second century the monarchical episcopal structure of the churches was universal. The New Testament does not provide canonical evidence for monoepiscopacy as an exclusive ecclesial polity, yet this system gained strong theological support in Ignatius of Antioch and became the practical norm in the course of the second century.[20] Although the development of this institution can be traced historically, that is, through historical influences and human decisions, it may also at the same time be understood as inspired by the Spirit of God. Insofar as God wills the being and well-being of the church, it is reasonable to infer that God wills the institutions that support and preserve it. But in a context of historical consciousness we are also able to understand how God could also will other institutions that perform the same function. In other words, the divine dimension of the church cannot automatically be presumed to be reflected in one form of church institution exclusively and for all time.

At the same time, one can understand particular divinely inspired institutions of the church as *historically* necessary for the church without invoking divine necessity. I will indicate further on how the New Testament confirms that more than one organizational structure of the church can be equally inspired. Thus, for example, it seems quite unlikely that episcopal succession and government in the church will disappear; it has simply been too successful. This success can urge it upon nonepiscopal churches, without any claim that episcopacy as it has been actually instantiated is divinely willed in an exclusive way and thus necessary for all churches. In sum, a historical and theological approach to the church views church structures as

---

19. CCH, I, 193–94.

20. The sociological fact that the bishop in the tiny churches to which Ignatius refers are the equivalent of a pastor in later and larger churches has theological relevance that will be brought out further on.

both divinely inspired and grounded, on the one hand, and, on the other, changeable and able to coexist with other different divinely inspired organizational patterns.

Institutional objectification. The visible church is an objective institution. But an objective institution consists in the routinized behavior of a community of people; human subjectivity in its action constitutes the groundwork. This process of objectification can be traced in the case of the genesis of the church, not in detail, but in large categories. In the earliest church certain needs of the community were met when particular persons with the talent or skill or inspiration necessary to meet them did so. They were teachers or prophets or leaders or enthusiastic witnesses. Later, perennial needs were matched with titles or offices that assured permanent provision of the ministry. This institutional objectification in its turn generated a theological conceptualization or theology of the church.

One can discern a significant theological development in Augustine's reappropriation of Cyprian's sacramental theology that illustrates the priority of historical behavior to the creation or reform of institutions. This particular theological development was wrought or at least occasioned by historical and cultural changes in the situation of the church. In Cyprian's sacramental theology, the minister had to possess the Spirit to communicate the Spirit. In other words, the minister had to be a sanctified person. In the church of Augustine's time, such a principle appeared to be impossible on a large scale. In Augustine's conception of the sacraments, they belonged to Christ, and Christ operated in the sacraments independently of the holiness of the minister.[21]

Other examples show the existential and at times fragile character of ecclesial institutions. This was demonstrated in a shocking way during the great schism in the Western church in the late Medieval period. Suddenly, as if overnight, Western Europe woke up to a church with two popes with allegiances on both sides. The very institution and office dedicated to holding the church together as one became a cause of division. Only an extraordinary international effort, at once

---

21. CCH I, 260–61.

theological, legal, and political, over a forty-year period was able to put the papacy back together again.[22]

These developments help inculcate attitudes that follow upon a historical consciousness. Objective historical institutions cannot be considered absolute; they are means, or vehicles, or mediations of something larger than themselves and can always be adjusted. No matter how durable they appear, they can break; they need constant tending. This is explicit in the next principle.

Tension between community and institution. The relationship between community, understood as the existential product of the spontaneous shared bonds holding a group together, and its objective institutional structure can be characterized as tensive. Tension carries no negative value here but indicates a polarity of forces that are dynamically united and generative by their pulling in different directions. Community suggests the creative energy of interacting subjects; institution suggests a controlling and channeling of energy in a common direction.[23] The historical life of the church constantly actualizes this abstract and formal principle. For example, churches spontaneously tend to become inculturated within the world, environment, and culture within which they exist. At the beginning of the twentieth century, many Catholic theologians began to enter into dialogue with modern philosophy, historiography, and science in their interpretation of Christian self-understanding and doctrine. Labeled "modernism" by Catholic authority, this movement was repressed. This represents an extreme form of the tension between the vitality of the community and the conservative tendency of control by institution.

Raising this dynamism up to the level of a formal principle and a heuristic devise, however, emphasizes that these two dimensions are unequal and bear an ordered relationship to each other. Institutions do not exist for themselves but in relationship to the energetic existential life of the community they serve by structuring it. The resolution of the crisis of the papacy during the Western schism taught this lesson on a grand scale. The terms of the crisis required theology

---

22. CCH I, 420–21.

23. CCH, I, 127. The polarity is heightened in the organic conception of the church of Friedrich Schleiermacher and Johann Adam Möhler. See CCH, II, 360–61.

to bring this principle to the surface and make it operative.[24] Institutions must continually be adjusted lest they negate their intrinsic function and become self-serving.

Tension between charism and office. This principle lies so close to the previous one that it may be no more than an analogous application or instantiation of it. Offices are generated out of needs that are first felt before the office is created. The structural character of offices gives them an objective place in the community's organization and this in turn provides a permanent addressing of the need. This fundamentally functional way of reading the offices of the church neither diminishes them nor undermines a certain "ontological" status. Since the being of the church consists in existential historical behavior, it cannot continue to exist over time without offices, making them constitutive of its existence. This functionality, however, suggests criteria for judging their effectiveness and guiding their reform. Offices should be such that they provide ministries that animate the life of the community.

Tension between progressive and conservative forces. That progressive and conservative forces encounter each other in the church seems too obvious to mention. But announcing this as a principle legitimates and gives positive valence to each pole. Neither can be eliminated; each has to engage the other. Sometimes it is obvious which is which. At other times a movement intended as conservative may unleash progressive effects. The Gregorian Reform is a good example of the heuristic character of these principles. Was the Gregorian Reform really a reform or did it set the church back by setting up the foundations for institutionalism and clericalism? Such a question cannot be answered absolutely; it requires contextual thinking and interpretation, and thus responses may vary. The larger point, however, lies in the necessity of there being different views in a community. A community generally and a church in particular proves itself healthy when these two forces creatively engage an issue and speak to each other about it. The church suffers when conservatives and progressives fail to engage the issues together but simply address each other about each other.

---

24. See CCH, I, 417–18.

Tension between continuity and change. This phrase announces another principle obvious to those who share a historical consciousness. Internalization of the perspective it encourages in its turn prevents characterizing a development as a "radical change" by encouraging attention to the substructure of continuity. Consider some examples of dramatic change in the church. Was the Reformation a reappropriation of the substance of the church or a break with its legitimate, developed institutional form? How different on the ground in terms of parochial life was the Roman Catholic Church in England at the beginning of the sixteenth century and the Church of England at the beginning of the seventeenth? The life of the church would be more peaceful if those who wanted things to remain the same were able to see how much they actually change over time. Implicit ideals neither of stasis in a changing world nor of complete reversal supply realistic alternatives. Understanding the church as a community constituted with certain social "habits" combines the dimensions of subjectivity or freedom and objectivity in a way that preserves continuity and identity and allows for creativity and newness as the church moves forward in time.[25]

Inculturation. Inculturation refers to the "incarnation" of the church in the culture in which it exists. It means appropriation or corporate cultural reception of Christian faith in such a way that it becomes an internalized part of a people's life. The word belongs to the twentieth century; the reality has being going on from the beginning, frequently unconsciously. Historical ecclesiology demonstrates that, while we can identify anthropological constants in a single human race, no single common human culture and no single transcultural church or doctrine or practice exist. Christian classics have to be interpreted; inculturation demands a unity of the whole church that is pluralistic.[26]

---

25. CCH, I, 127–29. I will return to this idea in the context of viewing the church as the sum total of the activities that are generated in and by the community and that in turn generate the community itself.

26. This is one of the principal theses of the first two volumes of CCH. Examples of the principle appear in every chapter. The process of the extended formation of the church, however, provides classical instances that bear continual analysis. For example, see the reflection on inculturation in the patristic church in CCH, I, 258–59.

The classic example of inculturation in Christian history lies in the transition of the church from its Jewish beginnings in Israel to its insertion into the Gentile world of Greek and Roman urban life and culture. The church gradually settled into and adopted Hellenic and Roman linguistic, social, and cultural forms. This transition is often taught as a smooth development that occurred spontaneously and without rough edges: the life and doctrine of the New Testament and the patristic churches are one and the same. Not so. Inculturation entails losses and gains; the original and the new are analogous and never identical.

As Christianity passes to non-Western cultures, the question of identity as measured by a tradition that is largely Western has become a profound problem that will continually reappear in different forms. For example, the Melanesian Council of Churches wrote in response to BEM: "We must also confess that many of the theological problems addressed in BEM seem foreign to us, since they arise out of the history of Christianity in Europe and thus do not appear relevant to our Melanesian concerns."[27] The debate over Hellenization in the nineteenth century became polemical and the term "Hellenization" was cast in negative terms. Today's historical and social-cultural consciousness allows a more subtle appreciation of the delicate problem of inculturation. On the one side, no one wants Christian revelation, faith, or the church to be absorbed by, compromised by, or reduced to any culture. The church should not be divided on the basis of cultural issues that distract churches from the unity they possess in a common faith. On the other side, church unity cannot be maintained on the basis of an imaginary universal culture. No one wants a church that is culturally alienated from the particular lives of its members. This is a crucial issue in the church today.

Church Structures as Human and Divine

The historical and developing church rests on continually dynamic divine foundations. The co-presence and interactive qualities of these two dimensions of the church, human and

---

27. BEMresponses, V.180.

divine, are not negative and antithetical but positive and constructive.

The question of the human and divine dimensions of the church keeps coming up. It points to the essential foundational principle of the church's being constituted in a double relationship to God and to the world, noted in the first orienting principle for analysis of the church. It is implicated in the way one understands the development of church institutions just alluded to: historical development lies over against what is willed by God, and churches construe "divinely willed" exclusively rather than inclusively. Richard Hooker transcended this limited view when he maintained that a church ordinance could be both divinely sanctioned and changeable, or that two different church orders could both be divinely willed.[28] Schleiermacher's ecclesiology offers a systematic way of putting these two dynamic relationships and forces together in a positive and constructive way.

The church's simultaneous relation to the world and to God as mediated by Jesus Christ and the Spirit allows Schleiermacher to set up a dialectical relationship between two forces that in the end constitute church life.[29] The relationship to God includes the dynamic impulses of God-consciousness that stem from Jesus Christ and the internal influence of the Spirit of God within personal Christian experience and corporate ecclesial subjectivity. The relationship to the "world" includes not only the active concerns of daily life but also resistance to the impulse of the Spirit. Both individual Christian existence and corporate ecclesial existence involve this interactive relationship so that these two dimensions cannot be separated.[30] As a result, one cannot expect to find a pure account or example of the will and purposes of God in the church, but only limited and mixed instantiations of freedom and grace that are played out by human decisions in history. The church embodies human and divine elements drawn from its twofold relationship, and one cannot neatly separate

---

28. See CCH, II, 214.

29. This report summarizes the description of this aspect of Schleiermacher's ecclesiology in CCH, II, 331–33, 362–63.

30. I will deploy this tension again further on in a discussion of the church-world relationship.

out one dimension from the other. This theological construct allows the ordinary Christian and the theologian to approach the various structures of the church realistically with critical reverence.

Catholicity: Distinction and Interaction between Whole and Part

A distinction between the whole church and parts of the church can shed light on the development of the church across its whole history. But the distinction becomes increasingly more important in the early modern period and thereafter as the church becomes increasingly more pluralistic.

I defined the principle of whole and part in the context of the post-Constantinian church and the Donatist crisis this way: "The principle says that the whole church exists in any given part: any local church can embody the whole church. But at the same time, the whole or universal church consists of a communion of churches. This means that the object of ecclesiology is always the whole Christian movement; no single church exhausts the church, even though the church subsists in principle in every church."[31] This principle, however, becomes more relevant as the church becomes more explicitly pluralistic. Thus Hooker especially drew out its relevance for the church of Western Europe in the wake of the Reformation. He wrote that "as the maine body of the sea being one, yet within diverse precincts hath divers names; so the Catholike Church is in like sort devided into a number of distinct societies, every of which is termed a Church within it selfe."[32] Hooker had internalized the historical situation of the church in Europe at the end of the sixteenth century. Once a situation of pluralism prevails, one particular church can no longer claim to be the "catholic" or universal church. All churches in such a situation become member churches in the catholic church. Hooker explicitly recognized that the actual pluralism of the churches had to be accepted in principle. He stated as

---

31. CCH, I, 262–63.
32. Richard Hooker, *Of the Laws of Ecclesiastical Polity*, I-III, ed. W. Speed Hill (Cambridge, Mass., and London: Belknap Press of Harvard University Press, 1977–81), III.1.14; cited in CCH, II, 214.

principle a formal characteristic of the whole church and its particular concrete embodiment in each part. "All people need language to speak, but they need not speak the same language: 'the necessitie of politie and regiment in all Churches may be helde, without holding anie one certayne forme to bee necessarie in them all.'"[33]

The implications of the whole-part distinction developed significantly after Hooker. Hooker recognized pluralism among churches in the whole of Western Europe, but not in a given local or unified region. The recognition of some measure of religious freedom and tolerance, although it was promoted by the Anabaptists and found in some cities or regions in the sixteenth century, was a seventeenth-century development. The historical consciousness that was exemplified in Schleiermacher's theology and ecclesiology opened a way beyond tolerance to a certain mutual acceptance that later characterized the ecumenical movement. In many quarters today, the influence of the World Council of Churches, various ecumenical conversations, and interfaith dialogue have mediated another stage of consciousness. This consciousness may be described as simultaneously pluralistic and transcendental. It recognizes the integrity of many different traditions and at the same time seeks and finds analogies between them or areas of similar if not shared conviction. This new consciousness correlates neatly with the part-whole distinction. What is distinctive of each tradition is particular; what is shared is the apostolic tradition that each church has appropriated somewhat differently.

Unifying Structures and Diversity

Fragmentation within the church in the modern and postmodern periods, especially at the present time when the majority of Christians live in the developing world, requires rethinking the dynamics of the organizational structures of the church. Institutional boundaries help maintain the unity of the church and preserve the integrity of diverse traditions. They also set barriers that divide churches. How should these two lines of force relate to each other?

---

33. CCH, II, 215, citing Hooker at *Laws*, III.2.1.

"Although no one in the sixteenth century saw either pluralism or division as necessities [in the Western church], the conditions for their breaking out openly were being prepared during the whole course of the late Middle Ages, geopolitically, politically, culturally, and religiously."[34] Various regions or nations were becoming more independent, self-consciously distinctive, and politically autonomous. It would be natural for these forces to be felt within the church. But the church did not successfully adapt to them, and the following principle seems to be relevant: "The more a large institution becomes diversified and pluralistic, the more flexible will the institutional administration have to become in order to preserve its unity."[35] The ecclesiology in place at the beginning of the sixteenth century was a product of reaction against conciliarism. It stressed papal sovereignty; it expected obedience to official papal directives. In hindsight, it seems inevitable that insofar as the center could not accept explicit differences within the whole body, it could not hold. "In brief, Europe had reached a point where, if unity were defined as uniformity without self-conscious respect for differences, there could not be a united Christendom."[36]

The pluralism introduced into the Western church with the Reformation calls for principles that can enable the church and the churches to deal with it. Looking back at Calvin's ecclesiology from a present-day historically conscious perspective provides one such principle. Calvin grounded his church organization in the New Testament; yet it was quite different from the organization of the church in place, which also rested on warrants in the New Testament. The principle I find operative in Calvin's ecclesiology comes from this clash between his ecclesiology and that of the Church of Rome. It stems more from his method than his explicit teaching. The principle is contained in a series of propositions:

> One is that the New Testament church continues to exercise a normative claim on the ecclesiology of the Christian churches. Churches should reckon with it. Another is that there is no clear

---

34. CCH, II, 78.
35. CCH, I, 419.
36. CCH, II, 212.

cut, consistent New Testament polity that can be applied today. The appropriation of the New Testament must include adjustments for the present historical situation and environment of the church. And third, the tensive unity of these two principles generates a third: the New Testament can be seen to validate different church polities at any given time. On the one hand, no version of the organization of the church in the New Testament can exclude all others; on the other hand, the pluralism of the New Testament witness to the church can stimulate different arrangements.[37]

In the ecclesiology of Schleiermacher pluralism is recognized as a historical necessity. The historicity of the church consists in the tension that was just reviewed between the church and the world, or, more accurately, the tension between the invisible power of God's Spirit and the reception of its effects in the finite and resistant world. Moreover, in a historical world where the church is always particular and limited, pluralism ceases to be a negative principle and takes on positive qualities. Since all churches are limited and none can command the field, diverse ecclesial forms become a positive asset for the people of God.[38]

In the twenty-first century theologians instinctively affirm that the only unity possible within the church must include a dimension of plurality and allowance for differences. This applies to the question of unity among the churches. It also applies within individual churches, communions, and denominations, and even to ecclesial existence within the parish or congregation. But despite the principle, the churches hesitate to act; a countertendency insists on narrowly drawing the boundaries of tolerance. The churches need definite structures that allow for diversity.

A revised conciliarist principle. Relative to the theme of structures of unity that allow for diversity, I want to bring forward an aspect of Hooker's thought that has bearing on our present situation. Hooker had a vision in which common laws shared among nations would allow for interchange among all peoples. Within this

---

37. CCH, II, 144.
38. CCH, II, 364.

uncommonly wide framework of thinking, he understood the whole church to be made up of the whole Christian movement including all the individual churches. If there were to be an institution that could represent the whole church, it would have to be conciliarist in principle. That is, the whole church could only be represented by some kind of general council that had representatives from all the churches. In effect, Hooker took the distinctions and discussion of conciliarism, which unfolded within a single though divided church, and transferred them to the great church, which after the Reformation in the West was made up of many churches.[39] In so doing he offered a framework for a worldwide structure of communication that bears some analogies to the World Council of Churches.

Communion ecclesiology. "Communion ecclesiology" is a deliberately vague phrase that opens up a creative imagination for ecclesiology in our time. The name means different things in different situations and ecclesiologies. But having experienced the ecumenical movement, the creation of the World Council of Churches, and Vatican II's opening up of the Roman Catholic Church to interchurch dialogues, communion ecclesiology can be seen to represent a common desire among most churches that they be in communion with other churches. What "communion" consists of is a major question, and it receives different answers. "But the new thing in all of this is the sense of communion itself that can absorb the dialectical tensions it entails: the corporate self-identity and local autonomy it presumes, the acceptance of a sense of being responsible to other churches in a way that recognizes a measure of authority of the others with whom each particular church shares communion, and the willingness to give the larger unity some institutional form."[40]

The ecclesiology of the Eastern Orthodox Church offers a prime model of communion ecclesiology that, with adjustments, can be appropriated universally with considerable relevance. The Orthodox ecclesiology of John Zizioulas presents the basic unit in the church as the eucharistic community assembled around the bishop. He recreates the tradition of the early church as reflected especially in Ignatius

---

39. CCH, II, 215–17.
40. CCH, II, 424–25.

of Antioch and Cyprian of Carthage. When he applies this to the present Orthodox Church, the "bishop and local church represent the basic unit and these units are held together primarily by a unity of faith through communication. The communication is downward to parochial eucharistic communities, laterally with other episcopal churches, and upward with heads of national churches or patriarchs, and worldwide through communions of communions."[41] But it is important to recall that, in the relatively tiny churches of Ignatius's time and the small churches of Cyprian's time, the bishop was essentially the equivalent of today's pastor of a parish or congregation.

With this model in mind, one can easily reimagine the church in such a way that the actual eucharistic assembly or parish congregation assembled around the word of God is the basic unit of the church existentially. The local church in the sense of the parish congregation is the church that mediates Christian faith on the concrete level of Christian life. But this ecclesiological revising of the fundamental unit of the church should not be understood in such a way that it negates the juridical church order of any denomination or communion. Universal apostolic ecclesiology does not operate on the same level as the particular ecclesiologies of specific church traditions. Rather, it provides a way to highlight the essential commonality in the role that particular churches play in mediating apostolic Christian faith to the Christian people.

MEMBERS OF THE CHURCH

The subject of the members of the church easily subdivides into the question about who the members are and the more abstract question of the meaning of membership. The latter question comes quite close to the subject matter of this whole book: what does it mean to be a member of the church? It points to a Christian social anthropology in the most existential way of conceiving it. Chapter 5 will take up the question of members of the church in the more specific terms of content for a transdenominational ecclesiology. This section attempts to

---

41. CCH, II, 488.

render thematic some of the implicit principles regarding the members of the church that become highlighted by a critical, historical description of the development of the church and its ecclesiology.

Membership in the church is not as straightforward a question as it may seem on the surface. The qualities expected of a member have varied considerably across time and cultures and continue to differ in different churches today. Because the church is constituted in and by its members, the responsibilities entailed in being a member are an important locus for ecclesiology.

A critical, historical approach to the church shows that the response to both questions, who are the members of the church?, and what does membership entail?, changes in the course of history. Membership in the relatively small churches of the second century, which stood apart from official Roman polytheism, required a different set of virtues than membership in the established church of the medieval period. Attention to social history and the church's being embedded in it shifts the focus of ecclesiological concern to the actual, changing church. This historically conscious ecclesiology brings more abstract theological language about the church down to earth. Analysis can recover a number of theological constants about the meaning of ecclesial membership, but it also undergoes significant historical changes.

Ecclesial membership has entailed wide cultural variations. Membership in the church in a culture where family and kinship bonds provide a fundamental structuring of human life, and where tribal or ethnic identity remains strong, will likely contribute strongly to personal self-identity. By contrast, in a modern or postmodern, fragmented, and individualistic culture, an intense identification with the church can be quite distinct from a person's public persona. In one culture, church membership may envelop a community's whole way of life; in another culture it may be one membership in a whole series of institutional commitments.

The quality of ecclesial membership can also vary greatly sociologically. Consider some extremes that allow for a range of differences in between. On the one hand, being a member of a small congregation of fewer than one hundred members will inevitably be a very conscious and intentional experience. It may entail personal demands. On the other hand, when one's congregation consists in seven thousand people, where there are ten different opportunities for Sunday worship, personal piety may still be intense, but the quality of participation will be different. Typical rural, suburban, and urban congregations within a single region differ considerably, and the economic stratum of the congregation also leaves a distinct mark on the meaning of being a member.

Still another major distinction can be discerned in the quality of membership within the single congregation according to variations among persons or personalities. One example of a distinction between two considerably different styles of membership can be discerned in the active in contrast to the passive member. Some churches encourage members to be aggressive in assuming responsibility for the community; it is their community along with others. For example, a church may downplay ordained ministry altogether and stress the unity and charisms communicated with baptism. The Mennonites in the Netherlands believe that "God's unilateral initiative does not necessarily require an ordained ministry but is linked to the proclamation that in principle is a task of each member of the congregation."[42] Members internalize and act out the mission of the church. By contrast, some churches form members as clients; for one reason or another, they belong to the church in order to receive from the church what it offers. One could develop this typology further, but the point is clear. Historical ecclesiology introduces a flood of distinctions that qualify the more general theological meanings of membership in the church. Transcendental categories can determine universal themes in ecclesial existence, but they are also constantly changing on the ground.

The intrinsically variable character of ecclesial membership makes the topic of the members of the church particularly important for the project of a transdenominational ecclesiology. In the final analysis, the church is constituted by its members, despite the impossibility of a group remaining together without structures and leaders. Members are slow to change and thus frequently provide a principle of continuity in the church during times of upheaval and innovation.[43] At

---

42. BEMresponses, III, 294.
43. See CCH, II, 204–05 on the parish during the course of the sixteenth century English Reformation.

the same time, the social sources of denominationalism may make it hard for leaders of the church to forge bonds of communion with other churches. But one has to ask whether the ordinary members of the church, as distinct from ministers or leaders, cannot also serve as a place where effort should be expended in the task of forging solidarity across ecclesiastical boundaries. Whatever the answer to this question may be, the members of the church should be the center of attention in the discussion of all the other topics. The church, finally, is the people of God after the pattern of Jesus.

This discussion has not transcended the level of broad general principle. Chapter 5 will take up somewhat more specifically the sacrament of baptism as the initiation of members into the church, the relationship of the members of the church or laity to clergy, and the distinction between the visible and invisible church, which is a legacy of the history of ecclesiology.

ACTIVITIES OF THE CHURCH

The fourth locus or topic in the study of the church embraces the church's activities. These may be divided roughly between those contained within the church and those directed outside it. This section focuses on the church's internal activities. A social organization consists in self-constituting activity: the church, as it were, constitutes itself historically and sociologically by certain foundational activities. I will consider the actual activities that so define ecclesial existence more specifically in chapter 6. This section, as others in this chapter, draws together some general principles from the history of ecclesiology that define a certain approach to church activity.

The church consists in a certain number of basic activities by which it posits itself in history. It is thus constituted by human freedom. At the same time, this freedom is both received as a gift and channeled in a direction by the social habits it has learned from Jesus of Nazareth and the history of its life in the Spirit. Regarding the church as a social bundle of activities opens a space for a sociological appreciation of it as a living community. Of all the church's activities assembly for prayer

and worship is foundational. Because virtually all the churches
assemble around word and sacrament, ecclesiology will include
a primordial theology of the word and a sacramental theology.

The church may be envisioned on a foundational level as a set of social activities. The church exists in a manner analogous to a living social organism. It is constituted by and consists in a set of actions that bind people together in relationships. This way of viewing the church appears most clearly in its genesis, but the principle also applies at any given time. In both cases the principle highlights the freedom of the social institution within history.

The narrative of the genesis of the church transposed into analytical terms makes the point. The first ecclesial community was constituted out of the stuff of disciples who found in Jesus God's salvation and acted out their discipleship in concert. Throughout the protracted genesis of the church, one finds consistent testimony to its relationship to God: the community rests upon divine grace, God's initiating gift in Jesus and of the Spirit or divine presence. The embryonic communities borrowed structures and developed indigenous habitual responses to new contingencies as they arose. The church emerges out of multiple vectors of force: Jesus, the Spirit, Jewish scriptures, traditions and patterns of worship, forms of relationship learned in Greek and Roman cities, in response to ever-new exigencies in an expanding and complexifying organization. Pierre Bourdieu's concept of a social *habitus* helps us to understand how the community freely meets ever-new situations and problems in history, while at the same time operating out of a social nature or personality that preserves the originating spirit. "The principle of contingency in historical development does not mean sheer randomness; response to the variations of environment is guided by the deep *habitus* provided by faith, traditions, and the memory of Jesus."[44]

The development of the church through history consistently shows how activity or practice lies at the foundation of the emergence of new

---

44. CCH, I, 132. See ibid., 131–32 for an expansion of this principle. Also Pierre Bourdieu, *The Logic of Practice* (Stanford, Calif.: Stanford University Press, 1990), 54–56, 80–97. The notion of social habits reinforces the fourth principle of orientation proposed early in this chapter regarding the sociological character of the organization of the church.

institutions, institutional claims, and thus new doctrines. The Reformation of the sixteenth century sets before us a clear demonstration of this principle. The Reformation also shows that the principle, when played out, can have pluralistic and fragmenting effects. But the developments of the eleventh-century Gregorian Reform were also quite radical. Old claims for the papacy in a new practical situation that allowed them to be implemented generated genuine novelty in the church.[45] In sum, principles from the sociology of knowledge remain crucial for understanding the church: all knowledge is tied to social context and historical situation. Perception, estimates of plausibility, and understanding all function in relationship with society and practice.

Among the many activities of the church, gathering together for worship constitutes the foundation of the church from a historical and sociological perspective. Here the human response to grace and revelation most intentionally and directly expresses itself. At the end of the day, the community called church most explicitly appears as church in its assembly for worship.

This principle, like the last, can be illustrated both in the origins of the church and in its ongoing life in history. Relative to the origins of the community, even though we have little direct testimony to the first twenty years, several pieces of evidence indicate that the primitive community of disciples shared common meals together and read and interpreted the scriptures in order to understand the event and ministry of Jesus of Nazareth. One has in these gatherings or assemblies a kind of kernel that remained a constant as organizational and institutional forms developed around it. So, too, in the historical life of the church across the millennia: the constant factor consists in communities of disciples assembled in prayer and worship, around scripture and sacrament, as new churches and new organizational forms are created around them, or they changed to meet new times and circumstances. This does not mean that any organizational form will do, but it does say that worshiping communities may demand new organizational forms in different times and circumstances.

---

45. CCH, I, 339–40.

Most churches incorporate into their patterns of worship the word of scripture and the sacrament, that is, the Lord's Supper or the eucharist.[46] It will be important, then, in chapter 6 to propose a theology of assembly around word and sacrament as integral to a transdenominational ecclesiology. These theologies will be intimately connected with concepts of ministry and church organization, which will be developed in chapter 3.

Finally, on the principle that the church is ultimately constituted by its activities, every church will have a host of diverse practices and customs that define its specific character. It is important to emphasize that the effort of dwelling on those activities that churches share in common does not undermine the distinctive tradition of each church. Because the subject of the common activities always remains a distinctive church community, the commonality of these activities will be analogous. The pursuit of the apostolic dimension in the many ecclesiologies of our time is neither reductionist nor intent upon uniformity.

RELATION OF THE CHURCH TO THE WORLD

Two relationships define the church, one to God and the other to the world. This means that the church does not have an existence independent of the world so that it may then enter into relationship with the world. Rather, the relationship to the world constitutes the church. This principle in ecclesiology gradually grows in importance in direct proportion to the gradual deepening of historical consciousness and the internalization of the implications of historicity. I divide this schematic presentation of principles culled from the history of ecclesiology into two parts: the first is theoretical in character, and the second enumerates some of the practical consequences of the church being embedded in the world.

The Ontological Character of the Church-World Relationship

The church in history is never pure church: it is constituted in a tension between the effects of the divine Spirit and the limiting

---

46. In chapters 5 and 6 I will attend to those churches that do not practice baptism or celebrate the Lord's Supper.

*and obstructing power of the world which remains an intrinsic
dimension within it.*

Few ecclesiologists in the history of the church formulated the relationship of the church to the world with more depth and nuance than
Friedrich Schleiermacher.[47] A common understanding of "the world"
makes it refer to a sphere outside the boundaries of the church; the
church would be related to something outside itself. Schleiermacher's
usage resonates with complexity and resembles that of St. John for
its subtlety. "World" refers to "human nature in the whole extent
in which it is not determined by the Holy Spirit" (CF, #126). "The
world" thus symbolizes the whole of human reality, the whole sphere
of human reach, insofar as it has not been caught up in the influence
of the Holy Spirit. On one side of the equation, then, the world is
good. But the theme of sin, of resistance to the effects of the Spirit,
adds to this a countertendency or force. As in John, the world is
simultaneously good, neutral, and prone to sin. The world in this
last sense contains a resistance to or drag upon the impulse of the
Spirit toward transcendence. Moreover, this world does not simply
subsist outside the church, because the church exists in the world
and the world is inside the church. The world thus constitutes a dimension of the being of the church. "The world is the natural and
historical 'prime matter' which is made church by the influence of
the Christian Spirit as form."[48]

The mutual interpenetration of the influence of the Spirit and the
world within the church creates a tension. A certain dynamic interaction between these two dimensions characterizes the church and
life in it. The world, which always includes a concrete and specific
time and place in history, specifies the church here and now and
always limits and determines its existence. At the same time the

---

47. I comment specifically on Schleiermacher's discussion of the church-world
relationship in CCH, II, 331–33, 363–64. This same construct was used earlier to
reflect on and explain the simultaneously human and divine dimensions of essential
ecclesiastical structures.

48. CCH, II, 363. Schleiermacher writes: "Hence church and world are not spatially
or externally separate; at each point of human life as we see it, wherever there is church,
because there faith and fellowship in faith are to be found, there is world as well, because
there exist also sin and fellowship in universal sinfulness." CF, #148.

power of God as Spirit is always operative in the church urging transcendence and victory over sin, ignorance, and division. Given these ontological terms describing the church's existence, one can formulate the mission of the church as the task of mediating the effects of God's presence as Spirit and as revealed in Jesus Christ to the world: to human consciousness, to history, and to society.

Practical Principles Stemming from the Church-World Relationship

The constitutive character of the church's relationship to the world provides a foundation for several operative principles. One is that the particularities of the world in which it exists helps to determine a church's character. Thus particular "worlds" help account for the diversity among the churches. Another is that a changing world entails a changing church. The symbiotic relationship of the church to the world, finally, pushes the churches to develop an explicit and sometimes distinctive social ethics.

Given the ontic character of this relationship and the ontological formulation of it just described, several practical principles flow directly from the church-world relationship. Each one adds a note of realism to any idealist theological account of the church.

First, the dynamic relationship of the church to the world in any given time and place represents a major factor in determining the identity and character of a particular church. In the light of historical consciousness "one has to expect that different churches will assume characteristically different relationships to the world at different times and in different places."[49] Using the analogy of hylomorphism, the formal theological understanding of the church will take on its specificity and particularity in the concrete history in which it is instantiated.

A good example of this particular principle can be found in the ecclesial polity of the church John Calvin organized in Geneva. On the one hand, Calvin explicitly relies on the New Testament in describing the four offices of ministry in the church. On the other hand, commentators acknowledge a certain rough parity between the

---

49. CCH, II, 81.

organization of the church in Geneva and the relatively new system of government of the city. Calvin preferred aristocracy to monarchy as an ideal. One sees in Calvin's polity conciliar principles and provisions for checks and balances in the exercise of ecclesial authority and power that bear some semblance with Geneva's city councils. This is what was called for in the new republic.[50]

Second, the relation of the church to the world accounts for changes in the church. The constitutive, interactive relationship of the church to the world means that just as time and process alter the world, so too must the church change. The church as a structure of history cannot not change. The correlation of the history of ecclesiology with the history of the church demonstrates this principle beyond all doubt. The ideal of an unchanging church, which tacitly operates in many ecclesiologies, does not correspond with reality. Because the church forms a part of history, it demands change to retain its identity. Major changes occur when a church tries to remain static as the world changes around it.

Third, the relation of the church to the world helps to account for diversity among the churches. The relationship to the world, when viewed diachronically, elicits the principle of change; the same relation to the world and history, when viewed synchronically across cultures, elicits the principle of difference. The church takes on different characteristics in relation to different places, societies, and cultures. Moreover, the same world may call out different reactions to itself from various groups within any church or various churches within the larger church. The types of various relationships to the world or to human culture outlined by H. Richard Niebuhr can characterize whole churches or represent sympathies that cut across churches.[51]

Fourth, because of its symbiotic relationship to the world the church has to develop a social-ethical policy defining its stance toward the world. Whether or not they explicitly formulate and adopt them as official policy, churches spontaneously develop certain ethical stances in relation to the world in which they exist.[52] Here the

---

50. CCH, II, 144–45.
51. H. Richard Niebuhr, *Christ and Culture* (New York: Harper & Row, 1951).
52. CCH, II, 426–27.

world refers to society and the way social values and behaviors are internalized within members of the churches. A good example of this principle was the social gospel ethic developed during the nineteenth and early twentieth centuries in Europe and especially North America. The liberation theology developed in Latin America in the 1960s and 1970s in reaction to widespread systemic destitution and other liberation theologies developed during the late twentieth century offer further illustrations. These late developments have analogies across the whole history of ecclesiology.

Chapter 7 will take up more specifically the meaning of "the world" and some specific issues that are common to the churches such as missionary activity and dialogue with society, state, culture, and other religions. The discussion here has been restricted to the lessons that a historical ecclesiology from below raises on a formal level.

To conclude, the ecclesiological principles that have been assembled in this chapter hardly transcend the obvious for one familiar with the history of the church. So gathered together, however, they add up to a fundamental orientation for the student or analyst of the church at any given time or place. They deconstruct a variety of absolutes about the church that have been erected by particular churches that are cut off from frequent traffic with other churches. Our current world is making such isolation more and more impossible. A better strategy for understanding the church will be to allow these principles to fashion a framework that opens up the imagination to appreciate analogous commonalities across the many different churches that make up the whole church. This is the task of part II of this work.

Part II

ECCLESIAL EXISTENCE

Chapter 3

The Nature and Mission
of the Church

In a world where people have become explicitly aware of how many different religions claim human loyalty, the phrase "Christian church" can refer to the whole Christian movement. Although Christianity lacks a single organized structure, a comparison of many of the largest bodies of Christians or different churches would reveal that they share a good deal in common. Except in some special cases, an outsider would have no hesitation in pronouncing them "Christian." What is the "nature" of all these churches? And can one characterize a purpose that they share in common?

This chapter proposes a statement that theologically characterizes the nature and purpose of the Christian church. It aims at a "defining" statement that will be accepted by the largest possible number of Christians. Such an effort seeks a fine balance between the description of a particular church that all others would not accept as their own and a bland statement of the nature of the church that has no real purchase on the many instances of its actual life. But the metaphor of "balancing" may misinterpret the strategy for reaching this common nature and purpose of the church. The chapter aims to set forth a deep dimension of the church that lies beneath the many churches and is measured against the normative sources of the church. If this description of the church expresses in theological language the depth that all churches can recognize in themselves and with which they can identify, it will achieve the goal of this chapter.

The success of this effort depends on a number of premises, some of which were considered in part I. But one supposition in particular needs to be highlighted. Because the whole Christian church is divided into so many different particular churches, the nature and mission of the church as it is proposed here will be actualized in a variety of different analogous ways. And the language used here will be appropriated differently in different churches, due to different sizes, ecclesial horizons, polities, and practices. The primary referent for the very term "church" differs among the churches. This means that the development of the theological conception of the nature and mission of the church that follows must be construed in terms of an iconic or symbolic language that takes historical form in analogous ways.

The chapter unfolds in four parts. The first is apologetic and in a brief way explains how human being itself bears an openness to ecclesial existence. The second part deals with the nature of the church by retrieving language that has characterized the theological self-understanding of the church, in some cases, from the beginning and across its history. The third part treats the purpose or mission of the church. The chapter closes with a characterization of ecclesial existence from the perspective of the church's nature and purpose.

THE ORIGIN OF THE CHURCH

It has become a commonplace in the study of the humanities that one cannot fully understand any corporate human practice or organization apart from the way it began and the context in which it unfolds. Therefore this description of the nature and purpose of the church begins with a sketch that situates its origins in the course of history.[1] But prior to that, it seems useful in our time to give an account of the origins of the church as a religious organization in terms of a philosophy of religion. In an age when religion itself is frequently called into question, a statement of how it relates to an understanding of the human will provide a wide context for the discussion that follows. Thus this abbreviated account of the origins of the church notes the openness of humanity to organized religion, the point of departure of the development of the Christian church in Jesus of Nazareth, the social-historical development of the church, and its deepest theological underpinnings.

---

1. This brief statement rests on a fuller explication of the development of the church during the first and second centuries in CCH, I, 69–139.

Anthropological Openness to the Church

Every presentation of the nature and mission of the church will rest on presuppositions of a kind associated with the philosophy of religion. Even where revelation is considered unconditional and an encounter unaffected by reflective human self-understanding, this understanding itself has the marks of a fundamental theology. A certain number of anthropological constants, then, will contribute to an understanding of the origins of the church. It is important for basic apologetic reasons to give an account of the background theory within which an understanding of the church is situated.

That human beings are prone to engage in a type of questioning that gives rise to religion seems to be an anthropological constant. Such questions concern the deep mystery that surrounds human existence. Just who am I and who are we as a species in this unimaginably large universe? Is there a deeper origin of our existence than the contingency and arbitrariness suggested by random selection? How should we imagine the destiny of each person, the race, the planet, and the universe? If there were answers to these questions, how would one know them or be engaged by them? These questions exist at various levels and intensities, to be sure, but they appear to be universal.

These questions give rise to answers. And religions offer the context in which answers from beyond the self are available. Religious experience is the source of answers to ultimate questions that are themselves transcendent: they deal with what is beyond empirical evidence and appear to come to us gratuitously, rather than being manufactured and projected by us. Often these religious experiences of a positive response to the questions that define humanity itself arise out of negative situations in which existence itself is threatened. Death is perhaps the prime example of a human experience that seems to negate human life radically with extinction or annihilation. A positive religious experience in contrast to death might appear as revelation of a power that transcends death and encompasses it with a promise of transformed existence. Such experiences as these lie at the foundations of religions that transcend a particular time, place, and culture.

Religious experience and the answers to questions of ultimacy give rise to the various religions. The sociality of human existence guarantees that responses to religious questions with penetrating relevance will be shared. Religious answers to the deep questions about life do not remain absolutely private. The importance and truth of transcendent concerns lend religion a universal relevance that constitutes in its turn a spontaneous orientation toward communication. Its depth gives religion the power to forge bonds of common identity and purpose. Religion that is universally relevant is intrinsically social; it aims at drawing human existence into a community that shares this religious truth and binds human beings together.

Religion may be regarded as a social and cultural space, a community, which is more or less organized, that provides the responses to ultimate questions. Religion is not understood here as a rival of revelation but comes into existence on the basis of particular historically mediated experiences of transcendence. Such experiences, from a Christian perspective, may be loosely understood in terms of revelation. All religions have a dimension of "being revealed" in the sense of being based on particular experience of transcendent reality. Such revelations are not to be understood a priori as hostile to or competitive with Christian revelation, but in Christian terms as simply "manifestations" of the closeness of God, creator of heaven and earth, to all human beings, especially in connection with their religious questions.

Because the object of religious experience and faith transcends empirical data, the experiences in which it is mediated can only be expressed symbolically. Religion bears an intrinsically symbolic character and can be considered a set or system of conceptual and practical or concrete symbols that represent and mediate transcendent reality, and disclose finite reality in the light of transcendence. The symbols also serve to introduce the constituency of a given religion into the sphere of transcendence and mediate in various ways that transcendence in the world and to history.

As a revealed religion Christianity arose out of a set of experiences that were mediated in history. Specifically Christian revelation and the Christianity that grew out of it were born and nurtured within Judaism. A basic bond ties Christianity to the scriptures and history of Judaism for Jesus himself was a practicing Jew. We thus move to the source of distinctively Christian revelation, Jesus of Nazareth.

Jesus

Jesus of Nazareth occupies the center of Christian revelation and faith that in turn ground the church. The central importance of the role of Jesus Christ in the Christian church seems self-evident. I will return to a fuller account of his place in ecclesiology in drawing out the nature and mission of the church. But two points relative to Jesus Christ and the origin of the church ground the whole discussion.

The first issue revolves around the question of whether or not Jesus is the founder of the Christian church. To reduce this question to an alternative, either Jesus did or did not found the church, oversimplifies the discussion. But at the same time it allows the logic of both lines of reasoning to appear. The differences lie along an axis connecting a doctrinal imagination and a historicist imagination. From a doctrinal perspective, that is, one that represents Jesus in terms of doctrinal language, it is evident that, given his divine nature, Jesus founded the church. Texts such as Matthew 16:18 are held up as a direct indication or the symbol of a sophisticated argument that Jesus founded the church. A more historicist imagination will be impressed by the historians' arguments that Jesus worked as a reformer within the horizon of Judaism and had no thought of starting a new religion.

It is possible and I believe quite useful to mediate these two positions with language that includes both understandings of the matter without deciding between them. Such would be the case in the proposal that Jesus constitutes the foundation of the church. While allowing for different ways in which being the foundation might be argued and thus understood, it affirms Jesus' intrinsic, essential, central, and commanding position in the church. It says, for example, that even if Jesus did not actually intend to found a church, still, in another sense that is not quite historically explicit or literal but nonetheless real and true, Jesus remains the founder of the church. Being its foundation means that Jesus is the central and centering mediator of the church's understanding of God. Specifically Christian faith in response to specifically Christian revelation caused the church to come into being.

A second spectrum of differences in Christian beliefs revolves around the way Jesus' relation to the church should be understood. I will seriously oversimplify two sets of such alternatives in order to develop a mediating formula. One alternative relates to the classic doctrine of the divinity and humanity of Jesus Christ. Some Christians spontaneously lean toward Jesus' divinity and fit his humanity into that centering focus. By contrast, others assume that Jesus was a human being in history and, beginning there, try to understand how they can affirm his divinity. These alternative approaches to christology will affect how people envisage the relationship of Jesus to the church, both historically at the origins of the church and systematically at any given time in the church's existence.

Another distinct but related issue, characterized by a wide spectrum of views, revolves around the mediating place or role that Jesus Christ enjoys within the structure of Christian faith itself. For those with a *christocentric* perspective, faith is mediated by Jesus Christ in such a way that Christ constitutes the center of reality itself. This centrality extends from the creation of the cosmos, in which Jesus Christ was the agent, to ultimate human salvation. For those with a *theocentric* perspective, God, the creator of heaven and earth, the one whom Jesus called Father, constitutes the center of reality even though Christian life and faith in this God is mediated by Jesus Christ. The alternatives are different but share much in common, and each alternative has an influence on how the relationship of Jesus Christ to the church is conceived.

It is possible and I believe quite necessary to mediate all these positions with language that includes them but does not draw mutually excluding lines between them. This is not to suggest that these different perspectives have no bearing on the nature, character, and mission of the church, for they surely do. Those holding these positions should constantly be in conversation with each other. Moreover, it is possible and desirable to understand the church in a way that allows these differences to coexist. Such language would recognize that for all Christians and hence for ecclesial existence as such Jesus is the central mediator of God. Jesus is the one in whom the Christian finds God's salvation. All members of the church place Jesus at the center of their relationship to God. With this unifying consensus in place, differences in understanding how Jesus is to be understood as Christ and savior today can remain open. Historically, the very recognition of the divinity of Jesus arose within the experience of his bearing salvation from God. That same unifying experience can sustain a plurality of christological conceptions today.

In sum, a great deal of pluralism in christology obtains in the churches today, even as there was in the New Testament period. Such pluralism need not divide but rather can be a rich source of growth, nourishment and even celebration.

Historical-Sociological Development of the Church

The historical origins of the church provide an important object of study today. The relevance of this historical study for a more open and pluralistic understanding of the church lies in the implications of historical development itself and certain sociological patterns that can be discerned in it. The New Testament accounts of early church development provide fertile ground for a multiplicity of views of church structure and organization, and the various contemporary churches all seek to find scriptural support for their particular perspective of organizational structure and form. The point to be made is simple: critical analysis of the church's organizational development argues against the idea that there is one exclusive God-given institutional form for the church.

Consideration of the historical genesis of the church contains valuable lessons. First of all, learning the story of the historical development of the church helps one to see the amount of human freedom and historical chance that were involved in developing the structures of the church. The story of the church's development moves from the primitive organization found in a movement to more complex organizational forms. Its growth involved continual adaptation and change over time. This appears in all the critical historical reconstructions.

Second, study of the development of the church shows the way in which sociological patterns and laws that govern the development of any institution also were at work in the formation of the church.

This enables a more concrete and historical view of the church, rather than attributing each step in the church's development to a unique intervention of the Spirit. One sees in this social development how, time and again, as the needs for the social well-being and activity of the churches arose, someone assumed responsibility for a particular ministry, and the community generated a particular office or role that guaranteed that the ministry would continue to be provided. The Spirit of God may be understood as working within this process, rather than as an extrinsic agent manipulating events from the outside.

Third, closer historical, social, and theological examination of the individual communities in the emerging church of the first century show the degree to which pluralism marked the whole church. In other words, there were considerable differences among these communities as they developed in distinct and differing contexts. On the strictly theological plane, one finds a host of different images and metaphors for understanding the church. Theological pluralism, then, characterizes the New Testament ecclesiology, and this in turn serves as an acceptable theological norm for understanding the church.

These three features of the formation of the church are crucial for understanding the possibility of a transdenominational ecclesiology. It does not matter whether one thinks of this development in terms of one movement with differentiations in the communities in the various cities, or if one sees the individual churches as each striving to remain in communion with the others. In either case, the church was pluralistic. The ideas of historical development, of social adaptation to context and need, and of pluralism held together in a deeper unity that can sustain within itself differences are thus demonstrated in the process and results of the formation of the normative apostolic church. The intensity of the value of unity in the early church was itself a function of the differences that it managed to hold together.

This analysis gives rise to a recognition of the church as a visible, social organization, even though it cannot be reduced to that. The New Testament does not allow a reduction of the church by what one might call ecclesiological actualism. This refers to the view that the church is pure event and only exists when people assemble, thus eliminating the dimension of ongoing social organization. Such an ecclesiology would be an extreme ecclesial existentialism that maintains that no church exists when people are not assembled. We will see that, while actual assembling is surely the primary activity grounding the church, the church also entails broader institutional structures.

Theological Underpinning of the Church

The historical and sociological vectors that channeled human decisions into the formation of the church do not fully explain that formation. As noted earlier, the very essence of the church's identity lies in its relationship to God and God's relationship to it. The collective faith in God, and the shared conviction that God takes the initiative in that very faith, constitute this historical community as church. God has acted in the formation of this church and is acting within it. "The Church is not merely the sum of individual believers in communion with God, nor primarily the mutual communion of individual believers among themselves. It is their common partaking in the life of God (2 Pet 1:4), who as Trinity, is the source and focus of all communion. Thus the Church is both a divine and a human reality" (NMC, 13).[2]

Behind the development of the church as a historical and social organization lay God's ongoing interaction with the people of Israel. Beneath the corporate impulse driving development of the church forward lay an experience of revelation and salvation, and of Jesus risen and present to the community. Within the actual decisions and actions that constituted the church lay a religious experience

---

2. The relation of the church to God lies at the heart of ecclesiology. But even at a fundamental level this dependence on God can conceal different conceptions of how this relationship is to be construed. Some ecclesiologies emphasize the church as prior to faith in God, for the organization that represents God's presence and activity is prior to each individual, and each one is dependent on the church for his or her faith in God as mediated by Jesus Christ. Others emphasize the priority of grace to any human instrument by which that grace may be mediated. Grace and faith are prior to the construction of a church; the church as human organization of a corporate faith is dependent upon Word and Spirit prior to any organization. Each of these background conceptions will be uneasy with a language that finds its center of gravity in the other. These differences of emphasis may be tolerated in a larger view in which they are both operative and related to each other not by mutual negation but by a tension of different dimensions and aspects of the church. They are not contradictory.

of God as Spirit and grace that gave coherence to the historical development and the social organization. These experiences, which
were sometimes directly and sometimes implicitly stated, suffuse the
whole account of the church in the New Testament writings. This
shared religious experience, that God provided the underpinning of
the church, constituted its most distinctive defining dimension in
each and all of its forms.

This theological conviction found expression in three, and more
distinctively two, related sets of symbols revolving around God whom
Jesus called Father, Jesus of Nazareth, and the Spirit of God. This
symbolic language will be the subject of the following section. All of
the three symbols are instances of a broader thesis that God is the
origin and source of the church. "The Church is thus the creature of
God's Word and of the Holy Spirit. It belongs to God, is God's gift
and cannot exist by and for itself" (NMC, 9). A theological understanding of the nature of the church will draw out the meaning of
the christological and pneumatological foundations of the church.

THE NATURE OF THE CHURCH

A definition of the nature of the church has to be essentially
theological. While other human elements constitute this historical
organization, and they will be considered in their turn, it is primarily in the theological domain that the distinctive nature and the
common possession of all the churches lie. The church's essential
characteristics flow from its relation to God and the way in which
that relationship takes shape. In the quest for what is normative
and apostolic, a description of that essence must stay close to the
Bible, particularly the New Testament. At the very outset, however,
I want to recall again that this common characterization will be
understood analogously. The analogy derives mainly from the differences among the primary "referents" of the language used by the
different churches today. For example, these churches are congregational, national, formed by communions or mergers, or "universal"
institutions spanning nations and continents. On that premise, this
description of the common theological nature of the church has

three parts: the first goes directly to the ways in which church self-understanding bears witness to its relationship to God. The second states the tension between the church's being related to God and to the world in a way that was perceived from the very beginning and is a constant that defines its life. The third part takes up what have become traditional "marks" or features of a true church.

The Theological Foundation of the Church

Theological understanding of the foundations of the church refers to ways in which the community expresses its experience of God bringing the church into being and being present to it in its historical life. The New Testament is filled with such expressions; across its history the community praises God for God's presence to or within the community. This presence resonates in millions of particular experiences of the people who make up the church. But a theological analysis of these experiences that tries to contain this corporate conviction in concise language that all will recognize has to use broad categories or symbols that are widely shared and familiar. I have chosen the essential Christian symbol of Trinity as closest to both the New Testament's language and the contemporary language of the churches. In the first part of each subsection I explain in theological prose how God, creator of heaven and earth, Jesus Christ, and the Spirit of God are involved in the foundation of the church. I then present and briefly comment on the corresponding biblical images for the church: people of God, body of Christ, temple of the Spirit.

The God of life. The relationship of the Christian church with Judaism has been a subject of intense interest since the very beginning and will continue to engage Christians and Jews. It remains a topic of significantly different views. However, I want to bypass this discussion and focus on a central conviction that the Christian church has inherited from its parent religion. This appears within our common monotheism and consists in a fundamental image of the "nature" of God whom I call here a "God of life."[3]

---

3. This is somewhat arbitrary as a single defining characteristic. It will appear in what follows that several other designations could also be chosen. These aspects of God that appear in Jewish testimony to their experience are not competitive but aspects of a whole history of religious understanding.

The Christian church began within the boundaries, culture, and religion of Israel; Jesus, its foundation, was a Jew, and the church's scriptures were the Jewish scriptures. It thus shared in the Jewish experience of God. This God acts in history; God is savior because God saved the Jewish people and continues to save in history. God is personal: God judges sin and forgives the repentant sinner. God creates and as creator continually gives life to creatures; God blesses and provides. God's wisdom accounts for the order of things. God enters into a covenant with people. God is a lover of all people because all are God's own; God responds to the prayer of people and acts on their behalf.[4]

In the Jewish scriptures God chooses people, and God has chosen Israel. In the New Testament one finds passages that indicate that the new communities thought of themselves as chosen. The idea of being chosen can have two distinct meanings that are opposed to each other: the one signifies "being chosen" in a simple, affirmative sense that is not necessarily exclusive of others; the other intends it with a negative connotation that God has not chosen or has even rejected others. It is clear that this second sense has played a major role in the history of Christian ecclesiology and may even be operative in some churches today.[5] But I use the term "chosen" in a purely affirming sense whose meaning still remains subtle and dialectical. On the one hand, the Christian and Christians as a people and a church experience themselves as chosen ones who have been incorporated into a covenant struck by God so that they are God's people. On the other hand, the very God who has so chosen Christians is the creator of all, so that the Christian message of God is implicitly critical of a tribal or particularist or possessive and isolating view of God. God is precisely God who created all, saw that it was good, and approached the sinner in loving forgiveness. Being chosen, then, cannot shrink God to the size of a given group of Christians or of all of them together.

---

4. This paragraph is drawn from Roger Haight, *Jesus Symbol of God* (Maryknoll, N.Y.: Orbis Books, 1999), 89–95, where I try to indicate somewhat generally the message of the scriptures about God which helped form the religious context in which Jesus was raised. This work is referred to as JSG.

5. This is of course a major question that should be addressed for a host of important reasons. But it need not be discussed here.

People of God.[6] "In the call of Abraham, God was choosing for himself a holy people. The recalling of this election and vocation found frequent expression in the words of the prophets: 'I will be their God and they shall be my people' (Jer 31:33; Ez 37:27; echoed in 2 Cor 6:16; Heb 8:10)" (NMC, 18). This choice of God of a people to do God's will and project in history is taken up in the New Testament witness: "But you are a chosen race, a royal priesthood, a holy nation, God's own people, that you may declare the wonderful deeds of him who called you out of darkness into his marvelous light" (1 Pet 2:9–10). With this symbol a deep reservoir of experience with a long history flowed into a text that still represents the conviction of the church. Each Christian feels related to God in a particular way. All relate to the church to which they belong as the particular community that has itself been chosen and subsists in a covenantal relationship with God. In the history of God's relationship with Israel the church constitutes a new people of God in parallel with the Jews.[7] In sum, an exegetical-hermeneutical analysis and interpretation of this symbol for expressing the nature of the church yields an understanding that this community is willed by God so that it is meant to reflect God's values and intentions for human existence in the world and history. But it absolutely does not mean that other peoples or communities are not chosen. Such an interpretation would contradict the church's understanding of God.

Jesus Christ. It was said earlier that Jesus Christ is the foundation of the Christian church. The God who acts in history acts through historical agents. Jesus of Nazareth became the historical medium through which God acted in the fashioning of the Christian church. This foundational influence flowered in the many ways in which the memory of Jesus Christ determined the development of the church. I implicitly incorporate or include the many expressions of Jesus'

---

6. The biblical images of the church are used by the Faith and Order Commission of the WCC to express a common understanding of the theological nature of the church in NMC, 14–24. It briefly develops the image of "people of God" in NMC, 18–19.

7. The discussion of one or two covenants, and, if two, the relationship between them, bears some importance for Christian self-understanding. Since such a debate goes on within almost all the churches, it should not be church-dividing but seriously engaged within the church and in dialogue with Jews.

power in forming the church in this consideration of the classic image of the church as the body of Christ.

The church depends upon Jesus Christ historically. The historical movement that culminated in the formation of a Christian church historically separated from Judaism began with the ministry of Jesus of Nazareth. One does not need to retrace that history here to affirm this historical relationship. But recognition of how the church is tied to the memory of Jesus' concrete ministry, to what he said and did, to the values and convictions he preached and died for, carries crucial consequences. Too often ecclesiologies leave Jesus behind, even though they read the gospels in their assemblies. Jesus revealed God and made God present in his ministry.

The church also depends on Jesus Christ sociologically. This does not mean that Jesus set up the organizational structure of the church; the weight of opinion among critical scripture scholars goes against this. But the sociological structures grew out of a community that was shaped by the person and message of Jesus Christ. One has to read the many different social forms as vehicles for the community to pursue the project they inherited from the teacher, the prophet, and the Christ. Jesus Christ shaped the community that created the structures of the community.

The church is dependent on Jesus Christ theologically.[8] Here the dependence of the church on Jesus Christ has to do with his divinity and his role as divine mediator. The whole New Testament implicitly witnesses to Jesus Christ as the bearer of salvation from God in human history. Everything about Jesus' role as prophet and teacher, healer, parable of God, and exemplar of human existence enters into this theological understanding of the church. God lies behind the whole thing, the history, the formation of the community, its development, through the mediation of Jesus Christ. Once again, in an effort at summary through an abbreviating formula that has become standard, one can consider the theological dependence of the church on Jesus Christ as prophet, priest, and king.[9]

---

8. I sketched more extensively some of the themes in the New Testament's theology of the church in CCH, I, 110–25.

9. Although the triple role or function of Christ can be found in the tradition before him, Calvin raised it up as a kind of standard summary statement.

Jesus of Nazareth appeared as the prophet of God who spoke the word of God. This represents an initial perception and recognition of Jesus during his ministry. Its meaning developed after his death and resurrection with the interpretation of his person and message. In the Prologue of John's Gospel, often considered a kind of climax of this development within New Testament literature, Jesus of Nazareth is the Word of God incarnate. Gradually the word "Christ" developed into a name and as a name was used as a synonym for the Son of God and the Word of God. Jesus Christ is the prophetic Word of God embodied in history. This interpretation of Jesus Christ transcends the historical dependence of the church on Jesus of Nazareth. God's presence and agency within Jesus are raised up and highlighted so that Jesus mediates God at work in the foundation of the church.[10] As a result the church has the historical function of continuing to announce God's wisdom and prophetic word.

Jesus of Nazareth was a healer and worker of wonders for the benefit of those in need. The gospels are filled with a variety of stories about Jesus healing and making whole; the incidents caused amazement and crowds of people came to hear him and seek his ministry. While scholars dispute whether Jesus himself baptized, there is no disputing that he presided at meals in which outcasts were welcome. Also not disputed is the fact that Jesus' disciples baptized others. The church took up these actions and they were gradually transformed into standardized ritual. Behind them and then within them lay Jesus now interpreted as the Christ. Ultimately, he was compared with the high priest as the eschatological mediator of salvation who is with God. Jesus Christ continues to play this role in history in and through the sacraments and other rituals of the church.

It is more difficult to find the dynamic within Jesus' ministry that led to his being conceived as the head and governor of the church. During his ministry the gospels portray him as rejecting the idea of being a king, and it is frequently displayed as a dramatically ironical idea. The sign above the crucified one announced that he was the

---

10. At certain stages in the history of ecclesiology, this influence of God as Word in and through Jesus was interpreted as though it were a direct and immediate founding of the church by God, even though such an interpretation is implicitly docetic. In other words, it downplays the historical mediation.

king of the Jews (John 19:19). Christ's rule of the church is more a function of his resurrection and exaltation into the life of God and his role as foundation and inspiration of the church and the model of its ministry. But in Paul's image of the church as the body of Christ, all are baptized into unity with Christ, and the author of Ephesians depicts Jesus Christ as the head of the body-church.

Body of Christ. "For as in one body we have many members, and all the members do not have the same function, so we, though many, are one body in Christ, and individually members one of another" (Rom 12:4–5). In Paul the body of Christ refers to the local community. The metaphor is self-evident: many make up one; differences are acknowledged and coordinated; divisions in class, rank, order, charism, ministry, gender, nation, and race are overcome. The many form a coordinated and dynamic unity *in Christ,* that is, by mystical or transcendent participation in his life (1 Cor 12:12–31). In Ephesians the author transposes the metaphor and refers it to the whole Christian movement. God, in exalting Jesus Christ, "has put all things under his feet and has made him the head over all things for the church, which is his body, and the fullness of him who fills all in all" (Eph 1:22–23; 4:15–16). This metaphor seizes the religious imagination and crystallizes it in a mystical and pragmatic way: the transcendent meaning of life is sealed and the criteria for practical community life are set out.

The Spirit of God. God as Spirit is another foundational pillar of the church. The church is grounded in the presence and activity of God as Spirit within the church. The symbol "Spirit of God" expresses the experience of the gratuitous, enabling, and transcendent power of God within history, human community, individual leaders, prophets, and kings. It refers to the power and might of God actually flowing into nature and human life, not just generally, but in this and that particular instance. The Holy Spirit of God from the beginning to the present supports the church as it did Jesus' own life and ministry.

The church thus depends historically and sociologically on the Spirit who acts within the members and in the community as a community, indeed, as the body of Christ. The Spirit constitutes the inner transcendent or divine dimension of the community. The

Spirit ultimately holds things together, not without human freedom, but precisely by working within human freedom and empowering it. This conception so radically shaped the imagination of the early church that the language of the Spirit implicitly and explicitly pervades the New Testament account of the church. A new outpouring of the Holy Spirit dramatically symbolized the authenticity of this new movement within Judaism.

Theologically, the idea of the church as a community of the Spirit envelops the church and provides the license and the divine dimension of many of its activities. The church knows the Spirit as the power of prophecy, the impulse for speaking in tongues, and the light of insight and interpretation; the unifying Spirit heals divisions and provides the wellspring of a common life together. The Spirit raises up charismatics, empowers ministers, and responds when invoked in the creation of new ministries or signified by a laying on of hands. The Spirit operates in and through the church when the church acts in the Spirit. The Spirit at work in the church provides grounds for a theology of preaching, a theology of sacrament, a theology of ministry, a theology of prayer, and a theology of Christian spirituality.

Temple of the Holy Spirit. The author of Ephesians writes: "you are fellow citizens with the saints and members of the household of God, built upon the foundation of the apostles and prophets, Christ Jesus himself being the cornerstone, in whom the whole structure is joined together and grows into a holy temple in the Lord, in whom you also are built into it for a dwelling place of God in the Spirit" (Eph 2:19–22). These metaphors of temple and house express the general corporate experience of Christians that the church provides a social space in which God can be encountered as immanent to human life in history. The Spirit is both prior to the community and made available through it.

To conclude, these theological foundations of the Christian church correlate with an analysis of the church from below and from a historical perspective. The church in and of history testifies in its scriptures that God has taken the initiative in the historical founding, development, and flourishing of the church. The whole institution, which will be described at greater length in the chapters that follow, has its being and ongoing existence as a consequence of God's transcendent presence and grace. This deep grounding and the mystical language of participation in God as Creator, Word, and Spirit are used by all Christians to describe their church. All else beyond this bond of unity among all Christians and with God, which bears so much ontological depth and density, pales in importance when compared with it.

The Church as Historical and Eschatological

As a historical organization the church actualizes a promise from God of transcendent and eternal fulfillment (NMC, 48–52). The Faith and Order Commission expresses this polarity in the following way: "The Church is an eschatological reality, already anticipating the Kingdom. However, the Church on earth is not yet the full visible realization of the Kingdom. Being also a historical reality, it is exposed to the ambiguities of all human history and therefore needs constant repentance and renewal in order to respond fully to its vocation" (NMC, 48). This thesis correlates with the intrinsic duality of historical and theological languages about the church.[11]

Faith and Order goes on to characterize this tension more fully. On the one hand, the theological images of the church reflect the eschatological or ideal dimension of fulfillment to which the church is called. These theological ideals also correspond to the real presence of God as Creator, Word, and Spirit at work in the church in history. The eschatological dimension holds out an ideal future and an effective presence in the historical church. On the other hand,

the Church, in its human dimension, is made up of human beings who — though they are members of the body of Christ and open to the free activity of the Holy Spirit (cf. Jn 3:8) in illuminating hearts and binding consciences — are still subject to the conditions of the world. Therefore the Church is affected by these conditions. It is exposed to: change, which allows for both positive development and growth as well as for the negative possibility of decline and distortion; individual, cultural and historical conditioning which can contribute to a richness

---

11. See the first orienting principle in chapter 2.

of insights and expressions of faith, but also to relativizing tendencies or to absolutizing particular views; the power of sin. (NMC, 50)

This foundational conception of the church can be explained in a more objective way and in the existential language of Christian experience. The objective statement of this tension uses terms that are analogous to the exegetical meaning of the kingdom of God. It refers to something that is ideal, utopic, eschatological, and thus not to be fulfilled before God's "time" or the end of time. And yet that which will be constituted by God in God's time is already breaking in and happening in this history of ours. It is seen only in fragments, but those fragments reflect its real presence. Schleiermacher uses a distinction analogous to this in explaining the role of the invisible church in the visible church. The invisible church is the power of God at work within the church, whether it be named the Spirit, the divine Word, or grace. The divine dimension in the church is really present and operative but not visible. The visible church is the historical church in its human actuality.[12]

Existentially, the rationale for these objective conceptions are found in dimensions of the way people experience the church religiously. The church in its human actuality presents itself overtly to the appraisal of all, whether it be common observation and public opinion or the method of historical science. But to the member who has experienced the community religiously from the inside and who by faith is drawn into transcendence by its preaching and sacramental ministries, the church participates in the transcendence it mediates. This is explained well in the iconic ecclesiology of John Zizioulas. The historical and this-worldly institutions that make up the church have a mystagogical power to draw the human spirit into transcendence. The eschatological dimension of the church consists in the transcendent order that is thus mediated to members, presented to them as being "of God," and pertaining to the absolute future.[13] This dimension of

---

12. Cf. ##148–49. See CCH, II, 332–33, 362–63. I refer to this distinction of Schleiermacher at several junctures in the course of this work.

13. John Zizioulas, *Being as Communion: Studies in Personhood and the Church* (Crestwood, N.Y.: St. Vladimir's Seminary Press, 1997, orig. 1985), 174, n. 11. See CCH, II, 442.

transcendence is integral to a religious or faith-filled perception of the church, that is, that upon which a theological conception is based.

This tension between the eschatological and the historical, the theologically ideal and the historically actual, has practical consequences in the expectations of members of the church. It generates practical attitudes that should govern Christian life. It militates against impatience with the human dimension of the church. It also militates against escape into a divine sphere detached from the world by bringing things back to earth and history. Finally, it sets up a tensive framework that is crucial for understanding the marks of the church.

The Marks of the Church

The church is one, catholic, apostolic, and holy. These marks of the church are four descriptive attributes of the church that authenticate it as the true church of Christ.[14] To the outside inquirer, honest and genuinely interested, they may appear to be a theological hoax. They do not, at face value, seem to correspond to the reality of the historical church or churches.

Rather, they are frequently used by individual churches in a polemical fashion to justify themselves over against other churches. This tends collectively to negate the very claims that are made. Are they of any use? Can they function constructively and realistically in a transdenominational ecclesiology?

I believe the traditional marks of the church can help to understand the church as it truly is and is called to be if they are interpreted in the following way: First, they have to be understood dialectically. As in all assertions of faith, reducing them to literal historical claims distorts the very nature of faith as a response to transcendent reality. Second, these marks have to be interpreted nonpolemically to describe the true church in all the churches. The marks of the true church primarily refer to the effects of the Spirit within the church that the churches share in common. Third, the marks of the true

---

14. Faith and Order outlines the four marks of the church at NMC, 53–56. See Hans Küng's discussion of the marks of the church, which he calls "dimensions" of the church, in *The Church* (New York: Sheed and Ward, 1967), 261–359.

church call the actual churches to the task of making them historically real across the boundaries of the churches. This scheme will be
the burden of the short commentary attached to each mark.

Oneness. The first mark of the church describes its unity. No one
can miss the paradox involved in this claim. The Faith and Order
Commission states it this way:

> The essential oneness which belongs to the very nature of the
> Church, and is already given to it in Jesus Christ, stands in con-
> trast to the actual divisions within and between the churches.
> Yet in spite of all divisions the unity given to the Church is al-
> ready manifest in the one Gospel present in all churches, and
> appears in many features of their lives (cf. Eph 4:4–5; 1 Tim 2:5;
> Acts 4:12). The unfortunate divisions among the churches are
> due partly to sin, and partly to a sincere attempt of Christians
> to be faithful to the truth. Working for the unity of the Church
> means working for fuller visible embodiment of the oneness that
> belongs to its nature. (NMC, 53)

The ideal of the unity of the church dominated twentieth-century
ecclesiology and released the enormous energy of the ecumenical
movement. This brief commentary of four points derives from it. The
first simply recognizes that the unity of the church comes from God;
Christians and churches are united in what they have received from
God's initiative in Jesus Christ and the Spirit and this transcends historical divisions. This transcendent and thus eschatological oneness
can be realized only partially in history.

Second, this unity appears in a new way due to globalization and
the confluence of the religions everywhere. That which unites Christians impacts consciousness much more strongly in a context of
religious pluralism and interreligious interchange than in a world
restricted to inter-Christian debate.

Third, the unity Christians actually share from the grace of God
impels a quest for greater historical unity. This seems so self-evident
and so strong an impulse that churches that do not in some way reach
out for communion with other churches have to be judged by this
mark of the church. A postmodern situation where few churches have

not internalized some measure of historical consciousness makes this all the more evident. There is no one historical or organizational form of unity; any number of formulas could work. Historical church unity is realized by degrees. Therefore to abstain from all interest in commerce with other Christian churches would raise questions about the authenticity of any given church.

Fourth, however, not only historical consciousness but also the apostolic witness and the apostolic church show that the unity among the churches does not necessarily involve uniformity but has to be pluralistic. Unity does not mean the destruction of diverse, rich, vital, and authentic Christian traditions that adhere to scriptural and apostolic norms. These many traditions have to be preserved in formulas for communion.

Catholicity. Faith and Order offers a good place to begin a brief discussion of the subtle concept of catholicity.

> The essential catholicity of the Church is confronted with divisions between and within the Christian communities regarding their life and preaching of the Gospel. Its catholicity transcends all barriers and proclaims God's word to all peoples: where the whole mystery of Christ is present, there too is the Church catholic. However, the catholicity of the Church is challenged by the fact that the integrity of the Gospel is not adequately preached to all; the fullness of communion is not offered to all. Nevertheless, the Spirit given to the Church is the Spirit of the Lordship of Christ over all creation and all times. The Church is called to remove all obstacles to the full embodiment of what is already its nature by the power of the Holy Spirit. (NMC, 55)

This statement presupposes rather than defines the meaning of catholicity. It requires interpretation of the meaning of this characteristic of the church.

Catholicity refers to the Christian church in its wholeness or full extension as distinct from a local community. It is the universal church of which Christ is the head in the metaphor from Ephesians. It also implies the universal relevance of the church, its openness to the entire world or *oikumene*. But in the course of the church's development, catholicity acquired other meanings and uses.[15] For example, Augustine used it polemically against the Donatist church: how could a local church be a true church if it stood against the church that geographically filled the world? Such a use by one church against another no longer convinces in a pluralistic situation, especially when there is a consensus today that the whole church may be realized in any given part. The defining quality of authentic catholicity, then, when applied to a particular church, lies in that church's embodiment of the substance of the whole church within itself. Catholicity has to do with a church's identity, its representation of the universal essentials in its particular individuality, not its extension or number of members. Catholicity is thus intimately related to the unity of the church just described and the apostolicity of the church to be described next.[16]

The catholicity of the church has to be understood today in the context that began to emerge in ecclesiology during the sixteenth century and has grown since. More specifically, our new ecclesiological climate provides a common recognition of pluralism among the churches that together make up the whole church, a much clearer sense of a whole-part distinction, and an increasing mutual appreciation among the churches. Many different churches today can claim apostolicity.

The dimension of catholicity that connotes the openness of the church to the entire world entails a missionary character of the church. It also implies inculturation in many different regions and cultures if it is to be genuinely applicable to all peoples.[17] And inculturation in its turn entails pluralism. The deep logic of catholicity, therefore, requires an effort at defining those dimension of the church that are precisely universal within the pluralism.

---

15. Küng discusses catholicity in *Church*, 296–319.

16. "The catholicity of the church, therefore, consists in a notion of entirety, based on identity and resulting in universality. From this it is clear that unity and catholicity go together; if the church is one, it must be universal, if it is universal it must be one. Unity and catholicity are two interwoven dimensions of one and the same church." Küng, *Church*, 303.

17. I prescind here from the question of the role of the church in the salvation of all peoples. This open question is better treated in christology, and it should not be one that divides the church. Nevertheless it remains an important issue with a significant bearing on missionary policy and activity.

Like the mark of unity, the imperative of catholicity must address ecclesial fragmentation so that division within and against itself does not negate the church's relation to the whole world. This imperative requires attention of particular churches to the whole church so that each church can better mirror the essential whole within itself. Each church should feel called upon to recognize other churches as parts of a truly catholic church.

Apostolicity. Apostolicity refers to the authenticity of the church as measured by its continuity with the norms of faith as they were constituted in the original formation of the church in what is called the apostolic period. The dates of this period are not clearly defined or agreed upon. Apostolicity is a quality of both the whole church and of individual churches. The Faith and Order Commission describes its relevance in this way:

> The essential apostolicity of the Church stands in contrast to shortcomings and errors of the churches in their proclamation of the Word of God. Nevertheless, this apostolicity is witnessed to in the many ways in which the Church, under the guidance of the Holy Spirit, has been faithful to the testimony of the apostles concerning Jesus Christ. The Church is called to return continuously to the apostolic truth and to be renewed in its worship and mission stemming from its apostolic origin (cf. Acts 2:42–47). By doing so it makes visible, and does justice to, the apostolic Gospel which is already given to it and works in it in the Spirit, making it the Church. (NMC, 56)

This quality of the church is not the same as the several institutional vehicles that were created to insure and preserve it, but neither would it have been possible to preserve apostolicity without some such historical means.[18] The question that apostolicity

---

18. Apostles, distinct from "the twelve," and prophets were the first public witnesses to the original revelation and faith. Apostolic succession does not refer to successors to the apostles, since there could be no further "original" witnesses, but to the ongoing task or commission to remain faithful to the original witness. The subject of this task was therefore not another group of individuals, but the whole church. The church is called to be apostolic, that is, to continue to witness to the apostolic faith. This fidelity was insured by institutional means which gradually evolved; several were in place by the end of the second century: monarchical bishops who were appointed in succession to

raises relative to the whole church concerns the degree of flexibility among the churches in recognizing different structures for preserving fidelity to apostolic faith. Recognition of apostolicity is central to unity and catholicity. More deeply and crucially, apostolic faith has to be preserved existentially, and different institutions can and have functioned to make this happen. Succession in the office of bishop represents a valid and, because of its historical success, a recommended office in the church.[19] But in itself it does not guarantee apostolicity, and apostolicity can be maintained without it.

Apostolicity too has to be understood tensively because historical process is marked by both continuity and change. The only way in which new forms can retain their continuity with the past involves adjustment, interpretation, and analogy. Apostolicity cannot exist apart from the tension between sameness and difference of any given church and its institutions relative to apostolic origins. Therefore, on the one hand, churches cannot simply reproduce the structures of the primitive apostolic church; they will always carry different meaning in a different historical context. But, on the other hand, churches have to make the case for the continuity between themselves and the apostolic faith contained in apostolic structures.

Holiness: the church and sin.

The essential holiness of the Church stands in contrast to sin, individual as well as communal. This holiness is witnessed to in every generation in the lives of holy men and women, as well as in the holy words the Church proclaims and the holy acts it performs in the name of God, the All-Holy. Nevertheless, in the course of the Church's history sin has again and again disfigured its witness, and run counter to the Church's true nature and vocation. Therefore in the Church there has been again and again God's ever-new offer of forgiveness, together with the call for repentance, renewal and reform. Responding to

---

churches and in communion with neighboring bishops, writings that were commonly accepted and read, and which had almost filled up the present canon, orders or manuals of community life and worship, creeds, catechesis, letter writing, travel and visitations among churches, synods. See CCH, I, 141–97.

19. BEM, "Ministry," 53b.

this call means fuller visible embodiment of the holiness that belongs to its nature. (NMC, 54)

A discussion of the holiness of the church requires preliminary clarifications of different ways of looking at the matter and different uses of language. Without some nuance, the church's claim to holiness may seem ridiculous to outsiders. For example, it is important to recognize a difference and yet a relatedness between sacrality and moral uprightness. Holiness is a quality of God and can only be predicated of created things insofar as they participate in and mediate God's holiness. There is a tendency to attribute moral uprightness within the church to God's grace, and thus the term "holiness" may suggest an existential union with God on the part of a person or a group. This rather extended sense is quite common.

The tension between the eschatological and the historical seems particularly taut in considerations of the church's holiness. The distinction between an objective and a subjective holiness of the church helps to clarify things. Objectively the church is holy insofar as it actually reflects and mediates God's gracious presence in its scripture, preaching, doctrine, forms of worship and sacrament. These institutions that mediate God's presence to human subjectivity as the effects of God's Spirit constitute the church. The action of God in scripture and sacrament is not strictly dependent upon the moral uprightness of ministers or people, but is known in God's promise and encountered in the objective forms and ministrations. Subjectively, the holiness of the church reflects the measure in which the existential life of the church and its members bear witness to the power of God's Spirit or grace in their lives. What Augustine referred to as the fruitfulness of the sacraments depended on or was mediated in the faith and charity of the faithful. But if this distinction of the church's objective holiness from its existential or subjective holiness were pushed to an extreme, where a loose-living church claimed holiness, it would lose credibility. The tension, and with it the existence of the mark, requires some correlation between the words and actions of the church.

Therefore, historically, one must reckon with degrees of holiness within the church. The objective ideal postulates that the church be a reflection of God's presence and activity in the world, that as a people the church's actions and general comportment correspond with its public message. It provides a historical sphere or "place" of God's being available as in the temple of the Spirit or the body of Christ or a people who reflect their covenant with God.

The holiness of the church leads to the topic of sin. "All the churches agree that there is sin, corporate and individual, in the Church's history (cf. Rev 2:2)" (NMC, commentary at 56). But the churches have different ways of understanding how sin affects the church and different linguistic styles. Faith and Order summarizes these positions nicely:

> For some, it is impossible to say "the Church sins" because they see the Church as a gift of God, sharing in God's holiness. The Church is the spotless bride of Christ (cf. Eph 5:25–27); it is a communion in the Holy Spirit, the holy people of God, justified by grace through faith in Christ (cf. Rom 3:22; Eph 2:8–9). As such, the Church cannot sin. The gift is lived out in fragile human beings who are liable to sin, but the sins of the members of the Church are not the sins of the Church. The Church is rather the locus of salvation and healing (cf. Is 53; Lk 4:18–19). According to this perspective one can, and must, speak only of the sin of the members of the Church and of groups within the Church, a situation described by the parable of the wheat and the chaff (cf. Mt 13:24–30), and by the Augustinian formula of *corpus permixtum*. Others, while they too state that the Church, as the creature of God's Word and Spirit, the body of Christ, is holy and without sin, say at the same time that it does sin. They say this because they define the Church as the communion of its members who — although they are justified believers brought to birth by the Spirit, and Christ's own body — in this world are still sinful human beings (cf. 1 Jn 1:8–10). (NMC, commentary at 56)

In the end, can there be a consensus among the churches about what the very nature of the church is? Although they live within that common reality, finding the words to state it plainly frequently fails. But all churches should be able to recognize themselves as the people of God, the body of Christ, and the house of God's Spirit. They should also be able to appropriate to themselves the marks of the church and be able to see them in other churches.

THE PURPOSE OR MISSION OF THE CHURCH

The last section addressed the nature of the church. The discussion of the purpose of the church that follows reflects the interaction between its nature and its mission. Together, the nature and purpose of an organization form a mutual relationship that determines the ontology of its being and the character of its existence. There is no nature apart from its purpose: the purpose teleologically determines the nature of the group; the nature provides the resources to accomplish the purpose. The two dimensions together and interactively constitute the church. In ecclesiology, it would be natural to expect that the purpose of the church be developed under the category of its mission and to some extent it has. But the category of mission has also been narrowed to fit the sphere of missionary activity. Moreover, in the late nineteenth and early twentieth centuries, missiology developed as a subdiscipline in its own right. As a result, a tension has emerged between ecclesiologies that stress the nature of the church and those that highlight the mission of the church. One tendency in ecclesiology is to look inward at what the church is called to become; the other tendency is to look outward at what the church is called to do in the world. This tension has generated a good deal of differentiation in the discipline of ecclesiology. It can also represent a healthy catalyst for thinking about the church.

The mission of the church has to accord with its nature, but no reflection on the nature of the church is adequate without concern for its mission. These two dimensions have to be held together so that they are always seen as interacting with each other. The recognition that this tension can be benign and creative will allow more room for openness to and acceptance of the emphases on both sides of the spectrum. With this in mind, the tension dictates the three-part structure of this section. The first section lays out and then develops more thoroughly the tension as it is expressed in Faith and Order's *The Nature and Mission of the Church*. Once the tension between these two distinct points of view on the church has been set up, the second and third parts deal with each side of the tension between community and mission from the perspective of the other side. Thus the second section will examine the idea of becoming "community" as a *goal* or mission of the church, and the third section the idea that "mission" defines the very *nature* of the church.

The Sign and Instrument of God's Design

Faith and Order has a subheading in its document on *The Nature and Mission of the Church* which is entitled "The Sign and Instrument of God's Intention and Plan for the World."[20] This short statement expresses well the polarity between the nature and purpose of the church. The polarity consists in a tension between the call to develop its nature as a sign of God's design for the world and the call to be an instrument advancing that design in the world. "The one, holy, catholic and apostolic Church is sign and instrument of God's intention and plan for the whole world. Already participating in the love and life of God, the Church is a prophetic sign which points beyond itself to the purpose of all creation, the fulfillment of the Kingdom of God. For this reason Jesus called his followers the 'salt of the earth', 'the light of the world' and 'a city built on a hill' (Mt 5:13–16)" (NMC, 43). More explicitly, the tension lies between being a "client" of Jesus, the object of Jesus Christ's mediation, and a disciple or follower of Jesus, the participating subject of Jesus Christ's mission to the world. The duality of the response, the way the two themes belong together, is expressed easily and without strain: "Aware of God's saving presence in the world, the Church already praises and glorifies the Triune God through worship and discipleship, and serves God's plan. Yet the Church does so not only for itself, but rather renders praise and thanks on behalf of all peoples for God's grace and the forgiveness of sins" (NMC, 44).

Another way of expressing the polarity consists in reading it in terms of two distinct facets or dimensions of one response to the initiative of God's grace in the event of Jesus Christ. One facet responds directly to God and renders thanks to God in the form of worship

---

20. NMC, 43–47.

and praise; another facet is directed under the impulse of grace to the world, history, and fellow human beings so that the church may be the instrument of God's outreach to all. The first response recognizes the transcendent and God-given character of its being. "Therefore the visible organizational structures of the Church must always be seen and judged, for good or ill, in the light of God's gifts of salvation in Christ, celebrated in the Liturgy (cf. Heb 12:18–24)" (NMC, 45). The other dimension of the response looks outward and sees the church as God's vehicle in the world: the church serves as the instrument of God's plan in history, sent to proclaim the Good News in work and action, thus making actual in history God's presence (NMC, 46). The language of the first dimension reflects human dependence and receptiveness in relation to God's grace and assumes the attitude of a community of worship and thanksgiving. The language of the second dimension is more active and outward looking. This response is formulated in terms of "discipleship" and "being sent," so that the church appears as an "instrument" of God's intentions and activity. "As instrument of God's plan the Church is the community of people called by God and sent as Christ's disciples to proclaim the Good News in word and deed, that the world may believe (cf. Lk 24:46–49). Thus it makes present throughout history 'the tender mercy of our God' (Lk. 1:78)" (NMC, 46). "The integrity of the Church as God's instrument is at stake in witness through proclamation, and concrete actions in union with all people of goodwill, for the sake of justice, peace, and the integrity of creation" (NMC, 47).

Summarizing this first point, the ecclesiology of Faith and Order uses the language of "sign and instrument" to reflect on the dual dimensions of the one response of the church to God's initiative in Jesus Christ. This action of God and human response constitute the church; it is the faith-response to God's initiative around which church as organization was and is formed. The faith response, however, has two dimensions that reflect the two-fold commandment of love of God and love of neighbor. The creative interaction between these two dimensions is so important for the self-understanding of the church that more commentary is necessary, first on a substantive and theological or ontological level, and then on how this gets played out sociologically.

Community and mission on a theological level. This first reflection on the tension between the nature and mission of the church on a theological level shows how the question of the church's mission transforms the initial understanding of the church's nature. Practically speaking, the whole church in all of its churches finds itself in the three theological images drawn from scripture: the people of God, the body of Christ, and the temple of the Spirit. All churches view themselves as a community of the people whom God has addressed in Jesus Christ and who respond in faith and love. The second dimension of the church, however, its mission, calls up a theological understanding that relates the organization called church to God's providence in history, to God's will for the whole human species, and the whole world. The question of the church's purpose, an answer to the question of what the church is for, often remains implicit in ecclesiology or receives a shallow answer in a treatment of its missionary activity. As crucial as that question is, it does not go to the deeper theological issue by critically reflecting on just what the role of the church in human history is within the large horizon of human existence itself. Does it have a part to play in the destiny of the human race as a whole? If so, what is it? Why did the church appear so late in history if it has such a role? And why has it not touched more human lives after two millennia if it has such a global mission? The issues of missionary strategy really depend on these much more basic considerations.

The New Testament contains no single theological response to the question of the constituting mission of the church. As a pluralistic collection of writings, the New Testament supports more than one conception of the mission of the church. Moreover, one can make the case that the mission of the church is to become ever more itself, and thus more strongly and clearly a people of God, a body of Christ, and a temple or house of the Spirit.[21] But at the same time, the New Testament proposes another distinctive response, namely, that the church is meant to continue in history the ministry of Jesus of

---

21. This is the implicit answer to the question of the purpose of the church by those who take the missionary mandate as an adequate response. To "go . . . and make disciples of all nations" (Matt 28:19) entails the simple purpose of growth and extension of what the church already is.

Nazareth. The church is the community of disciples who are called
and sent to do in history what Jesus did in his ministry now that
he is physically absent.[22] The signs of the Spirit of God were clari-
fied in the ministry of Jesus, and that Spirit continues to animate a
community so that it became an extension of Jesus' ministry and a
continuing visible presence of Jesus Christ's power in world history.
This response has the advantage of being not only a theological conception or vision, but also a description of the moving force in the
formation of the church.

A theological conception of the nature of the church as community and its constituting mission should form a perfect unity.[23] When
the foundational images of the church that in different ways capture
its nature are explicitly placed within the context of the mission or
purpose of the church in history, they broaden considerably the range
of meanings that these metaphors release. For example, the people
of God cannot be understood as a static community set aside from
society but must be understood in the light of this mission from God.
"Sent as Christ's disciples, the people of God must witness to and
participate in God's reconciliation, healing, and transformation of
creation" (NMC, 47).[24] The body of Christ is a symbol for a community within which Christ dwells and of which he is head. In the
context of mission, this body has to be understood as a body acting
in the world in the pattern of the ministry of Jesus of Nazareth. The
temple of the Spirit cannot be understood as having its doors closed
to the world. In the context of the mission and purpose of the church
under God's providence in history, the church sends out its members
as disciples into the world.

---

22. This structure appears rather plainly in Luke because he adopted an extended
narrative-historical framework for his writing and told the story of the Spirit of God in
two volumes in which the ministry of Jesus reached out into world history through the
Jesus movement and the gradual formation of the church.

23. In actual history there is and will always be a tension between these two dimensions that constitute the church. The more practical tension between these two
facets will be considered below.

24. What is being called into question here is not any portion of the church withdrawing from the world for prayer, contemplation, and witness to the world, but the
idea that being isolated from society could be normative for the church as such. Mo-
nastic life or other forms of withdrawal from society may be salutary for some, but this
cannot be a norm for the church as such.

Tension between maintenance and mission. The theoretical tension between the nature and purpose of a group contained in its self-understanding actualizes itself in the practical life of the church. The practical tension between the nature and mission of the church can be brought out with the sociological distinction between maintenance and mission.[25] Maintenance refers to the set of social operations designed to nurture and enhance the health of the organization. Mission refers to the set of social operations that are intended to put into effective practice the goals for which the organization was founded or created. The tension can be broadly described in terms of behaviors that are inner directed and others that are outer directed. These themes may be associated in Christian language with grace and freedom, with God's action in and on the church and the church's action in the world.

It was just shown that no theoretical conflict separates these two dimensions of any organization for together they define its being. But in practice the one or other set of operations can come to dominate its existence. There could be all sorts of legitimate reasons for this: the demands of the cultural context, the actual historical situation in which it finds itself, the particular condition or health of a church at a given time, and so on. It may be a matter of emphasis that requires a certain compromise or neglect of the other side of its comprehensive and integrated life. One also has to expect that different churches will have different characters with different emphases. The second and third parts of this section will describe how these two dimensions of the church can be integrated on a conceptual level.

The Goal of Being a Sign Community

Faith and Order's document on *The Nature and Mission of the Church* offers a concise statement of what it calls "The Mission of the Church."[26] I take up each side of the polarity between nature and mission separately in order to highlight the distinct focus that each

---

25. Gregory Baum, "Contradictions in the Catholic Church," *Theology and Society* (New York: Paulist Press, 1987), 230–46.

26. NMC, 34–42. This statement of the purpose or mission of the church sets up the section that follows it and further develops it: "The Church as Sign and Instrument of God's Intention and Plan for the World," NMC, 43–47.

pole contributes to an understanding of the church. But to highlight how the two foci reciprocally relate to each other, the subheadings are phrased in a paradoxical way. The *goal* of the church can be conceived as constituting its very being, and the *nature* of the church can be conceived as being a mission. We begin with a consideration of Faith and Order's text and then proceed to commentary on it.

The nature and being of the church can be understood by conceiving it as a crystallization of God's intention for creation. "It is God's design to gather all creation under the Lordship of Christ (cf. Eph 1:10), and to bring humanity and all creation into communion. As a reflection of the communion in the Triune God, the Church is God's instrument in fulfilling this goal. The Church is called to manifest God's mercy to humanity, and to bring humanity to its purpose — to praise and glorify God together with all the heavenly hosts. The mission of the Church is to serve the purpose of God as a gift given to the world in order that all may believe (cf. Jn 17:21)" (NMC, 34).

In this text the Faith and Order Commission emphasizes that the role or mission of the church in the broad plan of God for creation is to manifest or sign forth for the world the world's relation to God and God's relation to it. One could say that the mission of the church is to be itself authentically, because as such it becomes a sign that witnesses to the world its true identity in God's scheme of things. "In exercising its mission, the Church cannot be true to itself without giving witness (martyria) to God's will for the salvation and transformation of the world. That is why it started at once preaching the Word, bearing witness to the great deeds of God and inviting everyone to repentance (metanoia), baptism (cf. Acts 2:37–38) and the fuller life that is enjoyed by the followers of Jesus (cf. Jn 10:10)" (NMC, 37).

Expressing the goal and purpose of the church as a perseverance and strengthening of its nature underlines the point that the church does not require the conversion of every human being for it to fulfill its purpose in history. The quality, in the sense of the clarity, of the sign of God's presence and action in the world becomes far more important than that the church absorb the world into itself.[27]

---

27. Some ecclesiologists have grasped this basic point and conceive the church precisely as designed to be a minority that gives witness to the rest of the ultimate goal of

Of course too much concern with the internal life of the church in a self-conscious desire for perfection in the Christian life may subvert the very thing it seeks to accomplish. A missionary motivation is needed to prevent a narrow self-absorption. A church becomes a sign to the degree that as a community it communicates, that is, it actually reflects outside itself the grace and power of God's Spirit within itself. Its ministry places at the disposal of the members of the church what is needed to nurture their lives of faith. The church directs its ministry inward in order to build up the community into the likeness of a people of God, the body of Christ, and the temple of God's Spirit. Ministry encourages a church that praises and worships God: principal activities gravitate around doxology and other practices that nurture faith. Chapter 6 will develop the structured activities by which the church nourishes its internal life. But consideration of the church's mission shows that these activities also sign forth God's presence and power to the world.

Use of the term "sacrament" to designate the church. In connection with the church being a sign, Faith and Order takes up the use of the term "sacrament" by some churches to describe the church as a whole.[28] It indicates that while some churches use this language to harness together in dialectical unity the grace and human freedom that constitute the church and impel its mission, other churches see dangers in this concept. "The churches who use the expression 'Church as Sacrament' do so because they understand the Church as an effective sign of what God wishes for the world: namely, the communion of all together and with the Triune God, the joy for which God created the world (notwithstanding the sinfulness of Christians)." But other churches are skeptical for two main reasons: "(1) the need for a clear distinction between the Church and Sacraments: the Sacraments are the means of salvation through which Christ sustains the Church, and not actions by which the Church realizes or actualizes itself; and (2) the use of the word 'Sacrament' for the Church obscures the fact that, for them, the Church is a sign

---

all humankind. See, for example, Juan Luis Segundo, *The Community Called Church* (Maryknoll, N.Y.: Orbis Books, 1973), 78–86, 89–91.

28. NMC, commentary following 48. The citations of NMC in this extended paragraph are from this text.

and instrument of God's intention and plan — but it is so as a communion which, while being holy, is still subject to sin." Beyond that, different churches have developed the language of their sacramental theology differently so that the term "sacrament" carries diverse meanings and overtones.

Faith and Order resolves this problem simply by calling attention to it. Some churches use the idea that the church exists as a kind of primal sacrament that is not to be confused with the particular sacraments such as baptism and eucharist and that does not actualize itself but is the sign and instrument of God's activity. Therefore, if the dangers are avoided, such language is useful in describing the church. But churches are hardly bound to use it. Given the pluralism of the understanding how sacraments work, it would probably not be good for a transdenominational ecclesiology to use this language. The idea of a sign in the deep sense of a symbol can be useful here without employing the term "sacrament." But in every case, when the church is called sign, or symbol, or sacrament in the context of mission, the sense is transformed by a context that demands performance. The church becomes a sign in its actual signing forth or witnessing.

God's Mission Has a Church

Reflection on the mission of the church during the second half of the twentieth century gradually developed this formula that reverses the normal way of looking at things, namely, the church has a mission. Instead of establishing the substantial nature of the church and adding on to it a mission, study of the origins of the church gradually revealed anew the priority of God's mission in Jesus Christ to the church. Thus the proposition that "the mission has a church." This dynamic, historical way of understanding the church "turns inside out" all ideas of a static church that is established once for all.[29] God takes the initiative; logically and chronologically the mission is prior to the church. The church took shape around the originating impulse of God in Jesus toward the kingdom of God in history and finds its raison d'être in continuing to mediate God's empowerment and supply the social basis for this mission. This dialectic should not

---

29. J. C. Hoekendijk, *The Church Inside Out* (London: SMC, 1967), 30–44.

be construed in terms of community versus mission but of community as mission. The church is a mission church to the degree that as a community it manifests the grace and power of God's Spirit by its active life in the world.

This view of things can be discerned in the formulations of Faith and Order. "As persons who acknowledge Jesus Christ as Lord and Savior, Christians are called to proclaim the Gospel in word and deed. They are to address those who have not heard, as well as those who are no longer living according to the Gospel, the Good News of the reign of God. They are called to live its values and to be a foretaste of that reign in the world. Mission thus belongs to the very being of the Church." (NMC, 35).[30]

In its fullest statement of the engagement of the world in the sense of society, Faith and Order draws its inspiration from the ministry of Jesus.

> The Church is called and empowered to share the suffering of all by advocacy and care for the poor, the needy and the marginalized. This entails critically analyzing and exposing unjust structures, and working for their transformation. The Church is called to proclaim the words of hope and comfort of the Gospel, by its works of compassion and mercy (cf. Lk.4:18–19). This faithful witness may involve Christians themselves in suffering for the sake of the Gospel. The Church is called to heal and reconcile broken human relationships and to be God's instrument in the reconciliation of human division and hatred (cf. 2 Cor. 5:18–21). It is also called, together with all people of goodwill, to care for the integrity of creation in addressing the abuse and destruction of God's creation, and to participate in God's healing of broken relationships between creation and humanity. (NMC, 40)

---

30. This view is supported with dynamic, economic trinitarian language. "The Church, embodying in its own life the mystery of salvation and the transfiguration of humanity, participates in the mission of Christ to reconcile all things to God and to one another through Christ (cf. 2 Cor 5:18–21, Rom 8:18–25). Through its worship (leitourgia); service, which includes the stewardship of creation (diakonia); and proclamation (kerygma) the Church participates in and points to the reality of the Kingdom of God. In the power of the Holy Spirit the Church testifies to the divine mission in which the Father sent the Son to be the Savior of the world" (NMC, 36).

The conviction that the mission of God has a church responds directly to the question of the church's role in history. The church embodies and actualizes in history the mission of God, or God's will for history, that Jesus expressed as the kingdom of God. This kingdom ultimately has to be regarded as eschatological, but its power in history is mediated in an overt and explicit way by the church's response to God's initiative in Christ and the Spirit.

The church is carried and supported by a mission with universal relevance; the good news of God and God's grace revealed in Jesus is relevant for all humankind. This universal scope is expressed by Faith and Order in this way: "In the power of the Holy Spirit, the Church is called to proclaim faithfully the whole teaching of Christ and to share the Good News of the Kingdom — that is, the totality of apostolic faith, life and witness — with everyone throughout the entire world. Thus the Church seeks faithfully to proclaim and live the love of God for all, and to fulfill Christ's mission for the salvation and transformation of the world, to the glory of God" (NMC, 41). When discussion of missionary activity becomes more concrete and takes up the question of how the church reaches out to people of other faiths, one finds at least two conceptions of the church and its mission that conflict with each other. The one is most sharply defined as ecclesiocentrist; the other may be called pluralist. These views are closely related to positions in christology on the status of Jesus Christ relative to the savior figures in other religions or other religions themselves. These two positions make a difference in the way the church conceives its mission in the world and they will have to be discussed in chapter 7.

The church's ministry puts at the disposal of the members of the church what is needed to support them in their Christian lives. Some ministry focuses on building up the nature of the church; other forms of ministry and church activity support engagement in the world after the pattern of Jesus' public ministry. To be a member ideally entails not only being a client of Jesus, but also being a disciple, a follower of Jesus, one who takes up his mission by belonging to the organization of disciples who follow him. Chapters 6 and 7 will take up various activities of the church and the ministries that support them. Chapter 6 will focus on the ministries and activities that nurture the church as a community, and chapter 7 will address ministries and activities that express the church's mission to the world. The two forms of activity and ministry can be distinguished by their direction *ad intra* and *ad extra*. But they cannot be separated, because they mutually enhance each other, and should not be conceived as competing with each other in importance.

ECCLESIAL EXISTENCE

A Christian ordinarily belongs to the Christian church. To be a member involves internalizing the community and being responsible within it, for it, and to its ideals. In the tension between being an individual and a member, Christians can objectify the church and distance themselves from it, but never completely. For the experience of Christians, insofar as they are Christians, ultimately derives from church mediation. The church shapes the member's view of the world and existence. The last section of this and the next four chapters functions as a summary by describing in broad existential strokes the aspect of the church treated in the chapter. This is done by transposing the content of the chapter into the language of experience, conviction, and motivation.

The church is a religious organization. People participate in the church for religious reasons; it is a "place" that offers answers to ultimate questions of transcendence. Deep down in this commitment lies a conviction that true answers to these large questions about human existence cannot be merely individual; they have to be public and found in community. Moreover, they cannot be simply humanly generated, an individual or group projection, but must be revealed by and received from the source and goal of existence itself. The Christian community shares a common faith that God has revealed God's self as the fundamental logic of human existence in Jesus of Nazareth who is the Christ.

People who belong to the church know that it is a historical organization that had a beginning at a point in time and developed over the centuries. They also believe, however, that these beginnings and the church's history is a function of God's providential will and influence. The center and source of the church and its relation to God is

Jesus of Nazareth in whom God was present and acted on behalf of all humankind. The Christian community lives in a relationship to Jesus Christ as a mediation between God and human existence.

The nature and purpose of the church can only adequately be described in religious language. Such language is symbolic because it transcends empirical reference and points to, participates in, and discloses the relationship of the community to God that Christians have experienced from the beginning. Three standard images from the scriptures are used by Christians to express their conviction of the theological foundations of the church. The church is a people of God, in the line of the experience of Israel. This experience need not be interpreted exclusively relative to other religions; in fact many Christians are convinced that the Christian church is a continuation of Jewish revelation accommodated for Gentiles: Jesus was a Jew. From the very beginning the disciples of Jesus experienced God as Spirit at work in their movement, and Spirit language has consistently been used to express God's presence to the community. But this Spirit is not undifferentiated: Jesus reveals what is of the Spirit in the community, and the Spirit makes the risen Jesus present to the community and thus the body of Christ. This primary religious language about the church is used universally by Christians who subject it to a variety of theological interpretations. This symbolic language inevitably takes on different shades of meaning when it refers to churches of different sizes, shapes, contexts, and cultural styles of life.

All Christians are convinced that the church rests on the constant initiatives of God which in turn the church mediates or represents to the members. This experience and conviction lead spontaneously to an exalted language about the church bordering on hyperbole. But few are unaware of the fact that the church is a finite, limited, and sinful community in history. They know the difference between life in the world and in the promised sphere of God. Thus the traditional language of marks or signs of true church are, like all religious symbols, dialectical and tensive. Concretely, they point to finite and at times broken realities that communicate a promise of transcendent perfection; they also continually urge reform. The church is one, united in one Spirit, Christ, faith, baptism, and Lord's Supper, and yet divided.

Christians consistently and in various ways strive to retain the community's continuity with apostolic origins, and yet the whole church is ever new and plural in its forms. The church is catholic or universally relevant in several senses and potentialities, but never perfectly so. The church is holy in its structures and members when they effectively mediate and receive God's Spirit, but Christians know the sins of the church, as an organization and in its members, as they resist the power of the Spirit.

All Christians can affirm together a broad statement about the purpose or mission and goal of the church: the church is meant to keep alive in history the message and ministry of Jesus, indeed, to make them effective in the members' own lives and through them in the world, in society, and in history. All organizations share a certain polarity or dual urgency between concern for the community's existence and for its mission. These represent impulses that turn inward and outward respectively. The two thrusts, so to speak, have theological grounding. This results frequently enough in two distinct tendencies in the church affecting individuals and whole communities. In some churches a conception of Christian life will emphasize building up a community of worship and fellowship that grows in stature before God; other churches may look constantly on the needs of the world and orient themselves with a rhetoric of service to the kingdom of God in history. The mission of the church will best be served not in some neutral balance between competing forces. An integrated Christian community will allow these two dimensions to animate and reinforce each other. In the Christian conception of human existence, love and service of the other constitute a response to God.

Globalization and a new awareness of other vital and self-conscious religions in the world with which the Christian church must get along have set a new context for understanding the nature and mission of the church. The idea that the Christian church is a sign-community in and for the world integrates the themes of community and mission and defines the purpose of the church in the twenty-first century. Just as Christians are convinced that Jesus was a function of the will and mission of God, that mission continues to support the church. The church lives within the mission of God, which Jesus called the kingdom of God. The kingdom of God that Jesus placed at the center of his preaching refers to God's will for justice and reconciliation in the world. The church is most fully itself when it becomes a community shaped by the values of Jesus which it displays to the world by working for their realization.

The hard questions. In each of the five loci in the template for understanding the church used in this book one finds what might be called "hard questions." These are issues that have divided churches and continue to do so in a way that makes them appear intractable. I will not attempt to resolve them. But a description of ecclesial existence should include an appreciation of the terms of the problems and a description of attitudes that can accommodate both sides of the seeming dilemma.

Two sets of antitheses, directly related to the organization of the church and the division of its ministries, formally belong to the discussion of the chapter that follows. But these antitheses involve conceptions that are so foundational and all encompassing that they have bearing on the nature of the church as a community. I distinguish the two, but they are closely related, and they usually exist together and reinforce each other. The one consists in an antithesis between a gathered community and a hierarchical community; the other is an antithesis between a congregational church, one whose basic unit is the congregation, and a larger universal organization.[31]

Both distinctions represent a priori conceptions of the church that function as hermeneutical filters for appreciating language about the church and deciding practical issues. Regarding the origins of the church from the perspective of the first distinction, one group will see church structure emerging by development out of the group of the disciples in dialogue with the environment; the other side will see church structure determined during the ministry of Jesus, or in a rapid linear development that reflects an exclusive will of God. In this view the church originated as a structured community so that

---

31. In between these two terms one might locate a "denomination," if by a denomination one means a larger organization of federated congregations that leave some degree of autonomy to the congregation. It is not necessary to negotiate the organizational structures and language of the churches at this point. The antithesis lies at the two ends of the spectrum. I am trying to get at quite different "ideas" of the church.

people are drawn into a divinely established institution. The second antithesis flows from the first and is self-explanatory. A congregationalist imagination conceives of the church as a local parish or autonomous community, which enters into relationships with other ecclesial communities without surrendering its autonomy; the seemingly antithetical position sees the church as a larger institution of which the congregation is a member or part. The one position spontaneously interprets larger institutional forms of church as important but not essential to its integral being; the other locates the essence of church in the larger communion of which the congregation is a part. The problem lies in two different fundamental imaginative frameworks within which the church is conceived: the one works "from below," so to speak; the other works "from above."[32] These differences are reflected in an observation by the United Church of Christ (USA) on BEM. When the UCC authors read BEM they observed a clash at a fundamental level "in which authority flows in a different direction than it is deemed to flow in the United Church of Christ."[33]

An existential-historical approach to these deep differences consists in representing a perspective that can appreciate the consistency, integrity, and finally the theological validity of both ideas. The point is not to construct a mediating conception of the church as a polity that integrates these values organizationally.[34] From the perspective of an experiential ecclesial existence and an ecclesiology from below, both of these conceptions have coherence and integrity in what they affirm, as distinct from what they tend to deny of the other. These are different ways of being Christian church that protect certain distinct values on each side.[35] Building organizational and more exactly

---

32. The problem does not consist in the impossibility of combining these two dimensions in a workable church polity that respects and integrates these seemingly competing lines of force. A number of different church polities succeed in doing just that. The problem lies in how much change is required at the extremes for churches at one end of the spectrum to recognize churches at the other end. Or, to shift the question, how much tolerance of the other position is necessary and possible?

33. BEMresponses, II.333. This statement points to a source of problems that other congregational or evangelical churches had with BEM.

34. This can be done and frequently is when churches with these different proclivities seek to enter into full communion with each other. This lies far beyond the boundaries of this text.

35. The typology constructed in CCH, II, 276–88 represents the values enshrined in these two ideas of the church.

juridical structures for the whole church that mediate and subsume these two ideas seems to be out of the question at this time. But mutual recognition, which is often experienced more by the ordinary faithful than by the leaders of the churches, can provide a significant penultimate goal. In the final chapter of this book I will introduce the idea of "partial communion" that may reflect a careful but open conception of ecclesial existence.

Chapter 4

Organization of the Church

Theological discussion of the nature and mission of the church as an abstract enterprise can yield a good deal of agreement. By contrast, the organizational structure of the church actualizes its nature and purpose in history. The issues of organization are much more concrete and specific and account for a considerable degree of the distinction, difference, and division among the churches. In addition, organization goes further than theological language to define the specific identity of churches.

The logical progression from the last chapter to the present discussion moves along a line of proportionality and teleology. Some measure of rationality or coherence in an organization suggests a certain correspondence between the nature and mission of a group and its organizational structure. Ordinarily the organizational structure of a church will reflect its mission according to a broad logic of the relation of means to ends. Theoretically, this coherence will extend to the activities of the group or body that will be discussed in chapters 6 and 7. The same kind of coherence is expected of a systematic and constructive account of the church.

The chapter is divided into five parts. The first lays out some premises that are at work in the discussion. They are not meant to be contentious but simply to raise up, clarify, and make explicit certain commonsensical assumptions about church organization. The second turns to the forms of ministry that govern Christian life most concretely in the congregations and parishes. The third part takes up larger organizational units of the church and the churches, while the fourth considers the question of the authority of ecclesiastical office, that is, both the authorization of the office itself and the authority it enjoys within the church as a community. The chapter concludes with a description of ecclesial existence from the perspective of organization.

COMMUNITY AND STRUCTURE

The church is an empirical historical organization with a specific membership that is defined theologically. The theological determination stems from the community's relationship to God. This elementary human-divine duality provides a framework for reflecting on the interaction between the community's being related to God and its organizational structure. Four reflections will help create a context for an analysis of the structure or organizational form of the church.[1]

A first reflection is directed to what may be called the inner and outer dimensions of the church and their relationship to each other. The church's organizational structure governs its empirical behaviors, and it may be codified in law or custom. In addition to its outer dimension, the church also has an inner life carried in the subjectivity of its members, in the intentions and motivations of those who make up the church. Unlike purely secular organizations, the church from the beginning has experienced the presence and power of God in its midst. Across the wide variety of witnesses to the life of the emerging community in the New Testament, the role of the Spirit of God in individual believers and in the corporate life of the church commands attention. The inner dimension of the church therefore does not merely consist in the subjectivity of its members but also refers to the presence and power of God as Spirit who defines the community and gives life to its organizational forms.

Friedrich Schleiermacher highlights the interactive and complementary character of the inner and outer dimensions of the church. He shows on a theological level how the two inseparable dimensions dynamically influence each other in a reciprocal way.[2] On the one

---

1. These reflections draw upon and expand the principles collected in chapter 2 and, as an introduction, relate them directly to the discussion of the organization of the church in this chapter.

2. See CCH, II, 331–33, 362–63. Schleiermacher called the two terms of this distinction "the visible and the invisible church." He thus takes up a distinction which

hand, the church as a visible organization obeys the laws and follows the patterns of all organizations in history. On this side of the ledger, one can expect all the limitations and glitches that one finds in other institutions, whether they be small informal groups or larger bureaucratic agencies. Here we find the strengths and weaknesses of particularity and finitude, as well as the infections of sin and infidelity. On the other hand, the church confesses and sometimes manifests the effects of the power of the Spirit in its life. The Spirit of God, understood according to the revelation of Jesus Christ, constitutes the impulse toward pure truth, moral goodness, and unity in the church. In the end, however, the inseparability of these two dimensions of the church has to be highlighted; one can distinguish these dimensions, but they cannot be isolated or separated from each other. The tension between them is interactive and dynamic; together they compose an existential, historical community that moves with history.

Another reflection revolves around the way the church is both a function of its members and prior to its members. I draw this proposition from the sociology of knowledge and give it a theological application.

The relationship between an objective institution and the subjectivity of its members can be understood in three logical moments, as distinct from chronological steps. First, an institution or organization has no existence apart from the members that constitute it. Institutions exist precisely as the patterns of behaviors of the people who belong. But, second, the language, system of understanding, and behavior patterns that are projected by human subjectivity take on a type of objective social solidity independent of the subjectivity of any individual person in it. These remain the standard patterns of group behavior into which individuals are socialized. Thus, third, this corporate objectivity shapes and determines the subjectivity of

---

has a long history in ecclesiology going back especially to Augustine and gaining some prominence in the ecclesiologies of the Reformation. But whereas the meaning of the distinction between the visible and invisible church contains many variations, and whereas the distinction has been ecumenically contentious, Schleiermacher's usage co-opts the phrase and provides it with a meaning that is broadly acceptable across ecclesiological traditions. The distinction does not need to be called by the designation Schleiermacher assigned it.

successive waves of members in the community giving it a certain objective authority in defining the nature of reality. On the one hand, the objective institutions are still dependent on the subjectivity of the members; on the other hand, they are not easily altered. Change usually comes slowly and is wrought by a slow, steady shifting of the corporate consciousness of the whole group.[3]

A number of corollaries significant for this discussion can be drawn from this dialectical interaction between subjectivity and objectivity, or freedom and social structure. One is the axiom already announced that the church is both a function of its members and prior to its members. From one point of view, the members constitute the church. From another point of view, the church in drawing members into itself forms new members by its "objective" patterns of behavior and corporate structures. But this principle of reciprocity or mutual influence has an important theological application that mediates between two seminal but sometimes conflicting views of the church. The one views the church "from below," as being a malleable institution able to be changed and adapted by its members at any given time to meet historical exigencies. The other views the church "from above," as a more or less constant structure established on the basis of its theological pillars, Jesus Christ and the Holy Spirit. From this perspective the many dimensions of the origins of the church and their interpretations will carry an authoritative value. Members conform to the church, not the church to its members. A balanced view of the church would be able to hold these two conceptions together in tension by admitting the truth of both. Such a view would recognize that churches may emphasize one side of the polarity without ruling out the other side altogether.[4]

---

3. Karl Mannheim, *Ideology and Utopia: An Introduction to the Sociology of Knowledge* (New York: Harcourt Brace, A Harvest Book, 1985), 55–108, 264–311; Peter Berger and Thomas Luckmann, *The Social Construction of Reality* (Garden City, N.Y.: Doubleday Anchor, 1967), passim.

4. This polarity correlates with the two seemingly antithetical basic ideas of the church discussed in the last chapter and with two correlatively different conceptions of the grounds of ministerial office discussed in this chapter. This sociological contrast does not explain the different theological conceptions in a reductive way. But it helps show how they can both be held together as two aspects of a larger reality.

Another corollary flowing from the subjective and objective dimensions of an organization and hence the church is a tension between what may be termed "community" and "structure," or "institution."[5] In this context, these terms reflect two dimensions of the group called church. On the one hand it is a free collective subjectivity marked by spontaneous and direct communication. On the other hand, relationships also consist of patterned responses that are recognized as regulated by custom, norms, and sanctions. These two dimensions in some kind of balance and dialectical interaction produce energy, stimulate movement, and contain excess. This tension describes an intrinsic or essential quality of the church and thus a constant in the history of the church and its ecclesiology. It bears some importance in the consideration of actual organizational structures.

A third reflection may be stated in terms of the correlation of institutional structures with ministry. This correlation means that "office," or "position," within the church corresponds with some ministry that the office is meant to supply. Negatively, this principle runs counter to a static view of the institutional church in which offices are honorific positions, something contrary to the gospels' witness to the teaching of Jesus. Position in the church cannot be reduced to status or reward. Positively, the principle formalizes a recognition that office has to do with ministry. Positions of authority have to be understood dynamically and teleologically as institutional sources and guarantees of the ministry that is consistently needed by the community. This dynamic teleological relationship also implies an explanation of the logic by which new ministries are generated. The church as a community and an institution is self-actualizing; it contains within itself the means by which it exists. This should be understood not only historically and sociologically but also theologically; the community is founded upon Jesus Christ and animated by the Spirit of God. It therefore has within itself the power and the warrant to meet new historical contingencies and exigencies for new ministries by creating the new offices that will supply these ministries.[6] There is no reason to think that this process ended in the second or third

---

5. See CCH, I, 127.
6. See CCH, I, 93–125.

century when the history of the church and ecclesiology shows that the process has been continuous.

This reflection implies a recognition of the dynamic historical nature of the church; it is a historical organization. Understanding the church has to integrate into itself this recognition of historicity. This means that like every other institution or entity in history the church changes over time.[7] As it continually moves into new historical times and places, it consistently must adjust its ministries, create new ministries, and allow some ministries to evanesce. Some offices and ministries in the church are central and constitutive of the church. This does not mean that they do not change, but that a certain consistent "substance" and function endure over time. The next section will consider a few examples of institutions, offices, and ministries that have remained stable in the church over time. Other ministries are distinctive to different churches. The whole church is made up of organizations containing a considerable variety of offices and ministries, some more central and important than others.

Finally, despite the obvious character of the observation, it will not hurt to reflect on the correlation between the vitality of ministries and the quality of church life. From a historical perspective, ministry constitutes the church. In an analytical treatment such as this, ministries are defined and distinguished and related logically to the whole life of the church. Ministry is understood in terms of its function in the organic interrelationship among the people constituting the church. The observation intends to shift the imagination toward the concrete historical functioning of the church. Socially and existentially, ministry determines the actual quality of ecclesial existence. Energetic ministry engenders dynamic church life; sluggish

---

7. Postmodern culture enjoys a historical consciousness in which change is not a disvalue; it is simply a given, part of the way things are. Change does not require explanation, whereas consistency and sameness do. They are not evident but problematic. In fact, sameness and consistency within an organization in a changing world tend to connote being out of touch with reality and hence a disvalue. Historical ecclesiology demonstrates the tension between change and consistency within it. When faced with conflicting opinions, it is often helpful to determine whether they rest on a presupposition that privileges sameness or adjustment in the evaluation of church structures.

or deficient ministry entails sleepy church existence and potential attrition among the members. The point of this distinction, therefore, is simply to underscore the crucial existential role that ministry plays in concrete church life and thus to accent the importance of the topic of the organization of that ministry. Such organization will inevitably be pluralistic among the churches; but this by no means subtracts from the crucial role that attaches to it and by implication the importance of the way it is structured.

MINISTRIES TO CHRISTIAN LIFE ENABLED BY CHURCH STRUCTURES

The Christian community has elementary or primary needs, and the ministries of the church attend to them. The discussion of these needs and ministries moves logically "from below" in two senses. On the one hand, appeal is made to the historical and social origins of the Christian community because one can see fairly clearly how ministries were adjusted to the needs of the community in the genesis of the church. On the other hand, a structural primacy presides over the ministries being described here; they lie at the foundations of the community's existence. The logical framework for construing these foundational ministries is the congregation because the church originated in the formation of various communities within the Jewish Jesus movement. This premise does not undermine the conviction that the whole Christian movement shared a common consistency. But that unity is most accurately conceived as a communion of emerging urban congregations. The development of this section will entail returning to this assumption of the congregation as the basic ecclesial unit. The imaginative referent of the term "church" in this section is the local community where ministries directly affect the community.[8]

---

8. The idea of "basic unit" is situated in an existential and concrete historical context. Attention is focused on where ministry actually engages the ordinary faithful. Therefore the point does not apply to juridical or other theological construals of the meaning of "basic." I intend this use of language without prejudice to different arrangements in larger church organizational units such as dioceses or synods.

The best way to conceive the offices of ministry in the churches that are reflected in the New Testament writings situates them within a historical developmental context: they were emergent and fluid. "There is no single pattern of conferring ministry in the New Testament. The Spirit has at different times led the Church to adapt its ministries to contextual needs; various forms of the ordained ministry have been blessed with gifts of the Spirit" (NMC, 87). One can trace a chronological development in a shadowy fashion across decades and generations in different communities in a variety of contexts and circumstances. One can determine a variety of sources and models that influenced the emergent churches in various degrees: the household, the synagogue, other religious groups, certain professional and educational associations. It is generally agreed that the household, as a place where the earliest Christians met, would have had an especially significant influence on the shape of its organization. The data include categories or types of ministry, "offices" or roles that were commonly recognized: apostles, prophets, elders. One can also discern differentiated patterns of organization. Daniel Harrington finds two distinct "polities" from the first century, the one consisting of bishops and deacons, the other of presbyters/elders. At the time of the Pastorals, "it appears that [these] two distinct church orders had been in operation and were in the process of fusion."[9] But the New Testament does not yield a single organizational pattern for the structuring of the ministry of all the churches. In later history this pluralism allowed different churches to find analogies for their own organizational structures in the New Testament. It is more common today to look upon the pluralism of the New Testament as itself a normative situation and pattern. Pluralism as distinct from universal uniformity possesses a certain positive value; in the light of historicity and cultural difference, it suggests adaptation and appropriation in a variety of contexts.

---

9. Daniel J. Harrington, *The Church according to the New Testament* (Franklin, Wis., and Chicago: Sheed and Ward, 2001), 162. Eventually, the three offices of bishop, deacon, and elders or presbyters "came to exist side by side in the same community. In this arrangement, the bishops and deacons are active church officers who are responsible to the board of elders (some of whom may also perform pastoral tasks)." Ibid.

Four Kinds of Ministry

From the variety of specific ministries that are reflected in the New Testament, four kinds of ministry appear to be essential to the existence of the community as such. One kind of ministry is directed toward nurturing the faith of the community, especially when it gathers in assembly. This ministry is directed inward, *ad intra*, toward sustaining and building up the spiritual life of the church. It has two distinct forms: ministry of the word and ministry of the sacraments. A third kind of ministry is directed toward the material needs of the members: ministry to the sick, elderly, widowed, orphans, the poor. This attention, even when it is principally directed toward members of the community, may also be considered ministry *ad extra* insofar as it is directed toward the material needs of people in their lives in society, in the "world."[10] The fourth kind of ministry is administration, oversight, or governing. It consists in an authorized leadership and coordination of the activities of the community. All four of these kinds of ministry are abstractions. For example, while all communities have leadership or governance, the actual structure of that leadership differs among the New Testament communities and churches today. The reduction of the variety of different kinds of ministry exemplified in the churches of the New Testament to these four functions may appear arbitrary to some. But appeal can be made to the fact of consistency though the ages. Wherever the church exists, it seems that various forms of these kinds of ministry are part of it. Their perennial historical presence indicates their character as primal structures of the Christian church.[11]

Faith and Order firmly situates ordained ministry within the context of the ministry of all the faithful. The church is the body of Christians animated by the Spirit which urges the ministry of all.

---

10. The term "world" here refers to the sphere of nonchurch, that is, life in the secular sphere but not necessarily "outside" the church. This ministry may also be directed to people outside the church, *ad extra*, in the sense of people who are not members of the church.

11. Edward Farley, *Ecclesial Reflection: An Anatomy of Theological Method* (Philadelphia: Fortress Press, 1982), 299.

The Church is called at all times and in all places to serve God after the example of the Lord who came to serve rather than to be served. The idea of service is central to any biblical understanding of ministry. Every Christian receives gifts of the Holy Spirit for the upbuilding of the Church, and for his or her part in the mission of Christ. Strengthened by the Spirit, Christians are called to live out their discipleship in a variety of forms of service. The teaching of the faith and of its moral implications is entrusted in a special way to parents, although all the faithful are called upon to witness to the Gospel in word and deed. Catechists and theologians provide an invaluable service in handing on and deepening our understanding of the faith. The following of Christ, who came to bring good news to the poor and healing to the sick (cf. Luke 4:18–19), provides a powerful and specifically Christian motivation for believers to engage in other forms of service: education and health care, charitable assistance to the poor and the promotion of justice, peace, and the protection of the environment. Through their participation in Christ, the unique priest of the new covenant (cf. Heb 9:11), Christians are constituted a royal priesthood called to offer spiritual sacrifices (cf. 1 Pet 2) and indeed their very selves as a living sacrifice (cf. Rom 12:1) after the example of Jesus himself. This calling underlies the Church's potentially costly witness to justice and the duty of intercession. In this way every Christian, on the basis of the one baptism into Christ, should seek to serve the world by proclaiming good news to the poor, "release to the captives and recovery of sight to the blind" and setting at liberty those who are oppressed. In short, this is an obligation resting equally on all "to proclaim the year of the Lord's favor" in all the varied situations of need in the world throughout the ages (Luke 4:18–19). (NMC, 82–85)[12]

---

12. This passage responds to frequent complaints voiced by evangelical churches that BEM did not stress the ministry of the laity enough and placed too much emphasis on ordained ministry. Even though BEM did establish the ministry of the whole community as the framework for its discussion, and received considerable praise for so doing, it was still felt that BEM so dwelt on ordained and episcopal ministry that it leaned in some churches' eyes toward clericalism. See, for example, the view of the United Church of Canada, BEMresponses, II, 283.

Faith and Order finds the analogue for ordained ministry in the Twelve who assisted Jesus because the basic rationale of ministry lies in serving the community in its existence and mission.

> In calling and sending the Twelve and his other apostles, Jesus laid foundations for the ongoing proclamation of the Kingdom and the service of the community of his disciples. Faithful to his example, from the earliest times there were those chosen by the community under the guidance of the Spirit, and given specific authority and responsibility. Ordained ministers serve in the building up of the community, in equipping the saints, and in strengthening the Church's witness in the world (cf. Eph 4:12–13). They may not dispense with the ongoing support and the encouragement of the community — for whom they are chosen, and for whom they are empowered by the Holy Spirit to act as representative persons. Ordained ministers have a special responsibility for the ministry of Word and Sacrament. They have a ministry of pastoral care, teaching and leadership in mission. In all of those ways they strengthen the communion in faith, life and witness of the whole people of God. (NMC, 86)

Faith and Order continues: "There is no single pattern of conferring ministry in the New Testament. The Spirit has at different times led the Church to adapt its ministries to contextual needs; various forms of the ordained ministry have been blessed with gifts of the Spirit" (NMC, 87). At the same time, the four kinds of ministry to the needs of faith (in word and sacrament), to those in material need, and in administration, provide a useful classification.

The concept of ordination should be explicitly tied to ministry. On a historical level, ordination is authorization by the community of ministers to specific offices or roles of ministry. The statement that ordination is authorization by the community exemplifies the principle that the ecclesiological understanding always involves two languages at the same time, the one historical-sociological, the other theological. No one states this better than John Calvin in his sacramental principle. God uses human agents to do God's will and work. By this reasoning, authorization by the community *is* authorization by God.[13] This simultaneous agency cannot be understood in the competitive framework postulated by a question such as the following: is this God's action or human action? In the Christian conception of the divine-human relationship, God's initiative always anticipates and supports human response.[14] I will treat the ordination of ministers within the context of church membership in chapter 5.

Animating faith by word and sacrament. The first two kinds of ministry are related to the faith of the community; they consist in animating the community's life of faith. This form of ministry is directed inward to the community (*ad intra*) as distinct from ministries directed outside the community to life in the world (*ad extra*). The gathering of the community to express its faith as a religious community constitutes the bedrock foundation of the church from a theological and a sociological point of view. The Acts of the Apostles lists four activities that the assembled community engaged in during the formational period of the church, but probably reflecting a post-apostolic period: "they devoted themselves to the apostles' teaching and fellowship, to the breaking of bread and the prayers" (Acts 2:42). Other activities of the nascent communities could be culled from the New Testament. But of all these activities two emerged as fundamental, constituting activities that grounded the church's existence: the reading of the scriptures, including learning and being instructed by them, and participation in the Lord's Supper or what came to be called the eucharist or thanksgiving meal. Ordained ministry to the community revolved around these centering and defining activities. "The chief responsibility of the ordained ministry is to assemble and build up the Body of Christ by proclaiming and teaching the Word of God, by celebrating baptism and the Eucharist and by guiding the life of the community in its worship, its mission and its service. Essential to its testimony are not merely its words, but the love of its members for one another, the quality of their service to those in need, a just and disciplined life and a fair exercise of power and authority" (NMC,

---

13. See supra, 32.

14. This observation reflects a positive response to a consistent and pervasive reaction to BEM on the part of evangelical churches to any language that seems to undermine the primacy of God's grace. BEMresponses, passim.

88). Across the centuries and different church traditions the ministry of word and sacrament, with specific reference to the Lord's Supper, has grounded the church. The relative emphasis or prominence may vary among the traditions, but the ministries of word and sacrament appear to be constitutive dimensions of church organization.[15]

Ministry to those in material need inside and outside the church. I pass over ministry to those in physical need at this point because consideration of that ministry relates more closely to the activities of the church and its relationship to the world and society. These ministries will be taken up in chapter 7.

Administration and governance. The fourth kind of ministry, that of corporate leadership and administration, is also essential to the church; no organization can exist over generations without offices of administration endowed with authority. The ministry of leadership, government, and administration set the style of life and the tone of the church. The distinguishing mark of each church tradition is often carried within its overall organizational and administrative structure. There are few areas in the whole area of ecclesiology more in need of clarity than the origins and development of ecclesial structure. One may distinguish three phases in the development of what became the universal episcopal structure of ministry during the course of the first 150 years.

The first phase consists in the earliest development of the church through three generations up to approximately the year one hundred. This roughly corresponds with the period represented by the canonical writings of the New Testament. During this period government of the Christian communities was pluralistic; there was no standardized form, no universal set of offices and ministries. *Episkopé* frequently connoted function rather than a personal office. Thus, for example, a presbyter or elder may have exercised oversight in a given community; or a collegium of presbyters might have been the directorate within a specific church. The canonical literature, scripture, does not prescribe a single structure of authority for the whole church.

---

15. This statement raises questions about churches that have no sacraments such as the Salvation Army and the Religious Society of Friends (Quakers). The issue will be taken up in later chapters.

The second phase of development roughly corresponds to the second century and the specific institutional innovation of this period is represented in the letters of Ignatius of Antioch. Ignatius forcefully bears witness to an office of a monarchical bishop early in the second century, and during the course of that century this pattern became more or less universal. As Ignatius represents him, the bishop is the centering authority in the community; he draws his authority from God by divine appointment. He is the teacher and the leader of the eucharistic worship. This bishop has primacy in the congregation, and Faith and Order associates the idea of primacy with a personal mode of governing ministry wherever it exists, at a variety of levels (NMC, 102). The main function of this ministry relates to the unity of the congregation: it is specifically designed to hold the community together as one in belief and in love.

The size of these early second-century communities or churches has a bearing on how one conceives of episcopacy and the fundamental unit of administration. The communities to which Ignatius addressed his letters were small congregations. A larger church such as the one in Rome was made up of many churches with their own bishops. It is not clear when the whole church of Rome came under the authority of a single bishop. The office of bishop, then, began as a position that was sociologically the equivalent of the pastor of a congregation.

The third phase of the development of episcopacy stretched forward from the second through the third century after Ignatius. Episcopacy underwent considerable development simply by virtue of the enlargement of the urban church as a unit. Two more functions of the bishop, beyond guaranteeing the unity of the congregation, became important. One consisted in the temporal line of succession that faithfully linked a given church with its past. The other consisted in maintaining a link at any given time between a church and the other churches. Early in the church's history, during the course of the second century and into the third, the church relied on a succession of persons in the office of bishop as a sign and an institutional vehicle for guaranteeing fidelity to the apostolic witness. Bishops also communicated among themselves by letters, visitations, and meetings or synods. This preserved a certain unity and consistency within the whole Christian movement and helped prevent fragmentation. "The threefold ministry of bishop, presbyter and deacon had become by the third century the generally accepted pattern" (NMC, 87). This third phase of development will be discussed further in the section on larger organizational forms.

Shifting the perspective to the context of the whole church today, consideration of the ministry of governance and administration at the outset on the level of the congregation helps to show that different polities do not necessarily entail division among churches on the level of ecclesial existence. Monoepiscopacy began at the level of the congregation, having developed from some prior form of governance. Gradually, the church's expansion changed episcopacy into the ministry to larger organizational units, which will be considered in the next part of this chapter. Relative to that larger function, the office has continued to develop in far too many directions and presently exists in too many forms to permit the general statement that it must be divisive. Denominations without episcopacy preserve the function of governance in offices of administration that bear another name. Episcopacy is an analogous concept and office.[16] Whatever form the larger structures of administration that hold congregations and regional churches together may be, within them the basic unit of the church as congregation or parish or gathering community retains a certain existential autonomy. It has its own ministry of governance and administration. The fourfold ministry reflects this elemental structure. The ministerial function of oversight at the congregational level guarantees what the church requires: unity within the community, continuity through history, and communion with other churches. With respect to unity the of the congregation and continuity with apostolic tradition and communion among congregations, the ministry of governance and administration is essential.

Theological Interpretation of Church Structure

The last chapter drew attention to the nature and purpose of the church as a whole. Theology provides the predominant matrix for

---

16. See Edward LeRoy Long, *Patterns of Polity: Varieties of Church Governance* (Cleveland: Pilgrim Press, 2001), for a comparative study of episcopal polities of different churches.

understanding the church's existence and reason for being. Although ministries and organizational structures developed historically, religious and theological convictions play a role. Theological premises operate in the analysis of church structures, and theological values are at stake in the way ecclesial polity is constructed. The theological foundations of the church, that is, sovereign God, Jesus Christ, and God as Spirit, have to be factored into a theological account of ministries in the community.

One way of correlating christological underpinnings with ecclesial offices and ministries used by both Protestants and Roman Catholics is drawn from Calvin's language of the three offices of Christ: prophet, priest, and king.[17] This division distinguishes ministries of word and sacrament within the ministry of animating the faith just considered. I add "healer" to accommodate the ministry to those in material need. These four offices of Jesus Christ, prophet, priest, healer, and king, correlate with the church's ministries of word, sacrament, healing, and administration or jurisdiction. These analytical categories are not meant in a reductive sense to limit ministries in the Christian community.[18] Ministries in fact are always being added and subtracted as the needs require. All sorts of different ministries coordinate and define church activity which can in turn be analyzed in a host of different ways: professional or volunteer, public or informal, and so on. But distinguishing these four generic forms of ministry and showing how they complement each other help to define ecclesial space. Surely these kinds of ministry exist in a variety of styles and formats in different churches, and this will contribute considerably to different tones of Christian life or ecclesial existence. But the point here is to try to grasp what the *ministerium* of all

---

17. Calvin, Institutes, 2, 15.

18. Note how the ministry of service could be conflated with administration, and ministry of word and sacrament could be conceived as one office of ministry. This shows the arbitrariness of this fourfold division. This is confirmed by different offices and structures supplying analogous forms of ministry. The variations of responsibilities among the offices of bishop, presbyter, and deacon in different traditions and over the years in the same traditions also show that these "stable" offices are not entirely consistent. The forms and organizations of ministry have developed historically in complex ways so that later forms of ministry cannot be identified directly with "the will and institution of Jesus Christ." BEM, M, 11 commentary.

the churches shares in common, how it is consistent with apostolic origins, and how it is grounded in Jesus Christ and the Spirit.

Ministry is the service in and for the community reaching inside and outside the community. Church polity at bottom arranges the church's ministry. Responses to BEM showed that most churches understand that the whole church is intrinsically ministerial; the community should be regarded as a community of ministers according to the New Testament image of the priesthood of all the faithful.[19] The sum total of designated ministries can be differentiated in various ways. The idea of dividing them according to the common idea of the three offices of Christ plus one has some merit. As Jesus Christ was prophet, priest, healer, and king, so too the church should have ministries that teach, lead at prayer and sacramental worship, care for those in need, and govern the community. All Christians find that their churches are communities of teaching, worship, and caring for people's needs that require leadership and administration; the vitality of all of these activities usually depends upon the effectiveness of the offices of ministry however they are organized.

The Christian looks for the ideals of Jesus' teaching and practice in the ministerial structures and behaviors of the church. Church members expect a reasonable appeal to freedom rather than dominating power in the exercise of authority. This authority is possessed by the minister, after all, because it is received by the community. More and more Christians recognize that the church is a voluntary organization and cannot be run on the basis of spiritual coercion. All Christians appreciate wisdom in interpreting the word of God in the particular circumstances of today's world. Parishioners desire effective leadership in prayer and presiding at the Lord's Supper, whether they expect an energetic, charismatic minister or one who all but disappears in the ritual provided by the church.

Faith and Order raises up three ideal qualities in the leadership and administration of the church and the exercise of authority within

---

19. These themes appear in Roman Catholic ecclesiology in Vatican II's forceful statements that the whole church is missionary by nature, that the laity share responsibility for that mission, and that ministerial responsibility conferred with baptism includes the laity's contribution to the internal spiritual and temporal well-being of the church and especially to the church's relationship to the world. CCH, II, 387–400.

the given polity: those exercising authority should exhibit a personal touch, should cooperate with other leaders collegially, and should engage the whole congregation or wider church communally. But these qualities can be actualized according to a range of different styles that are embedded in different organizational arrangements. Different central concerns or identifying marks characterize different churches. The bond that unites one church or family of churches may be a highly developed and distinctive liturgical tradition. Other churches may enjoy a certain flamboyance and eclecticism at their assemblies including dramatic preaching. Another church and its ministers may self-identify as a community who witness to God's grace by living according to a strict moral code. Still another set of Christians distinguish themselves by a certain allegiance to a set of beliefs that enshrine God's revelation in Jesus Christ. Some churches set their ministers apart; they may be distinguished by careful training or other marks such as celibacy. Other churches carefully protect the lay status of ministers and their equality with the rest of the faithful.[20]

A focus on the parish or congregation as the existentially basic unit of the church helps to sort out the way Christians may regard the larger administrative divisions of the church. I suggest that this can be done without prejudicing the particular jurisdictional arrangements of the churches. The specific concrete congregation is where the ordinary Christian most radically participates in the church. From that perspective how may Christians make sense of the maze of different church organizations, the contradictory convictions about the styles of ministry, and the locations of authority? Educated Christians increasingly have an open attitude based on several factors. They know that the New Testament recommends no single church order, that different orders developed and continue to develop, that the one Spirit of God can inspire more than one way of doing things, that when churches may be divided juridically the members of these churches need not be divided from each other personally or spiritually: they can be friends in Christ. They are also

---

20. It is important to recognize these differences. But I will show in the last chapter that it is a mistake to locate the identity in the sense of the integral character of a church in one or a few specific characteristics.

convinced that the church in history will never be united juridically in a single form of government, and that this is probably a good thing because it provides many different styles in which people may participate in the church. Aware of this, people move much more easily from one church to another than in the past. Does this mean that the church will always be divided? Perhaps, due to sin, that may be the case, but it is not necessarily so. Explicit mutual recognition and all sorts of different bonds can be forged across administrative differences. I will take up the question of full and partial communion in the final chapter.

LARGER ORGANIZATIONAL FORMS

We move from a consideration of the church in its most basic social-existential unit, the parish or congregation, to the church considered as a collection or communion of churches. This topic correlates with the historical development of the church during the course of the second and third centuries. After making that correlation, I will discuss some conditions for the possibility of larger organizational patterns that can be commonly acknowledged as structures for various levels of communion.

Historical Development of Larger Organizational Forms

During the course of the expansion of the church during the second and third centuries, the need for formal structures to hold the whole Christian movement together became more exigent. The other functions of the bishop, besides symbolizing and administering the unity of the congregation, became evident during this second phase: principally to preserve continuity in the apostolic tradition on a wider scale and to actualize union among the churches by remaining in communication with other bishops. "In the course of the first centuries, communion between local congregations — which had been maintained by a series of informal links such as visits, letters and collections — became more and more expressed in institutional forms. The purpose was to hold the local congregations in communion, to safeguard and hand on apostolic truth, to give mutual support and to lead in witnessing to the Gospel. All these functions are summed up in the term *episkopé."* (NMC, 91). This communication between the churches developed into communal, or synodal, or conciliar practices that further guaranteed the unity of the whole or greater church. The communal life of the church "implies unity in diversity and is expressed in one heart and one mind (cf. Phil 2:12). It is the way in which Christians are held in unity and travel together as the one Church, and the one Church is manifested in the life of each local church" (NMC, 96).

"The specific development of structures of episkopé varied in different regions of the Church: this was true of both the collegial expression of episkopé in synods, and its personal embodiment in the individual bishops. The crystallization of most of the episcopal functions in the hands of one individual (episkopos) came later in some places than in others. What is evident in every case is that episkopé and episcopacy are in the service of maintaining continuity in apostolic truth and unity of life" (NMC, 92).

Another development of episcopacy occurred during the third century, and the writing of Cyprian of Carthage bears witness to it. Cyprian conceived of episcopacy as constituting a *collegium,* a group that as a group bore primary responsibility for the unity of the church. The one ordained as a bishop became a member of this collegium; participation in this collegium implied a corporate responsibility for the whole church. The communication among bishops and churches, therefore, was not simply occasional and arbitrary; it was an exercise in corporate responsibility. Cyprian's view of the collegiality of church leadership is classic.

In the course of the church's history still other distinct forms of supracongregational episkopé arose. The styles of episcopal and patriarchal leadership differed in the East and the West. The papacy was solidified as a result of the Gregorian Reform. And the Reformation of the church in the West introduced a radical pluralism of church polities. "In the 16th century, oversight came to be exercised in a variety of ways in the churches which took their identity through the continental Reformation. These Reformers . . . accepted a break with the overall structure of the Church, including the ministry of universal primacy. Nevertheless, they continued to see the need for a ministry of episkopé, which the churches which went through the Reformation ordered in different ways. Some exercised episkopé in synodal forms. Others kept or developed ministries of personal episkopé, including, for some, the sign of historic episcopal succession" (NMC, 93).[21]

The twentieth century also witnessed major developments in the possibilities for various levels of mutual recognition of larger structures that can mediate various levels of communion. One was the ecumenical movement, which was driven by various associations such as Faith and Order; another was the formation of the World Council of Churches; and still another was the entry of the Roman Catholic Church into the ecumenical movement at Vatican II. Many interchurch dialogues have been going on for decades. When these advances are situated in the new worldwide cultural situation of globalization, where churches are both closer together and more differentiated and fragmented than ever before, consideration of such large structures seems opportune.[22]

Conditions for the Usefulness of Common Structures

For common structures across denominational lines to be considered useful, they must respect the organizational structures of churches

---

21. "The term 'local church' is used differently by different traditions. For some traditions the 'local' church is the congregation of believers gathered in one place to hear the Word and celebrate the Sacraments. For others, 'local' or 'particular' church refers to the bishop with the people around the bishop, gathered to hear the Word and celebrate the Sacraments. In some churches the term 'local church' is used of both the diocese and of the parish. At another level, 'local church' can refer to several dioceses or to regional churches gathered together in a synodal structure under a presidency. "There are different ecclesiological concepts behind these usages, yet most Churches agree that each local church, however it is defined, is united to every other in the universal Church and contains within it the fullness of what it is to be the Church. There is often a discrepancy between theological description of local church and how the local church is experienced by the faithful." NMC, 66 box.

22. "The Church, as the body of Christ and the eschatological people of God, is built up by the Holy Spirit through a diversity of gifts or ministries. This diversity calls for a ministry of co-ordination so that these gifts may enrich the whole Church, its unity and mission. The faithful exercise of the ministry of episkopé under the Gospel is a requirement of fundamental importance for the Church's life and mission. The responsibility of those called to exercise oversight cannot be fulfilled without the collaboration, support and assent of the whole community. At the same time, the effective and faithful life of the community is served by a ministry of leadership set apart to guide its mission, teaching and common life." NMC, 90.

that have fruitfully existed over time. To make this point we look, first, at the diversity of organizational structures that currently obtain in the church at large and, second, at the need for a framework or mindset among the churches that respects this pluralism.

A spectrum of ecclesiologies. In the second volume of this work I developed two ends of a spectrum of organizational structures ranging from "free church" polity to a "universal institutional" church structure.[23] These generalizations were drawn from the ecclesiologies of Menno Simons and John Smyth, on the one hand, and the Roman Church as exemplified in the Catechism of the Council of Trent, on the other. The two ecclesiologies, called "free church" and "universal institution" respectively, were set up to function as types that represent two ends of a whole series of actual and potential ecclesiologies. Each ecclesiology embodied a set of principles that were consistent among themselves and in some respects polar opposites of those of the other set. Each of these ecclesiologies could appeal back to the origins of the church and the canonical literature for embryonic foreshadowings of themselves; each was consistent with the New Testament or a development from it. Each embodied a series of values that should be prized by a church. The coherence of these ecclesiologies and the depth of these values have proven themselves to be solid enough to provide the backbones of traditions that have lasted centuries and nurtured innumerable Christian lives.

The requirements for larger ecclesiological forms. These two poles of existing ecclesiologies function like bookends that contain what seems to be a library of options in ecclesial polity worldwide. From that perspective they set the problem. But they also set the conditions for a framework within which Christians can think about solutions. They set up parameters that allow for constructive thinking. And the parameters suggest some directions in thinking about large ecclesiological forms.

Whatever organizational structures exist above the congregations or parishes, they must respect the congregation as the basic existential unit of the church. Actual Christian life is lived in the

---

23. CCH, II, 276–88.

congregation. The fostering of ecclesial existence in the congregation provides a fundamental criterion for judging whether a larger ecclesial unit is functioning properly.

Seen from the perspective of the multiplicity of congregations in an area or region, Christian communities spontaneously relate to other Christian communities, so that the isolation of churches or the lack of communion among them represents an abnormal situation. Here the direction of accountability looks outward. The degree of openness of a given congregation to others around it is a sign of its health.

The names and forms of higher organizational structures or ministries are not agreed upon among the churches. They take different forms or have different offices, and the languages describing agencies differ. It is quite important to recognize the analogies in the various larger church structures and to recognize similarity of functions.[24]

Institutional structure or organization always exists in tension with the more concrete and spontaneous actual life of the community. This tension should be such that the positive values of institution and communitarian spontaneity are not at odds but mutually enhance each other. This means that the higher or larger institution should never supplant or interfere with those aspects of church life that can be accomplished on their own.[25] This brings to bear the theological principle of whole and part: the whole exists in the part, so that the assistance of the larger institution is needed only to support and assist in the relatedness of the churches among themselves. In many cases regarding a variety of issues this assistance may require juridical authority.

It is natural that there be some institutional structures that reach out to encompass the whole Christian movement. What applies among churches in a region in principle applies globally to all Christian churches. Such an institution or organizational network has never actually existed in the church, but globalization makes it appear possible for the first time. Thus, beyond the local and regional

---

24. Long's typology of ecclesial polities in *Patterns of Polity: Varieties of Church Governance* is very useful here. He distinguishes three forms of governance among ecclesial bodies: episcopal, synodal, and congregational. Each of these types contains variations or subtypes.

25. In Roman Catholic social thought this is called the principle of subsidiarity.

levels, "ecumenical dialogue has led the churches to ask whether and, if so, how they may function within the church as a communion existing throughout the whole world" (NMC, 99).

Faith and Order has no ready solution to the question of different church orders.

> One of the most difficult issues dividing Christian communities concerns this form of ministry and its relation to the apostolicity of the Church. To focus the question in a very precise way: churches remain divided about whether the historic episcopate — in the sense of bishops ordained in apostolic succession back to the earliest generations of the Church — is a necessary component of ecclesial order as intended by Christ for his community; or is merely one form of church structure which, because it is so traditional, is particularly advantageous for today's community but is not essential. Still other communities see no special reason for privileging episcopal structure, or even believe it is better avoided, for they see it as prone to abuse. (NMC, 93 box)

In the earlier draft of this document, Faith and Order asked the churches to attend to the functional equivalence of episcopal, synodal, and congregational governance in the overall ministry of episkopé and preserving apostolicity (NPC, 93 box). BEM, however, recommended episcopal structures for all the churches in order to facilitate unity among the churches.[26]

Communion, Collegiality, and Primacy

Three functions of episkopé beyond the life of the congregation or parish or episcopal unit are to help preserve apostolicity, to serve as

---

26. BEM's suggestion that all churches consider adopting an episcopal form of polity occasioned a good deal of reaction from nonepiscopal churches. These churches do not measure apostolicity by episcopal succession. They argue that the office of bishop cannot be established from scripture to be divinely willed, is not a guarantee of apostolicity, and has not prevented division in the church. Some churches would be more open to the office of bishop if it were recommended as a sign of continuity and unity rather than a substantive and normative office of the church. One church stated: "In this respect our church also can ask whether it should not introduce the apostolic succession and give approval in principle to common 'signs of unity.'" BEMresponses, V, 54.

the link for communion among the churches, and to enable collegial cooperation in governing a larger segment of the church. Faith and Order defines the function of maintaining communion and collegiality in descriptive, nonjuridical terms. It also characterizes this kind of ministry as having these qualities: "episkopé both belongs to the whole church and is entrusted as a particular charge on specific persons. For this reason it is frequently stressed that, at every level of the Church's life, the ministry must be exercised in personal, communal and collegial ways. It should be remembered that 'personal,' 'communal' and 'collegial' refer not only to particular structures and processes, but also describe the informal reality of the bonds of koinonia, the mutual belonging and accountability within the ongoing common life of the Church" (NMC, 94). Personal means that this ministry should not disappear into a bureaucracy but be exercised by people with a personal touch. Its collegiality means that it performs its tasks by collaborating with other leaders in the pattern of Cyprian. The church of North Africa of the third century provides a model of churches coming together in the persons of their bishops gathered in synod for a "corporate, representative exercise in the areas of leadership, consultation, discernment, and decision-making" (NMC, 97). The communal dimension of this ministry of leadership "refers to the involvement of the whole body of the faithful in common consultation, sometimes through representation and constitutional structures, over the well-being of the Church and their common involvement in the service of God's mission in the world. Communal life sustains all the baptized in a web of belonging, of mutual accountability and support" (NMC, 96).[27]

---

27. The qualities of being personal, collegial, and communal are three dimensions that should mark all ministry of oversight. The qualities are drawn from the most prominent quality of the three major types of governance in the church today, episcopal, synodal, and congregational. BEM puts it this way quoting Faith and Order at Lausanne in 1927: "In view of (i) the place which the episcopate, the council of presbyters and the congregation of the faithful, respectively, had in the constitution of the early Church, and (ii) the fact that episcopal, presbyteral and congregational systems of government are each today, and have been for centuries, accepted by great communions in Christendom, and (iii) the fact that episcopal, presbyteral and congregational systems are each believed by many to be essential to the good order of the Church, we therefore recognize that these several elements must all, under conditions which

Few people today realistically think about the unity of the whole church organized by the juridical authority of the papacy. The plurality of traditions in the church is too firmly established for this to happen. Indeed, the papacy never enjoyed this universal authority in historical actuality. Today, however, a new cultural situation opens a space for discussion of a ministry of primacy over the whole church. One element of that situation is the recognition that *koinonia* entails precisely communion among different churches. Another is the ecumenical movement. "In recent years . . . both ecumenical rapprochement and globalization have created a new climate in which a universal primacy can be seen as a gift rather than a threat to other churches and the distinctive features of their witness" (NMC, 103).

It is helpful to distinguish two levels of papal functioning, the one inside the Roman Catholic Church and the other relative to the whole Christian movement. Inside the Catholic Church the pope enjoys juridical authority.[28] Another kind of authority, which may be called symbolic leadership, is applicable to the way the pope could relate to all the churches of the world. This would not be possible without dialogue between the papacy and the other churches. The pope would have to listen to the other churches before this symbolic leadership could be plausible. In recent years, despite disagreement, "there seems to be an increasing openness to discuss a universal ministry in support of mission and unity of the church and agreement that any such personal ministry would need to be exercised in communal and collegial ways. Given the ecumenical sensitivity of this issue it is important to distinguish between the essence of the primacy and any particular ways in which it has been or is currently exercised" (NMC, 104).

The Marks of the Church from an Organizational Perspective

From a theological perspective of the nature and mission of the church, the marks of the church are the result of God's presence and activity within the community. But God as Spirit acts in history

---

require further study, have an appropriate place in the order of life of a reunited church." BEM, M, 26 commentary.

28. The way this authority is exercised will be modified in the future under the impact of globalization and the gradual influence of regional pluralism in the church.

through historical means, that is, human agents and ministers who attend to the marks of the church. "Those who exercise oversight have a special duty to care for, and recall the community to, the unity, holiness, catholicity and apostolicity of the Church" (NMC, 95). In the concrete life of the churches, the organizational or institutional structures have to be realistic, pliable, and able to support tensions.

Unity open to pluralism. The order of the church, in the local congregation but especially in ascending levels of organization, has to be able to enfold within itself the diversity of its constituents. Faith and Order has a worldwide outlook and thus a good feel for difference. "There is a rich diversity of Christian life and witness born out of the diversity of cultural and historical context. The Gospel has to be rooted and lived authentically in each and every place. It has to be proclaimed in language, symbols and images that engage with, and are relevant to, particular times and particular contexts. The communion of the Church demands the constant interplay of cultural expressions of the Gospel if the riches of the Gospel are to be appreciated for the whole people of God" (NMC, 61).

Diversity has to be read in the positive terms of enrichment and enhancement. The unity of the church is meant to bring together different charisms and make them available to the community as gifts toward a fuller expression of faith and life. "Diversity is not the same as division. Within the Church, divisions (heresies and schisms), as well as political conflicts and expressions of hatred, threaten God's gift of communion. Christians are called to work untiringly to overcome divisions, to prevent legitimate diversities from becoming causes of division, and to live a life of diversities reconciled" (NMC, 63).[29]

Catholicity of communion. The quality of catholicity forces the imagination to envision the church as the whole Christian movement, and thus to think of the local or regional or denominational church in a wider context of other churches. But "other churches"

---

29. "Diversities in expression of the Gospel, in words and in actions can enrich life in communion. Particular emphases today are carried in the life and witness of different churches. How far are the different emphases conflicting positions, or rather an expression of legitimate diversity? Does the weight placed upon the different emphases obscure the fullness of the Gospel message?" NMC, 63 box.

entail differences that in some cases may seem to be quite radical. Catholicity as a quality, therefore, has to be understood in such a way that it presupposes those differences and tries to embody ways in which different traditions can be in communion with each other. The paradigm is drawn from the canonical literature: "From the beginning contact was maintained between local churches by collections, exchanges of letters, visits and tangible expressions of solidarity (cf. 1 Cor 16; 2 Cor 8:1–9; Gal 2:9ff; etc.). From time to time, during the first centuries, local churches assembled to take counsel together. All of these were ways of nurturing interdependence and maintaining communion" (NMC, 64).

Faith and Order expresses in utterly simple terms the ways in which churches that are different can be in communion with each other: "The communion of the Church is expressed in the communion between local churches, in each of which the fullness of the Church resides. The communion of the Church embraces local churches in each place and all places at all times. Local churches are held in the communion of the Church by the one Gospel, the one baptism and the one Lord's Supper, served by a common ministry. This communion of local churches is thus not an optional extra, but is an essential aspect of what it means to be the Church" (NMC, 65). The value of the notion of *koinonia* for the self-understanding of the church lies in the premise that communion presupposes differences among those who commune. The power of one faith in one gospel and one baptism and ministry to Christian life consists in the ability of these bonds to transcend differences.

Various levels of communion, when these are placed in the context of catholicity, can build broader bridges across which actual interchange can be negotiated and realized. "The goal of the search for full communion is realized when all the churches are able to recognize in one another the one, holy, catholic and apostolic Church in all its fullness. This full communion will be expressed on the local and universal levels through conciliar forms of life and action. In such a communion of unity and authentic diversities, churches are bound in all aspects of their life together at all levels in confessing the one faith and engaging in worship and witness, deliberation and action" (NMC, 66). The single most important step toward breaking down barriers to unity and fostering a communion that trusts the power of faith is the recognition of the authenticity and validity of the ministry of other churches. Barriers to this step are usually of two kinds: a failure to achieve a historical consciousness that justifies the positive value of real difference, and the residue of a competitive spirit that thinks recognition of the other somehow compromises self-identity.

Apostolicity as continuity with origins. Faith and Order makes two essential statements about the apostolicity of the church: it is a characteristic of the whole church, and it consists in the whole way of life of a given church that cannot be reduced to a single specific criterion or institutional means of preserving it.[30] "The apostolic tradition of the Church is the continuity in the permanent characteristics of the Church of the apostles: witness to the apostolic faith, proclamation and fresh interpretation of the Gospel, celebration of baptism and Eucharist, the transmission of ministerial responsibilities, communion in prayer, love, joy and suffering, service to the sick and needy, communion among the local churches and sharing the divine gifts which have been given to each" (NMC, 71).

The apostolicity of the life of the church requires institutional forms for preserving the authenticity of Christian faith and practice through successive generations and across cultures; it also requires openness and flexibility in measuring the living tradition of the church. Thus, on the one hand, "the Church has developed several means for maintaining its apostolicity through time, in different circumstances and cultural contexts: the scriptural canon, dogma, liturgical order, structures wider than the level of local communities" (NMC, 89). To this should be added the succession of bishops in their office of oversight. This is surely not the only way the church sought to preserve apostolicity, it has not been perfect, but it has been highly successful. On the other hand, the apostolic faith "transmitted through the living tradition of the Church is the faith evoked by the Word of God, inspired by the Holy Spirit and attested in scripture. Its content is set forth in the Creeds of the Early Church and also testified to in other forms. It is proclaimed in many Confessions

---

30. "The apostolic faith does not refer to one fixed formula or to a specific phase in Christian history" (NMC, 70).

of Faith of the churches. It is preached throughout the world today. It is articulated in Canons and Books of Discipline from many periods and stages in the lives of the churches. Thus the apostolic faith is confessed in worship, in life, service and mission — in the living traditions of the Church" (NMC, 70).

Objective and subjective holiness. The holiness of the church depends on the quality of its relationship to God since God alone is the Holy One. By various transferences, the church is called holy either in the media by which it communicates a relationship with God (scripture, preaching, sacraments) or by the effectiveness of God's grace in human lives (divine forgiveness and sanctification) (NMC, 54). What is to be said of other organizational means for preserving the "holiness" of the church, such as the power of the keys and excommunication?

The power of the keys and the practice of excommunication and reconciliation in the church will be implemented in different ways, degrees, and proportions in different churches. In every case, however, the church should strike a balance between the poles of objectivity and subjectivity. Some churches may think of a high degree of moral uprightness when they use the language of holiness. But members will always fall short of perfection. Other churches may refer the language of holiness to the symbols of faith, to doctrinal beliefs and the sacraments. But this language limps when the behavior of the community appears wicked or no different than that of anyone else. In some churches people have formed associations in order to focus energy on a faithful living of the Christian life and service of others. In other cases, these same motives have lead to the formation of independent churches. The history of the Christian church contains an extraordinary treasure house of various spiritualities that nurture Christian life and channel it to service of the neighbor. These spiritualities should not compete with but should complement each other.

CHURCH ORGANIZATION
AND GOD'S WILL FOR THE CHURCH

The discussion up to this point has dealt with elements that are common among many churches and potentially acceptable to all.

But the actual condition of the church remains pluralistic on the level of organization; the church is divided into churches, some of which are seriously different from others. The premise for this work is that difference ordinarily is legitimate and not necessarily a cause of division. But this in its turn raises a series of issues that have to be engaged. Is there a limit to the differences among the churches that can actually be held together? Is there a true or truer church? What is the authority of the polity of any given church? What kind of claim does a particular provision of the church's organization make on individual Christians in terms of authority? Are we to regard the organizational structures of the church as equally human historical developments or do some more than others correspond to God's will for the church? In sum, how are we to situate the church's institutional structures in relation to the gospel, God's will, and the Christian life of discipleship?

I propose to discuss this tangle of issues on the level of principle or in terms of some essential attitudes that have a bearing on how these questions might be answered in a fuller discussion. In principle it will be helpful to examine the provisions of church organization on two distinct levels, the level of the local community and that of the wider regional, national, or universal church. This distinction is clear at its extremes, the congregation as distinct from a denomination, national church, or communion of churches. It is less clear and remains fluid where a unit larger than a congregation or parish, a diocese, for example, functions as a local church.[31] In this discussion the imaginative referent of the local church is the existential unit of assembly. The "larger church" refers to an organized worldwide church, or national church, or denomination, or an organized communion of parishes or congregations, or possibly a large archdiocese or diocese, all of which do not have the same existential impact on believers as the congregations.

On the basis of this distinction between the local and the larger church, I take up the issue of normative church structures in three stages: first, the normativity of the New Testament; second,

---

31. See supra, n. 21 of this chapter.

normative patterns on the local level; and, third, the authority of larger church structures.

The Normativity of the New Testament

The New Testament is the central and most important authority in the church. Although there are historical, sociological, and especially theological reasons that justify the position of the New Testament relative to the church, the fact is that this status is practically speaking universally accepted by the churches. The classical doctrine states that scripture is the *norma normans non normata* of Christian faith and thus of the church convened in that faith. The New Testament especially contains or bears witness to the Christian faith vision. The New Testament provides access to the person of Jesus, the medium of God's self-communication and revelation. The New Testament also represents the "apostolic faith" in its classic form.

It is important especially in the present time to recognize that while scripture, especially the New Testament, constitutes normative or canonical literature for the churches, it is itself pluralistic and bears a diversity of witnesses to the content of faith. In other words, the content of the normative and constitutive document that grounds the church is a pluralistic text. This means that the New Testament prescribes some measure of pluralism within the church. The whole church is founded upon diverse expressions of the one grounding faith. I should repeat here that the term "pluralism" refers to diversity held together within a field of unity, or unity within diversity. The new deep recognition of the historicity of the scriptural writings and the differences among them entails important premises for understanding the whole church and the relation of the churches to each other.

The New Testament is the church's book. It was written within the church and by the church. This should not be understood as subtracting from the doctrine of inspiration, for God as Word and Spirit account for God's authorship of the scripture. This inspiration, however, has to be understood in conjunction with the historical genesis of the texts. Because the church inspired by its new faith produced the scriptures, the church is the interpreter of the text. But the whole church today consists in a collection of churches with different interpretations of their founding document. No single church can impose its interpretation on all the others any more than some New Testament writings can cancel the authority of others. Instead of the New Testament being a contentious document, it might better be taken simply as it is, the place where the churches can come together and converse so that they may hear not themselves but God's word in and through the texts. God speaks through the scriptures in an ever-new voice in every present situation. The interpretations of the churches only collide when they turn from the text and face each other, as it were, independently of the text. Instead of trying to prove by debate that each church's interpretation of the scripture is prescribed for all, it seems more intelligent to allow the different meanings of the word of God to emerge in conversation about the scriptural witness and to be receptive to its many teachings.

Normative Structures on the Local or Congregational Level of the Church

I now direct attention to the organizational structure of the basic existential unit of the church. This may be called loosely the local church; it is defined on the organizational level as the place where Christians existentially experience their being a member. Concretely this usually turns out to be defined spatially in terms of where the church assembles and is called the assembly, the congregation,[32] the parish, the eucharistic community, the "place" where people come together to hear the word of God preached and to respond in worship.[33] A discussion that aims at determining some fundamental parameters or norms for the church at this level amid the extravagant diversity of such congregations has to take historical and social conditions into account. This discussion cannot be decided univocally by an appeal to scripture or pure theological reasoning. Whatever is said here must be laid against the background of the social and historical differences between congregations.

---

32. The term "congregational" is used here in a descriptive sense and should not be understood in the technical sense of "congregational polity."

33. The "church" is not the place, but the unity of those assembled which most often and obviously occurs in a church. It is not the place because these people remain a unit, as Richard Hooker observed (CCH, II, 172 n. 54), even during the time when they are not gathered.

History and sociology bear witness to the enormous differences among Christian congregations; that differentiation or fragmentation of polities is increasing not decreasing. Great differences among continents, cultures, and nations account for some diversity. Many churches are more or less homogeneous and thus differences among them arise out of ethnic, national, or linguistic factors.[34] One can fairly expect that a local church of peasants who lack formal education and a highly educated congregation of city dwellers might require a different style and probably a different form of church polity. Different cultures and different groups within a given culture harbor differences in the way they estimate and relate to authority. In an individualist culture where self-actualization, personal conscience, and religious freedom are prized, authority will have to be exercised in a less autocratic and more democratic fashion. Fundamental political postures and provisions, such as the separation of church and state, bear significant influence on ecclesial polity, and this can be demonstrated by the contrast between churches in different cultures or amid different groups in a pluralistic society. The church will occupy the time of people in more traditional and less differentiated societies differently than the church in the suburbs of a complex Western industrial society. Differences do not make as much difference in a pluralistic society as they do in closer, less mobile cultures and societies. The relative ease in developed societies with which one may change his or her religious congregation and affiliation contains new social instruction about what is essential and what is less important in a church. Nothing in today's church, not the scriptures, not history, not sociology, and not theology, dictates a single congregational polity for all Christians.

---

34. H. Richard Niebuhr's *The Social Sources of Denominationalism* (New York: World Publishing, A Meridian Book, 1972) explores the many social and historical factors of differentiation that transcend doctrine or theological matters. This is not to deny that diversity of beliefs can offer grounds for division among churches. But most theologians accept a distinction between the human response of faith to revelation and the formulations of theology and doctrinal beliefs. This elementary distinction opens up space for unity in faith amid differences in belief that is analogous to the pluralism of church polities. See Roger Haight, *Dynamics of Theology* (Maryknoll, N.Y.: Orbis Books, 2001), passim; also supra, xii.

Diversity is a given, and it is understandable. The point, however, is not simply to let a thousand different churches bloom, for they are already in full flower and their petals are scattering in the wind. The question for ecclesiology is whether one can delineate some common structure to the Christian congregation, not in order to overcome diversity, but to find what the churches share in common. This requires a noncompetitive view of Christian congregations on the primary social existential level. Differences are to be expected and commonalities sought within the differences.

Such a process might begin with attention to the standard norms of theology. These include fidelity to scripture and more generally the history of the church's tradition. The equivalent of congregational polity constituted the framework for the development of the church during the New Testament period. The church began in small communities, most likely breakaways from the Jewish synagogues. One cannot quite replicate that particular past existence today, but some connection with scripture and tradition is needed to authorize a specifically Christian order. Church organization must also be intelligible and coherent with general theological understanding of the nature and purpose of the church and its relation with the world in which the church exists. Finally, the empowerment of the Christian life that a given church polity implies should be factored into the organization of a local church.

Another step in constructing a template for church organization on the local level can employ a functional analysis that mirrors the process of the formation of the church in the earliest period. The functions that are considered here are drawn from the history of the church. A more or less common way of designating these offices and ministerial functions since the early modern period is to relate them to what Calvin called the offices of Christ and to look for organizational structures that mediate these ministries to the community. I recall here the four offices considered earlier: teacher-prophet, priest, minister to the poor, governor or administrator.

In this way of thinking, each church should have an office or a minister or a provision that enables the whole community to assume responsibility for these ministries. The church should have a ministry of the word, an office endowed with responsibility and authority to preach, to criticize in the name of the word of God, and to teach. A church should have a minister of the sacraments, a presider of the eucharist, an office that receives people into the church through the sacrament of baptism, and a leader of prayer, worship, and the devotional life of the church. The church should have an office and ministers who assume responsibility for assisting those in society who are in need, both inside the community and outside it. The church requires an office of administration, of leadership, a governor or overseers with various differentiated levels of authority. It seems evident that the functions of these offices and officers are more important than their names. How ministry is delivered and how the offices are internally structured are less important than the ministries themselves. If the churches can overcome a certain tendency to a nominalism that looks no deeper than the name to find the ministry, one might find much more congruity among the churches than is apparent at first sight.

Finally, given the extensive and structured differences among local churches, it might be useful to characterize some essential attitudes that all the churches could adopt in their consideration of other churches. One such attitude is drawn from Calvin who considered the divine authority of various ecclesial arrangements. In principle, human arrangements cannot bind the conscience before God. But God wills for the church its well-being and this implies some order. By indirection, then, various church orders, while not directly willed by God, indirectly reflect and manifest God's will for the community's well-being.[35] Moreover, some forms of government have the sanction of centuries of service. The church cannot quite be imagined without them. Though their exact form may not be prescribed, they merit the consideration of all churches.[36] Another essential attitude is one that regards the various ecclesial arrangements from a noncompetitive perspective. Diverse forms of offices and ministries need not be negative but can be a positive sign that a church has become an inculturated part of a particular people. Conversation and

---

35. Calvin, Institutes, 4, 10, 4–5.
36. BEM, "Ministry," 53–54.

a common search for bridges between the churches should lead toward mutual recognition across diversity. Only rarely would some difference prohibit all forms or levels of communion among local churches; such communion should rather be constantly fostered by pastors and ministers.

The Normativity and Authority of Larger Organizational Structures

What may be said of the normativity and authority of larger church institutions such as denominations, structures that govern regional communions, national churches, or universal communions? How can we begin to understand or assess the quality of the unity that is predicated of the whole church? The historically realist assumptions contained in the premises of an ecclesiology from below rule out the binding normativity and authority of a single church structure that unites all Christians. A realistic consideration of history does not allow the possibility of the whole church becoming unified in a single institution.[37] The approach to this topic has to retain a delicate balance between historical realism and principles that seem to challenge the historical data with normative language. The extensive range of differences that characterize the pluralistic situation of the world church today speaks for itself. The three levels of discussion that follow, dealing with descriptive reflections, constructive reflections, and theological attitudes, will hardly solve the issues. But they help define the state of the question.

1. An observer of the church has to be impressed by the fact that pluralism so characterizes the polities of the world church on the macro level that it is difficult or impossible to claim that any single church polity can or should subsume all the others. There is certainly room for discussion of whether any given institutional form is better for this or that church in its concrete situation than another. But the history of ecclesiology practically demonstrates that a pluralism of churches is not an evil but demanded by history itself. There is more to be said about this because the quality of unity pertaining to

---

37. The universal jurisdiction of the pope over the whole Roman Catholic communion is not contested here. But its claim that it bears the same authority on members of other churches does not seem realistic.

the whole church cannot be jettisoned, even though the ideal of the uniformity of a single institutional Christianity has disappeared.

The history of Christianity and its ecclesiology seem to indicate another maxim: the larger the institution, the less direct authority it possesses relative to the individuals in the local churches. This seems contradicted by the gradual growth over two centuries of the direct juridical authority of the pope over individual members of the Roman Catholic Church.[38] But the actual authority of the pope in the lives of individual Catholics may be overestimated. It is certainly differentiated.[39] The point here is not to undermine the authority of the pope within the Catholic Church or the role of Petrine ministry in the church at large, but to suggest that on the macro level this ministry requires less juridical authority and more symbolic religious authority. This latter appeals to a religious response and freedom by evocation of gospel values relative to the present situation; it cannot be reduced to legal power. Genuine religious authority does not control but enters into dialogue, exhibits transcendence, and persuades. "Authority is relational and interdependent. The ecclesiological theme of reception highlights the relation between authority and communion (cf. Jn 1:1–12)" (NMC, 106).

Another lesson may be learned from the fragmentation of denominational churches and the relative ease with which people change their denominational identity. This indicates that a competitive evaluation of churches has diminished. People in developed societies have come to expect a pluralism of churches, so that generally speaking such a pluralism provides positive options. Individual churches or denominations no longer share an absolute character but have been and are subsumed under some undefined higher umbrella of Christianity itself. This should not be taken as an attack on denom-

---

38. Another way of reading the history of the papacy sees the pope gaining more and more authority over fewer and fewer constituents. Each time the pope claimed more juridical power, the church lost communicants, in the East in the eleventh century, in the West in the fifteenth and sixteenth centuries, and in the West today by attrition.

39. Pluralism in the Roman Catholic Church is increasing on a variety of planes. This church is no monolith. Surely, the details of this general statement need to be filled in by cultural and regional studies. Surely, too, certain behaviors can be legislated and codified. But there is no single uniform response on the religious level of reception and commitment across the whole church.

inational identity or a suggestion that they have no important role. The new awareness of the pluralism of religions may enhance their importance. It is their absoluteness that has succumbed to a more pervasive historical consciousness.

2. If the descriptive reflections seem deconstructive, the same generalized historical consciousness that mediated them also supplies constructive ideas. They need only to be listed rather than described, for they have become self-evident in the wake of the ecumenical movement of the twentieth century. The relativity, not relativism, mediated by historicity and the particularity of every church leads churches to be more open toward other churches. The ecumenical movement was dependent upon the rise of historical consciousness and continues to reinforce it. This openness to and dialogue with other churches has encouraged a general recognition of the offices and ministries of other churches. Of course, such recognition always operates within limits assigned by the ecclesiologies and theologies of any given church. But the movement is headed toward more openness to other churches and acceptance of their distinct identities. Still further, the degrees and forms of possible communion between churches are potentially unlimited. Once mutual respect among traditions can be assumed, so that various forms of association and communion are not threatening but mutually enhancing, churches can enter into agreements among themselves that are less tense and legalistic. A good deal of communion among churches goes on in the informal levels of the laity as distinct from pastors so that church bodies are often far ahead of their leaders.

3. Schleiermacher's historical consciousness allowed him to recognize the limits of any church structure and its ecclesiology. His theological method when applied to the church distinguished the church and the world, but held together the divine activity of Word and Spirit in the human institutions of the church through which divine agency worked. This allowed him to make some fundamental distinctions and articulate principles that negotiated the unity of the church and the plurality of churches. The invisible dimension of the church is God as Spirit at work in it; the visible dimension makes real and tangible the effects of the Spirit. Relative to truth and error, all branches of the church are particular, limited, historical, and

marked by some degree of error; but the truth is never absent from the church and always at work countering error. His belief in the power of the Spirit urging the church toward unity elicited several maxims that are appropriate to the situation of pluralism.[40]

ECCLESIAL EXISTENCE

The organizational form of the church helps define the identity of its members. The range of different forms of ministry and polity among the churches produce different attitudes and convictions about the church. Yet a clear and unmistakable nucleus of common beliefs, ministerial goals, and interpretative language characterize the great majority of Christians across the whole church. If the Spirit is operative in the whole church, one can expect that this consensus will not be far from the apostolic faith.

Ministry creates the space in which ecclesial existence happens and flourishes. That ecclesial space should be christomorphic; it should help transform its participants into the form of Jesus Christ. For this to happen, ministry should be patterned on the ministry of Jesus. Thus the kinds of ministry that correlate with the fourfold offices should find some parallel in all Christian churches. We are at the heart of ecclesial existence here even though the analysis remains discursive and abstract.

Ecclesial existence is shaped by the word of God. The various forms of the church's ministry of the word mediate the word of God to the community. Preaching at Sunday worship has become an almost universal practice. Such preaching takes a variety of forms and styles: it may be didactic, hortatory, or prophetic. All sorts of other ministries of the word from teaching to publishing characterize the Christian church. This ministry aims at so communicating the word of God that the object of Christian faith comes to provide the largest vision of reality and encompassing set of values within which Christian existence unfolds. The word of God provides Christian existence with meaning and coherent vision.

---

40. Several of these principles or maxims were enumerated earlier; see supra, 6–7.

Ecclesial existence is nurtured at the meal of disciples, the Lord's Supper. The invitation goes out to all to come in for the banquet. Jesus Christ is present in the eating of this meal in community and consequently present to each communicant. This is a true and real presence but appreciated by faith alone. At this communal meal Christian life is truly and really sustained and nurtured in the direction of outward-oriented love that unites the community and stimulates social concern and service. Baptism and the eucharist are the two main sacraments. Some churches recognize more rituals as proper sacraments. But all churches have various rites and spiritual practices that loosely fit the broad notion of sacramental mediation or the principle of accommodation by which God's presence and grace is mediated to the faithful in history.[41] The "priestly" ministry of Christ mediates God's salvific presence in manners other than preaching and interpreting.

The community of ecclesial existence is a place for healing, and a great variety of ministries stimulate this seminal experience of being made whole. Healing, after the pattern of Jesus' ministry, can be spiritual, psychological, material in the sense of being an ultimate security against deprivation of the necessities of life, and physical in the sense of the Samaritan's binding of wounds. One cannot be a member of the community and leave these dimensions of human existence behind. The space provided by this ministry reaches out to every phase of human existence, to being itself, and then extends outward into society by the agency of the members of the community. Ecclesial existence entails being a disciple of Jesus Christ. The disciple patterns his or her life on that of Jesus and takes up his ministry according to the capacity of each and the external context, circumstances, and possibilities. Ecclesial existence implies service.

Ecclesial existence should be a communitarian existence. Oversight coordinates the activities of the community and aims at promoting the unity of the community through recognition and reconciliation of differences and marshalling resources, that is, leading. Any given church may actually be a community held together by a balance of

---

41. According to this broad principle of sacramentality, a community sitting in silence and attending to the Spirit of God would constitute a communal sacramental act. A rudimentary sacramental theology is outlined in chapter 6.

power, by oppositions in tension with each other, by tacit agreements to disagree forged in some hostility. But it is not meant to be so. Ecclesial existence is intended to be harmonious, reconciling, based on love. Surely this is utopian language, but surely too is Jesus' language of the kingdom of God. On that premise, the possibility of this aspect of ecclesial existence having some actual purchase on the community depends on an ecclesial administrative authority. In one way or another the headship of Christ has to be mediated historically and socially. True, the New Testament itself suggests various forms of church polity, and ecclesial organization has become considerably more variable than ever before because of the multiplication and fragmentation among the churches. But in this situation centripetal forces are signs of grace. Deep social harmony in a given church, accompanied by the other facets of ecclesial existence, usually reflects the power of the Spirit in an authentic church of Christ. It will be rare if such a community lacks a clear line of administrative authority.

The fourfold ministry in the church should be aligned with the movement of God as Spirit in the church. The emergent church of the first century experienced the Spirit of God at work in its various members and collectively in the community. That experience ought to be available to Christians in their churches today. Jesus Christ provides the norm for discerning the authenticity of the Spirit for the Christian community. Speaking broadly here, Jesus and the Spirit provide the values and the inspiration for creating new and sustaining old ministries in the church.

A fitting conclusion to this discussion might be directed back to fundamental premises and attitudes. The Holy Spirit can be operative in different forms of these four kinds of ministry. The Spirit of God cannot be reduced, restricted, or limited to the inspiration of one form of ministry. This foundational assumption has to be matched by an openness to read the same Spirit in the different forms of these four kinds of ministry. There is no exclusive form of church administration and polity, no single human language for preaching God's word, no single theology of the eucharist, no single definition of the order of deacon or theology of development. To think of the ministries inspired by the Spirit in competitive terms contains a paradoxical denial of the biblical witness to God as Spirit.

Authentic Christian experience of the Spirit simultaneously releases the Spirit from the prison of human confinement and in so doing releases human freedom from narrowness and arrogance.

The hard questions. Three sets of different positions on matters relating to ministry raise the hard question of whether or in what degree they should divide the church. The first difference stems from the different "ideas" or fundamental conceptions of the church outlined in the last chapter. They elicit different conceptions of the grounding, the language, and the appraisal of the status of the office of ministry and the person of the minister. The one conceives ordained ministry derived from the Spirit but mediated through the common priesthood and ministerial responsibility of all the faithful and delegated to a few; the other understands ministry "as derived directly from the priesthood of Christ" and forming a structure that is constitutive of the life of the church.[42] BEM tried to hold these two together, but the responses of the churches were mixed on whether it succeeded. The degree and significance of the differences between these two views shows up in the second hard question: how is it conceivable that nonepiscopal churches can come to accept an episcopal ordering of church and ministry? Churches in congregational, free-church, or generally nonepiscopal traditions have internalized the strong positive values that their polities serve and protect; they also harbor deep suspicions about where personal episcopacy and hierarchy may lead. On the other side lies a deep respect for order and the stability of Christian identity in history which are preserved by traditional institutions. These sets of values seem to conflict and are not easily combined. A third area of overt disagreement relative to ordained ministry concerns the access of women. A good number of churches use strong language expressing a conviction that refusal to open up ordained ministry to women is simply theologically wrong and church dividing, while others try to explain why they are not there.[43]

---

42. BEMresponses, III.50. The first of these two positions does not represent a humanistic and antitheological reduction. Broadly speaking the position rests on faith in and experience of the presence and activity of the Holy Spirit in the ecclesial community.

43. Some of the responses to the failure of BEM to take a stand on this issue are fairly sharp. The United Church of Canada says "the text is sexist" (BEMresponses,

Without trying to negotiate or mediate these differences institutionally or theologically, three reflections can soften them. The first has to do with establishing a particular level of discourse distinct from and more expansive than that of declared doctrine. One can describe existential attitudes appropriate to ecclesial existence, attitudes shared by many Christians that do not contradict but transcend the public positions of their churches, and that reach across the divisions between churches. I am speaking here within the framework of ecclesial existence. Second, the positions of each church on these matters usually form part of a larger theological, organizational, and behavioral complex that has an internal logic which is on balance quite coherent, and which in any case cannot be shifted all at once. Each church has to try to appreciate the integrity of the organizational world and culture in which the other church lives. Often church members can do this more readily than official church representatives. Third, the identity of a church cannot be reduced to a single characteristic, trait, doctrine, or practice. This includes especially the dominant traits of particular churches mentioned earlier. The relationships between churches are secured by a rope of innumerable threads, and it cannot be severed by breaking one or other of those threads.[44] Christians agree on innumerable issues across and at variance with official church boundaries. To so identify a church by a specific difference, a single practice, form of ministry, or belief that one can break all communion with that church is a logical, political, and religious mistake that prevents the mutual influence that would allow development on one side or another. Churches that exist in pluralistic and democratic societies should readily internalize these fundamental principles that govern so much of the rest of their lives.

I conclude with a characterization of ecclesial existence from the perspective of church organization. Paul Tillich defines one of the fundamental ontological tensions of human existence as a polarity

---

II.283); the United Church of Christ, USA describes it as equivalent to overt racism. BEMresponses, II, 331–32.

44. Jeannine Hill Fletcher develops this principle relative to the problems of interreligious dialogue and relationships in *Monopoly on Salvation? A Feminist Approach to Religious Pluralism* (New York: Continuum, 2005), 82–101. I will return to this principle in the final chapter.

between being an individual and being a member of a community.[45] This may be translated into the description of ecclesial existence as a tension between being freed by the Christian message and being dependent upon and responsible to the community for the mediation of this salvific freedom. Through the community one receives from God a mode of existence that is theonomous; that is, dependence on God through the community is maximum freedom from ontic fear and heteronomy. The organizational structures of the community do not imprison freedom but communicate and sustain it through faith and ministry. Across the many organizational structures of ministry can be discerned a consistent and constant pattern of four kinds of ministry: teaching/preaching, leadership of worship/sacramental activity, caring for those with material needs both inside and outside the community, and oversight/administration. All these ministries are meant to enhance human existence, to "save" it from self-destruction. All members of the church, and hence ecclesial existence itself, participate in this ministry as both clients and at some level responders and cooperators; ministry is a form of imitation of Christ. Larger church structures bind the most basic units of the church to one another in a vast array of different constellations or patterns of organization. The first criterion of the effectiveness of higher offices is their success in nurturing Christian life on the ground in the parishes, assemblies, and congregations. They do not exist for themselves but for the people of God. They also keep the whole people of God in communion with each other, and success in this task constitutes a second criterion of their value. Finally, the whole Christian church across the many churches, denominations, and communions forms a vast phylum of humanity that shares a common vision of reality and set of values. Ecclesial existence is being a member of this huge communion of saints that far outstrips the often petty rivalry of the churches.

---

45. Tillich describes the tension between being an individual and participation in a community as part of the larger polarity of being which he calls "Individualization and Participation." See Paul Tillich, *Systematic Theology,* I (Chicago: University of Chicago Press, 1951), 176–77.

Chapter 5

Membership in the Church

Consideration of membership in the church opens up another entrance into an understanding of ecclesial existence. Who are the members of the Christian church? Potentially, of course, they are everyone. Very early in its history the church discovered that membership had no restrictions of territory, nation, or culture. "All are welcome." But more focused attention on initiation into the church and what membership entails leads more deeply into the nature of ecclesial existence. The meaning of ecclesial existence will only appear by increment in the course of all the chapters of this book and then only fragmentarily. But this chapter provides a place for looking into a series of issues that have perhaps unnecessarily divided churches over the years and asks whether they might be less important than the elements that are shared in common.

The historical significance of church membership varies widely. Consider on the one hand the membership in the church of a newborn baby in a medieval European town of a thousand people served by a single church and a single priest. The baby was baptized almost immediately, for, should it die, it would be lost. His or her membership in the church was then taken for granted; no one was not a member. The church comprehensively encompassed the experienced world. How different is the membership of the educated adult convert to the Christian church in an urban environment in a non-Western culture today? What is going on in that baptism? Both the acts of becoming a member and the memberships themselves, which are negotiated and ratified through baptism, seem to be as different as the time, space, and cultures that separate them. Yet Christians would ordinarily affirm that both involved the same sacrament of baptism and that it accomplished essentially the same thing in both cases.

160

This tension between sameness and difference structures a series of common elements and questions that pertain to membership in the Christian church, which will be discussed in this chapter. Some of them are as follows: how are we to understand the relationship between faith and baptism? The issue transcends the merely theoretical because it lies embedded in different practices in the administration of baptism. Another tension exists between laity and clergy, both conceptually and practically. This polarity helps explain different church polities and patterns of life. Still another nettlesome issue in ecclesiology revolves around the concepts of a visible and an invisible church. This long-lived distinction has taken on a host of different meanings in various polemical situations. Can it be useful today?

The following chapter addresses these issues by looking at membership in the church under four headings. The first focuses on baptism as the sacrament of initiation. Can there be a common theological understanding of baptism that defines the deepest meaning of being a member of the church while at the same time being able to absorb different baptismal practices among the churches? The second section deals with general principles for understanding the relationship of laity and clergy in the church membership they share together. The third tries to make common sense out of the notion of an invisible church especially in relation to the question of the linkage between salvation and the church. In the fourth I will characterize ecclesial existence from the perspective of the issues of membership together with the hard questions they present to the Christian churches.

BECOMING A MEMBER OF THE CHURCH

Faith and baptism, an internal human response and a public sacrament of the church, are the requirements of church membership. A consideration of the relation between baptism and faith is a good place to begin a discussion of church membership.

Faith

The universal appeal of Augustine makes him a credible authority for establishing some principles on the relation between faith and baptism. I look to his life story and his theology. Augustine came to view his whole life as one in which God's providence and Spirit were continually operative. According to his testimony, his early years were marked by his consistently ignoring the signals of God's saving grace, until he reached a crisis and underwent a conversion. He then converted his own experience into the doctrine of the priority of grace. Somewhat later, faced with Pelagian teachings, he honed that doctrine still further. Augustine felt that from the beginning his life consisted of a restless search for something to which he could commit himself absolutely. In the end he realized that even the restlessness and the search were gifts, the effects of a fundamental teleological pull and a push from God as Spirit. Augustine's experience and theology mirror a pattern found in the New Testament: the way one becomes a Christian and a member of the church begins with an impulse from the Spirit. The positive response to that movement gradually takes the form of faith, and it leads to baptism.[1] In short, baptism follows as a consequence of the saving action of the Spirit and faith.

This narrative generates a second reflection: the primary analogate of the various types of baptism lies with an adult who in faith requests it. The case for infant baptism will be made below, but despite its prevalence infant baptism does not provide the model of the sacrament. On the contrary, baptism follows upon and confirms a previously conceived faith. Baptism presupposes faith rather than creating it from nothing. Even in the case of infants, baptism should not be perceived as a magical act that effects something in a child independently of an active faith community outside of or apart from which the material activity would be meaningless. One must understand the activity of baptizing within a framework of faith-filled subjectivity and not in merely objective terms.[2]

A third point has to be added to the first two: baptism is a public, ecclesial action that entails an initiation into the church. It is not,

---

1. The pattern is illustrated in the story of Peter and Cornelius in Acts 10. It culminates with Peter saying: "Can anyone forbid water for baptizing these people who have received the Holy Spirit just as we have?" (Acts 10:47).

2. This principle should not be read as contrary to the traditional doctrine of the objectivity of the sacraments which I will mention further on and treat more fully in chapter 6.

by contrast, a private action or ceremony, but one that is performed in the name of the church and ordinarily in a public fashion.[3] One has to marvel today at the seriousness with which the early church took the preparations for baptism: a background check, a two- to three-year instruction period, ascetical testing. This does not mean that these practices should be held up as normative for the church in other times and places; baptism has more commonly been treated as something to which there is relatively easy access. But immediate baptism on demand is no ideal either. Rather, because baptism is an ecclesial action that initiates persons into membership in the church, it should reflect the depth and seriousness of ecclesial membership itself.

Baptism

This representation of the sacrament of baptism presupposes that differences between churches and traditions obtain with respect to its nature, function, and ritual form. They extend to "the sacramental nature of baptism; the relation of baptism to faith; the action of the Holy Spirit; membership of the church; infant baptism and baptism of those who can speak for themselves; the baptismal formula; the mode of baptism" (NPC, 77 box).[4] But this list should not be discouraging; it is not certain that these differences need be divisive, and the same documents testify to an increasing willingness of Christians to recognize each other's baptism. What follows takes the

---

3. This prescription does not rule out the possibility of clandestine baptism. It simply declares that such is not the ordinary case or norm.

4. NPC of 1998 was a draft of NMC. It was updated as follows: "the difference between churches which baptize infants, and those which baptize only those able to offer a personal profession of faith; the inability of some churches to recognize baptism performed by others, and the related practice of 're'-baptism; the different starting points and historical development of the terms 'ordinance' and 'Sacrament' (although both are understood as describing the act by which people are brought to new life in Christ); whether baptism is best understood as effecting the reality of new life in Christ, or as reflecting it; the difference between the churches which baptize insisting on the Trinitarian formula according to the command of Jesus (Mt 28:19–20), and those which insist that baptism 'in the name of Jesus Christ' is more consistent with the practice of the apostles (cf. Acts 2:38); the difference between churches which employ water as the instrument of baptism, and those which believe that Christian baptism does not require any such material instrument; those communities which believe that baptism with water is necessary, and those which do not celebrate baptism, yet understand themselves as sharing in the spiritual experience of life in Christ." NMC, 77, box.

lead of BEM in presenting a commonly accepted account of baptism that is attentive to scripture.

The institution of baptism. Baptism is associated with the very foundations of Christianity in the public ministry of Jesus of Nazareth. Most scripture scholars accept on historical critical grounds that John baptized Jesus. While they debate whether Jesus baptized others, it is virtually certain that Jesus' disciples baptized people into repentance and faith in the kingdom of God either during or after Jesus' lifetime. Surely it took time before baptism became recognized as an initiation rite into a distinct Christian church. But the practice reaches back into the time of Jesus and in a variety of ways it is associated with his ministry. Thus serious historical and theological reasons justify its being a foundational Christian practice.

The multiple meanings of baptism. Faith and Order's BEM synopsizes in an impressive way many of the earliest theological interpretations of the rite of baptism. Together they suggest the many positive ways in which the churches can share the deep theological rationales that accompany this rite of initiation into the faith community.[5]

> Baptism is the sign of new life through Jesus Christ. It unites the one baptized with Christ and with his people. The New Testament scriptures and the liturgy of the church unfold the meaning of baptism in various images that express the riches of Christ and the gifts of his salvation. These images are sometimes linked with the symbolic uses of water in the Old Testament. Baptism is participation in Christ's death and resurrection (Rom. 6:3–5; Col. 2:12); a washing away of sin (1 Cor. 6:11); a new birth (John 3:5); an enlightenment by Christ (Eph. 5:14); a reclothing in Christ (Gal. 3:27); a renewal by the Spirit (Titus 3:5); the experience of salvation from the flood (1 Peter 3:20–21); an exodus from bondage (1 Cor. 10:1–2) and a liberation into a new humanity in which barriers of division whether of sex or race or social status are transcended (Gal. 3:27–28; 1 Cor. 12:13). The images are many but the reality is one.

---

5. What follows is cited directly from BEM, B, 2–7.

Participation in Christ's Death and Resurrection. Baptism means participating in the life, death and resurrection of Jesus Christ. Jesus went down into the river Jordan and was baptized in solidarity with sinners in order to fulfill all righteousness (Matt. 3:15). This baptism led Jesus along the way of the Suffering Servant, made manifest in his sufferings, death and resurrection (Mark 10:38–40, 45). By baptism, Christians are immersed in the liberating death of Christ where their sins are buried, where the "old Adam" is crucified with Christ, and where the power of sin is broken. Thus those baptized are no longer slaves to sin, but free. Fully identified with the death of Christ, they are buried with him and are raised here and now to a new life in the power of the resurrection of Jesus Christ, confident that they will also ultimately be one with him in a resurrection like his (Rom. 6:3–11; Col. 2:13, 3:1; Eph. 2:5–6).

Conversion, Pardoning and Cleansing. The baptism which makes Christians partakers of the mystery of Christ's death and resurrection implies confession of sin and conversion of heart. The baptism administered by John was itself a baptism of repentance for the forgiveness of sins (Mark 1:4). The New Testament underlines the ethical implications of baptism by representing it as an ablution which washes the body with pure water, a cleansing of the heart of all sin, and an act of justification (Heb. 10:22; 1 Peter 3:21; Acts 22:16; 1 Cor. 6:11). Thus those baptized are pardoned, cleansed and sanctified by Christ, and are given as part of their baptismal experience a new ethical orientation under the guidance of the Holy Spirit.

The Gift of the Spirit. The Holy Spirit is at work in the lives of people before, in and after their baptism. It is the same Spirit who revealed Jesus as the Son (Mark 1:10–11) and who empowered and united the disciples at Pentecost (Acts 2). God bestows upon all baptized persons the anointing and the promise of the Holy Spirit, marks them with a seal and implants in their hearts the first installment of their inheritance as sons and daughters of God. The Holy Spirit nurtures the life of faith in their hearts until the final deliverance when they will enter into its full possession, to the praise of the glory of God (2 Cor. 1:21–22; Eph. 1:13–14).

Incorporation into the Body of Christ. Administered in obedience to our Lord, baptism is a sign and seal of our common discipleship. Through baptism, Christians are brought into union with Christ, with each other and with the church of every time and place. Our common baptism, which unites us to Christ in faith, is thus a basic bond of unity. We are one people and are called to confess and serve one Lord in each place and in all the world. The union with Christ which we share through baptism has important implications for Christian unity. "There is . . . one baptism, one God and Father of us all . . ." (Eph. 4:4–6). When baptismal unity is realized in one holy, catholic, apostolic church, a genuine Christian witness can be made to the healing and reconciling love of God. Therefore, our one baptism into Christ constitutes a call to the churches to overcome their divisions and visibly manifest their fellowship.[6]

The sign of the Kingdom. Baptism initiates the reality of the new life given in the midst of the present world. It gives participation in the community of the Holy Spirit. It is a sign of the Kingdom of God and of the life of the world to come. Through the gifts of faith, hope and love, baptism has a dynamic which embraces the whole of life, extends to all nations, and anticipates the day when every tongue will confess that Jesus Christ is Lord to the glory of God the Father.

Baptismal practices. These theological interpretations gathered from the New Testament provide in principle a common set of understandings which most Christian churches share. They are not

---

6. BEM comments on this last point as follows: "The inability of the churches mutually to recognize their various practices of baptism as sharing in the one baptism, and their actual dividedness in spite of mutual baptismal recognition, have given dramatic visibility to the broken witness of the church. The readiness of the churches in some places and times to allow differences of sex, race, or social status to divide the body of Christ has further called into question genuine baptismal unity of the Christian community (Gal. 3:27–28) and has seriously compromised its witness. The need to recover baptismal unity is at the heart of the ecumenical task as it is central for the realization of genuine partnership within the Christian communities." BEM, B, 6, commentary.

polemical; they draw out various ways in which Christians who constitute the church are consciously drawn into the sphere of God in the rite of baptism. But, at the same time, different churches practice this common baptism in different ways. In its presentation of a common understanding of baptism BEM strives to highlight those elements of common belief that might allow mutual recognition among the churches of the baptism performed in each church. Most churches, but not all, recognize that "baptism is an unrepeatable act. Any practice which might be interpreted as 're-baptism' must be avoided" (BEM, B, 13). Comparative ecclesiology strives to make that conviction practicable across denominational lines. And for this to happen, churches have to be convinced that the baptism of other churches is real baptism. In what follows I note theologies and practices that have divided churches and then present some considerations that bridge the differences.

Three relatively sharp disagreements arose during the history of the church that include an intricate correlation between theological understanding and the practice of baptism and define an ecclesial life-style. One occurred during the third century, and the writings of Cyprian bear witness to it.[7] Involved in the baptismal controversy between Cyprian and the bishop of Rome was the question of how one church could recognize the baptism of another church if the first church did not recognize the authenticity of the second or accept its ministry as valid. The underlying premises to this issue included various conceptions of unity, schism, heresy, and division. A second issue has to do with the understanding and practice linking baptism with the conferral of the Spirit. It is clear from the biblical witness and the earliest practices of baptism that the ritual dramatized or actualized a mediation of the Holy Spirit. But different churches have ritualized the connection differently.[8] A third problem has to do with the understanding and practice of adult or believers' baptism,

---

7. See CCH, I, 174–76.

8. "Christians differ in their understanding as to where the sign of the gift of the Spirit is to be found. Different actions have become associated with the giving of the Spirit. For some it is the water rite itself. For others, it is the anointing with chrism and/or the imposition of hands, which many churches call confirmation. For still others it is all three, as they see the Spirit operative throughout the rite. All agree that Christian baptism is in water and the Holy Spirit." BEM, B, 14.

on the one hand, and infant baptism, on the other. The Anabaptist movement during the Reformation highlighted the conscious, intentional character of sacramental action.[9] More specifically, can the case for infant baptism be made in a way that adequately represents the necessary role of faith in the practice of baptism?

A series of considerations drawn from the history of ecclesiology and BEM, especially when they are taken cumulatively, help to mitigate the divisive force of these differences. In other words, the point is not to wipe out differences but to establish a larger framework of shared faith that can absorb them into itself as legitimate and even positive and enriching differences. To that end, one might begin with a simple reflection on the historical consciousness that has been internalized by the churches across the world today. In a globalized and pluralistic world, where differences have become less resisted and more accepted and even valued as part of historical existence itself, it becomes considerably harder, even though not impossible, to brand the understanding and practice of another church as schismatic or heretical. Modernity and postmodernity have imposed a certain modesty on the churches.[10]

The majority of Christian churches baptize infants but also baptize adult believers. By contrast, churches that baptize only believers tend not to recognize infant baptism, partly because it lacks positive backing in the scriptures. In response, BEM notes that the dominant New Testament pattern of baptism involves a "personal profession of faith"; but it adds that "the possibility that infant baptism was also practiced in the apostolic age cannot be excluded" (BEM, B, 11). Some argue that reports of whole families becoming Christian point in the direction of a possible infant baptism.

Certain theological reflections on the ritual of baptism go some way in softening or mitigating what otherwise may appear as hard

---

9. See CCH, II, 238–39, 257–58.

10. This is reflected in the following commentary of Faith and Order: "As the churches come to fuller mutual understanding and acceptance of one another and enter into closer relationships in witness and service, they will want to refrain from any practice which might call into question the sacramental integrity of other churches or which might diminish the unrepeatability of the sacrament of baptism." BEM, B, 13, commentary.

and competing differences. One is the common consensus arrived at in the West in the thought of Augustine that the prime agency of the sacraments does not lie with the minister or even the church. It is rather God who acts in the sacraments. Another consideration, almost in tension with the first, is that this action of God transpires within and through a faith community. Whoever baptizes is not acting as a private individual. Baptism is a corporate action insofar as it reflects the faith of a community.[11] These two considerations set the meaning of baptism firmly within the context of a faith community and make it an action of faith and a trust in God's action. "The differences between infant and believers' baptism become less sharp when it is recognized that both forms of baptism embody God's own initiative in Christ and express a response of faith made within the believing community" (BEM, B, 12 commentary).[12]

These considerations have not met the fundamental objection that understands baptism as a sacrament that can only be fruitful when it is engaged by the personal faith of the one being baptized. But this too could be agreed upon by all with the recognition that "when an infant is baptized, the personal response will be offered at a later moment in life" (BEM, B, 12). In the case of infants, the community as it were assumes responsibility for the nurture of children in the faith that leads in the direction of such a commitment. Baptism of a child represents a corporate act of faith that God remains active within the church's process of educating young people in the faith.

---

11. This is why baptism "is normally administered by an ordained minister, though in certain circumstances others are allowed to baptize." BEM, B, 22.

12. Several evangelical churches complained about language of BEM that appeared to make baptism itself, in the sense of the ritual, the agent of what the sacrament effects. The criticism includes Catholic theology's formula *ex opere operato*, the effectiveness of the sacrament "in the positing of the sign." In response these churches "prefer statements which spoke of God's action in baptism" rather than statements where baptism is the grammatical subject (BEMresponses, IV.156). Although this will be discussed in the next chapter in reflections on sacramental theology, it is critical in the case of infant baptism. Augustine is the prime author of the doctrine of the "objectivity" of the sacraments in his *De Baptismo*. The point is that the sacrament is effective not because of the minister, and not because of the rite, but because of God alone through Christ. This defines the essential meaning of *ex opere operato*. The doctrine is entirely consistent with Augustine's later ferocious anti-Pelagianism. These objections seem to neglect this classic doctrine which actually supports the convictions from which the objections come. See CCH, I, 229–31.

It becomes finally effective when a person responds to God's action in faith.[13]

The discussion over the legitimacy of infant baptism and how faith becomes operative in the sacrament has so focused the question on the human response of faith (*fides qua*) that the role that the objective content of faith (*fides quae*) plays in the sacrament and in the life of the person baptized is neglected.[14] The object of faith as contained in the belief system of the Christian churches represents the vision of the community, the worldview as that has been revealed in Jesus Christ and appropriated by the church. Obviously this vision has been and remains the subject of myriad interpretations, and subdivided into a wide variety of traditions, and subdivided again confessionally, regionally, and congregationally. But none of these interpretations undermines the relevance of creeds, classical formulas that summarize the scriptural message in one form or another and stand as public representations of the Christian view of reality. The cognitive dimension of faith is meant to be appropriated by the one baptized when he or she is received into the community. The content of this faith vision cannot be incidental to the meaning of baptism. It contains the symbolic worldview into which the new infant member of the church will be socialized. This vision of reality will supply newly baptized adults with the basic principles of their existence.

---

13. This too corresponds with Augustine's doctrine of sacramental fruitfulness. While some churches think that BEM does not make the case for infant baptism strongly enough, the United Methodist Church [USA] believes that a failure to recognize the validity of infant baptism stems from an individualistic conception of faith. Baptism is not simply an act of an individual or for an individual; it is a community act in a communal context. The faith necessary in baptism cannot be reduced to "a personal confession of faith." Infant baptism relies on the indispensable factor of the *corporate, communal* faith of the church. Failure to appreciate this originates in a "typically Western, voluntaristic [individualistic] understanding of human personality and church community rather than the biblical concepts of covenant faith and corporate personality." BEMresponses, II.185.

14. The Orthodox Church of America seeks to retrieve for the sacrament of faith the relevance of the content of faith into which one is baptized. "We believe that the adoption of a single creed to be used throughout the universal church for baptism, as well as for other solemn occasions of creedal confession, has become an inalienable part of holy Tradition and represents today for the Orthodox Church a major criterion for recognizing or not recognizing the legitimacy of baptismal practices employed in the various Christian traditions" (BEMresponses, III.16–17). In fact the OCA recognizes the baptism of some churches but not all.

Together these reflections set up a common framework that can support variations in the symbolisms and rituals that make up the sacrament of baptism. Baptism with water in the name of the Father, the Son, and the Holy Spirit can be administered by immersion, by sprinkling, by pouring, and so on. "As was the case in the early centuries, the gift of the Spirit in baptism may be signified in additional ways; for example, by the sign of the laying on of hands, and by anointing or chrismation" (BEM, B, 19). It seems important to state categorically that Christian sacramental actions are not something that human beings accomplish. Nor is this magical action: secret formulas that contain power within themselves to accomplish supernatural effects. Sacramental action is based on and remains throughout a prayerful appeal in trust that God be present and active in the Christian community according to the promise made in Jesus Christ. The vast majority of Christian communities practice baptism and share this same existential faith: baptism initiates one into a community of faith in God's constant forgiving presence within the community as Holy Spirit after the pattern of Christ. Baptism symbolically represents, signs forth, and mediates the structure of the life of faith of the Christian, and that faith-life unites one to Christ and leads one in trust through death to resurrection. Given this common theology and spirituality, BEM can urge communion in baptismal understanding and practice: "Churches are increasingly recognizing one another's baptism as the one baptism into Christ when Jesus Christ has been confessed as Lord by the candidate or, in the case of infant baptism, when confession has been made by the church (parents, guardians, godparents and congregation) and affirmed later by personal faith and commitment. Mutual recognition of baptism is acknowledged as an important sign and means of expressing the baptismal unity given in Christ. Wherever possible, mutual recognition should be expressed explicitly by the churches" (BEM, B, 15).

CLERGY AND THE PEOPLE OF GOD

A major factor differentiating the churches lies in the relation between the members of the church at large and the clergy or corps of ministers. The differences here are both theological and practical. They run deep because they help establish an ecclesial culture that becomes a spontaneous second nature shaping ecclesial existence. Compare, for example, the ecclesiology of Richard Hooker in which he insists on an ontological differentiation of the ordained priest from the layperson, and the ecclesiology of Friedrich Schleiermacher where he carefully circumscribes the power of the clergy with an essentially congregational polity in order to avoid clericalism.[15] The difference between a hierarchical and a congregational view of the relation between the clergy and the people of God extends far into ecclesial life, especially to a theology of the sacraments. Another problem lies in the way hierarchically structured church polities clash in modern democratic societies with the views of highly educated church members. The tendency to define members of the church condescendingly as "lay" or "nonclergy" may be alienating the most talented members of some churches. By contrast the fragmentation entailed in pure-form congregationalism seems to undermine the authority of historical tradition. The aim of this section is not to resolve these tensions and problems, but to show how baptism as initiation into ecclesial existence can help to establish common principles that can serve to open lines of communication between different churches and ecclesiologies.

Baptism and the "Order" of the Laity

Baptism is more than initiation into an organization. Baptism constitutes a mode of being in Christ, in the church, and in the world. I appeal to the ecclesiology of John Zizioulas in an effort to explain the status of the baptized and thus the people (*laos*) in the church.[16]

Zizioulas's conception of membership in the church counters a superficial or pragmatic conception of organizational identity. The church, as the body of Christ animated by God as Spirit, exists as

---

15. See CCH, II, 185–86 and 325–27 for the views of Hooker and Schleiermacher respectively.

16. It may be important to note that Zizioulas has a hierarchical conception of the church. The church is constituted by four orders: the laity, the deacon, the presbyter/priest, and the bishop. The object of the appeal to Zizioulas is not this hierarchical structure, but his conception of the "place" of the laity in the hierarchy of the whole church.

a corporate mode of being in the world. To be drawn into membership in the church entails taking on a "higher" or "deeper" and more humanly authentic mode of being. He expresses this with the term "order" indicating a place or status of being. Baptism for Zizioulas becomes a kind of "ordination" because it defines a person's place or position in a community in relation to others. For Zizioulas, there is no "ordinary" member of the church, as in the phrase "mere laity." Laity are not defined negatively as nonclergy, but positively as those who participate in a mode of being as a result of receiving an ordained position within the ecclesial community. In Zizioulas's thought-world, this conception flows from a broadly Platonic and iconic imagination that understands ecclesial existence as participating in a divine archetype. This background may not be generally shared. But the resultant language still rings true across churches and cultures. Being baptized entails being drawn into a mode of ecclesial being-in-the-world.[17]

In addition to constituting a mode of being in the world, being a member of the church involves responsibility. The church professes the doctrine associated with baptism and the status of the laity or people of God called the priesthood of all the faithful. This doctrine appeals most explicitly to 1 Peter 2:9: "But you are a chosen race, a royal priesthood, a holy nation, God's own people, that you may declare the wonderful deeds of him who called you out of darkness into his marvelous light." Luther elaborates the doctrine at some length.[18] In Luther's ecclesiology the doctrine contains several aspects and implications but essential to them all is the status of the people of God, their rights and powers, as a congregation and as individual members of the community of saints. Luther breaks down the powers of ministry into seven. "Mostly the functions of a priest are

---

17. As an example of crosscultural analogous understanding, one might appeal to Schleiermacher's ecclesiology and conception of membership in relation to Zizioulas's. Even though Schleiermacher was also a Platonist, his explanation of the church is thoroughly historical. And yet Schleiermacher too would affirm strongly that the church is the body of Christ, animated by the Spirit, so that members by baptism and regeneration are drawn up into a new form of historical existence by their union with Christ in the Spirit.

18. Martin Luther, "Concerning the Ministry" (1523), *Luther's Works*, 40 (Philadelphia: Muhlenberg Press, 1958), 7–44; Paul Althaus, *The Theology of Martin Luther* (Philadelphia: Fortress Press, 1966), 313–18; CCH, II, 45–46.

these: to teach, to preach and proclaim the Word of God, to baptize, to consecrate or administer the Eucharist, to bind and loose sins, to pray for others, to sacrifice and to judge of all doctrine and spirits."[19] These rights and powers derive from union with Christ, so that the members of the church united with the Word of God take on the priesthood of Christ. This understanding has roots in Luther's conception of the wonderful exchange between Christ and the member of the church who is justified by grace through faith.[20] There is more to be said organizationally about the ecclesial regulation of these rights and powers. But the appeal to Luther draws the analogy between the status and "place" of the members of the church in both Orthodox and Evangelical theology and ecclesiology.

Finally, the shared status of all the members of the church who are initiated by a common faith and baptism is expressed forcefully with the phrase "a discipleship of equals." But this requires a more extensive commentary.

Discipleship of Equals

The Christian community or church is composed of the disciples of Jesus. In recent times the theme of equality in the church has assumed considerable importance. What does it mean to say that baptism initiates one into a community of the discipleship of equals? The response to this question goes some distance in getting to the heart of ecclesial existence.

I draw the phrase "a discipleship of equals" from feminist theology. Elisabeth Schüssler Fiorenza argues in *In Memory of Her* that Jesus in his ministry and the earliest Jesus movement promoted a discipleship of equals that later succumbed to patriarchal culture.[21] In other words, the Pauline maxim "There is no such thing as Jew and Greek, slave and free, male and female; for you are all one person in Christ Jesus" (Gal 3:28) was a realistic Christian ideal. It

---

19. Luther, "Concerning the Ministry," 21.
20. "Therefore when we grant the Word to anyone, we cannot deny anything to him pertaining to the exercise of his priesthood." Luther, "Concerning the Ministry," 21.
21. Elisabeth Schüssler Fiorenza, *In Memory of Her: A Feminist Theological Reconstruction of Christian Origins* (New York: Crossroad, 1983).

expressed the essence of the gospel and was implemented in embryonic ecclesial forms. Elizabeth Johnson formulates the goal of feminist liberation theology in terms of an equality that "does not obviate differences either between women and men or among the vast diversity of women."[22] I appeal to feminist theology at this point in order to show that its deep foundational insight into the theological sources of equality apply generally to Christian ecclesial existence.

To make this case as convincingly and as radically as it must be made, one has to begin with the counterintuitive character of the claim that all human beings are created equal. No lesson of human life can be clearer or more obvious than the fact that human beings are not equal. They differ in size, shape, weight, intelligence, talent, every kind of ability, character, temperament, and so on. Human beings are measured and judged, hired and dismissed, loved and hated, welcomed or shunned, exalted or humiliated, because they are different and unequal. Every individual is different; each one is unique; no two are equal; and that's a fact. Part of the glory of God lies precisely in God's infinite capacity for creating through natural processes difference and inequality. God has written inequality into God's own creation, and marvelously so.

The Christian appreciation of the equality of all human beings rests on resources that expand the doctrine of creation in the boundless love of God.[23] One facet of God's love for human beings is particularly applicable to the Christian conception of the relationship between God and human beings at this point. God's love for human beings raises them up to a new status of being the friends, the beloved, of God. Martin Luther and Søren Kierkegaard developed this relationship with pointed analogies.[24] In the marriage of two persons of unequal social standing or condition, the authentic and

---

22. Elizabeth A. Johnson, *She Who Is: The Mystery of God in Feminist Theological Discourse* (New York: Crossroad, 1982), 31–32.

23. One cannot separate God's creating from God's love; God creates out of love, and God loves what God creates. But one can mentally distinguish these two aspects according to a human framework, and the device releases insight into different levels of the creature's relationship to the creator. The logic that follows lies beneath the theological tradition of double gratuity, the freedom of God in both creation and redemption.

24. See Martin Luther, *The Freedom of the Christian, Selected Writings of Martin Luther*, II, ed. George Tappert (Philadelphia: Fortress Press, 1967), 27–28; Søren

thoroughgoing love of one spouse raises the other spouse to his or her level. In this view of things and in this Christian experience, identity is not wiped out, nor is the original negated. But the whole person is transformed by the love of the other and elevated, so that he or she participates in the dignity that is shared by the spouse. Such love can be called re-creative love because it transforms the beloved. Such is the redeeming love of God that is revealed in the event of Jesus Christ, and in many cases it plays itself out historically. People who share a new being in Christ often act differently. The father in Jesus' parable of the Prodigal Son represents this kind of love on God's part; its effects are frequently acted out in the altruistic lives of the saints.

Another teaching of the New Testament relative to the human response of love for God is contained in Jesus' joining of the two commandments of love of God and love of neighbor. The two commandments are linked together as the summation of the whole law: they are the two great commandments (Mk 12:28–34).[25] This was not an uncommon teaching in Jesus' time. But in Matthew's account of the "Great Judgment" (Mt 25:31–46), responses to disciples of Jesus are equated with responses to Jesus himself, now in the role of eternal judge. This parable or allegory of the final judgment about what is important in human life has consistently been interpreted as representing a kind of conflation between the love of God and the love of neighbor. This means that love directed to God implies love of God's own, of those who belong to God, all the persons whom God has created and loves. Shifting the direction, it also means that love of one's fellow human being for his or her own sake transcends its immediate object and implicitly reaches the author of that other, God. True love of God is, in the sense of entails, love of neighbor, and authentic self-transcending love of others implicitly includes God as its object.

On the basis of these conceptions of love, the church has frequently been depicted as a community that reflects the love of God for

---

Kierkegaard, *Concluding Unscientific Postscript* (Princeton: Princeton University Press, 1941), 438–40.

25. Luke appends the story of the Good Samaritan to the linkage of love of God and love of neighbor in response to the question of who is my neighbor. Jesus' pointed reply is that neighbor includes the enemy. See Luke 10:29–37.

human beings and the return of that love to both God and one's fellow human beings. This is particularly strong in Johannine literature: "A new commandment I give to you, that you love one another; even as I have loved you, that you also love one another. By this all will know that you are my disciples, if you have love for one another" (Jn 13:34–35). It seems obvious that the Christian community at large has never fully realized this injunction. It remains an ideal of which the actual church forms a Platonic shadow. It seems obvious to note that Christians behave like just about everyone else. And yet the intentionality becomes a conscious part of being a Christian and acts as a judge. Moreover, the dynamics of genuine love of God and love of neighbor actually do manifest themselves from time to time in varying degrees. In countless communities differences among people are acknowledged and received as blessings from God; frequently enough love transcends cultural, racial, and social boundaries. In some communities and churches this happens spontaneously; other churches urge with more insistence a code of ethics that respects the neighbor. But when equality is recognized and acted out so that it becomes a characteristic of actual social life, this is perceived and received as grace.

Ecclesial existence designates life within a religious community, life as a member of a church and the church. Every human being is constituted by a polarity of being an individual and being a member of a given community or communities in a specific time or place. This community is structured by certain ideals that are realized only fragmentarily and with considerable variation. The level of participation of any given individual in this community varies. But one has to say that in every authentic ecclesial community the ideal of love becomes real in some measure, for such love is one of the signs of the authenticity of the community itself. This does not refer to the love of God for each individual and for the community: this is a given, a premise on which the community is founded. It refers rather to the responding love for God that is proven genuine by love of neighbor. When equality is affirmed and respected across diversity, when love raises up the other to an equality of personhood, there God is effectively present. This happens in the church fragmentarily, but more frequently than is apparent in the obvious demeanor of the large organizational structures. It is much more likely to be experienced locally.

God's personal love establishes the identity and equality of each member of the community, and self-transcending love that recognizes this equality becomes a sign of a church's authenticity. From this it follows that communities should be suspicious of every institutional structure that even hints at discrimination. Differences that signal or lead to inequality are what authentic church overcomes. Late modern Western culture has gradually become aware of sexism as a system of radical injustice. It was gradually unmasked within its various systems as blatant abuse of power. This accounts for the strong reactions of some churches to BEM's tolerance of churches that disallow women's ordination and hence a place in the ministerial roles and the administration and government of the church. For many Christians and many churches this attacks at the roots the discipleship of equals that Paul named explicitly: "there is no such thing as male and female . . . ; for you are all one person in Christ Jesus" (Gal 3:28). This idea of the discipleship of equals, in a place where people come together in the gift of equality, raises the question of hierarchy, of a ranking of members with divine sanction. This can be examined at two points, the event of ordination and the kind of authority the minister of the gospel possesses or mediates. The next two sections take up these issues.

Ordination for Ministry

What goes on when a church ordains a person for ministry in the church? Churches interested in the unity of the church have to engage the question of the mutual recognition of church ministries and ministers. And this entails reflection on essential standards according to which ministers are accepted by a given church. Because ministry often corresponds with the style and character of a church, the understanding of ordination may differ greatly from church to church. We need a broad understanding of ordination, including what happens in ordination, and a common structure of the rite. BEM addresses that.

According to BEM, "ordination denotes an action by God and the community by which the ordained are strengthened by the Spirit for their task and are upheld by the acknowledgement and prayers of the congregation" (BEM, M, 40). This definition of ordination remains open to a good many variations in interpretation. But BEM appeals to scripture to further circumscribe the act. "The Church ordains certain of its members for the ministry in the name of Christ by the invocation of the Spirit and the laying on of hands (I Tim. 4:14; II Tim. 1:6); in so doing it seeks to continue the mission of the apostles and to remain faithful to their teaching" (BEM, M, 39).

BEM intends an understanding of ordination that can be affirmed by the greatest number of churches. It carefully describes what the church does in this ritual and what happens because of it. First of all, ordination is "an invocation to God that the new minister be given the power of the Holy Spirit in the new relation which is established between this minister and the local Christian community and, by intention, the Church universal" (BEM, M, 42). Churches disagree on what that new relationship is but together hold that a new minister is authorized in this public act. Second, ordination is "a sign of the granting of this prayer by the Lord who gives the gift of the ordained ministry" (BEM, M, 43). Confidence that this is the case rests on the promise of God's grace in Jesus Christ. The priority of God's grace underlies the very invocation of the Spirit. In this understanding ordination brings to a coherent conclusion the priority of grace in the personal experience of the ordained of a call from God and the ratification of a call through the church community. Third, ordination is "an acknowledgment by the Church of the gifts of the Spirit in the one ordained, and a commitment by both the Church and the ordained to the new relationship" (BEM, M, 44).

These large parameters for understanding ordination of ministers still leave room for a good deal of different practices within the churches. In fact most churches are very careful about the selection of candidates and the whole process leading to ordination. Many of the different instantiations of call and ordination are also described in the portrait supplied by Faith and Order, and these will be considered in the next chapter. At the same time this language also conceals some deep differences that run parallel to the divergent ideas of the church discussed in chapter 3 and the understanding of the office of

ministry alluded to in chapter 4. These result in two different conceptions of the relationship between the ordained minister and the
rest of the faithful. The references to Hooker and Schleiermacher at
the head of this part of the chapter supply good examples of the two
typical views. Some churches see ordination by the church as setting
the minister apart from the faithful; others reject that and, fearing
clericalism, take precautions that that idea not break the egalitarian
character of ecclesial existence. Some churches see ordination as a
sacrament; others reject the idea out of hand. Some churches see the
minister entering into a new relationship to God and to the community as a result of the action of the Spirit, a new relationship that
can be considered ontological and, analogous to baptism, perduring.
Others see ordination establishing a new juridical and functional relationship with the community, one that will be acted out in the
exercise of ministry itself.[26]

These two types of view, and they are outlined here only loosely
as types, may not be as severe in the way they are acted out as in the
metaphysics that underlie them. Moreover, there are positions on
the issue of defining this relationship between minister and faithful
that combine the best features of both. Consider the formula of the
United Methodist Church [USA]: "We assert the parity of dignity of
all members in the common priesthood; and yet we do set persons
apart by ordination for word, sacrament, and order. We believe the
ordained ministry is more than a division of function, and consequently agree that ordination is not to be repeated; and yet, we are
not willing to claim that in ordination something primarily ontological occurs" (BEMresponses, II.196).[27] What they are clear about is

---

26. There is a tendency to associate these two views with Protestantism and Ca-
tholicism/Orthodoxy. "The Protestant tradition has generally held that the distinction
[between ministry of the laity and the ordained] is functional, that is, the ordained are
set apart for special functions. The Roman Catholics as well as the Orthodox have made
ontological distinctions between the ordained and the laity." BEMresponses, IV.11.

27. One should notice a tendency in this discussion to construe the category
"ontological" in a way that approaches the idea of "physical." For something to be
ontologically real suggests that it has its basis in a physical reality. Certain aspects of
Aristotelian metaphysics can give this mistaken impression. By contrast, I take it that
ontology refers to being and that one's being is affected by one's being-in-relationships
that are acted out. Social existence does not pertain to nonbeing but affects people
ontologically.

that "ordination is more than ceremonial recognition of professional competency for ministry and more than bestowal of a special status in the church. We believe that because ordained ministry is more than a commitment to certain functional responsibilities, the concept of 'representative ministry' in United Methodism must never be allowed to perpetuate the perspective that ordination is merely a function" (BEMresponses, II.196).

This example shows that ontology and social functional existence are not necessarily antithetical and that these two ways of thinking can be mediated. There is no need for social function to be characterized as "merely" and reduced to something negligible. We are ontologically constituted by our action and our reception or constitution by the community. In any case, the language adopted by the Methodist Church shows how these two typical conceptions of the effects of ordination and the resultant relationship to the community can be subjects of meaningful discussion.

Clergy and Religious Authority

This chapter is about the members of the church. Most churches have clergy who are also members of the church; they are called and usually ordained to lead the community in various facets of ecclesial life. The ideal of a church called to be a community of equals in discipleship raises the question of religious authority. What is religious and specifically Christian authority and how does it function in the church? Because the issue is vast, it should be clear that what follows touches only certain selected points that are quite elementary, but they are not without value in a consideration of ecclesial existence. I will highlight the complexity of the issue, raise up foundational principles relative to religious and Christian authority, and show that these urge a pluralism of churches.

Any discussion of religious and specifically Christian authority today has to stipulate the complexity of the topic. The complexity holds on every level: psychological, social, cultural, and theological. Every individual relates to authority in slightly different ways, and every attempt at generalization runs into cultural, social, racial, and class distinctions. Some whole cultures are more authoritarian than

others; some authors describe a complete breakdown of the traditional structures of authority in contemporary developed societies.
What is authoritative for one is not so for another.

The concept of authority and attitudes toward it take on a variety
of forms in the churches themselves. At the extremes, for example,
the sources of authority are mediated in significantly different ways
in a large hierarchical church and a small congregational church.
Every church in between these poles develops a cultural framework
within which various kinds of administrative and spiritual authority
are negotiated. Even within a specific church with a tightly defined
authority structure, some groups will be more comfortable with a
fundamentalistic or legalistic exercise of authority while others will
lean toward openness and freedom. Given this complexity, what follows simply highlights selected general principles that encompass
the diversity and have some implications for a common ecclesial
existence.

It is difficult to limit a discussion of religious authority. But these
four considerations have bearing on ecclesial life in all the churches.
To begin, authority may be regarded as a social relationship in which
one person or agency has the power, ability, or capacity to influence,
direct, command, or move the thought or behavior of others.[28] This
social relationship depends on two factors: in the person with authority it presupposes some form of competence, and in the one
influenced by authority some form of recognition or acknowledgement of or trust in the competence of the one in authority. Offices
of authority are based on a public recognition that those who usually
hold those offices have the competence that goes with them.[29]

Second, it may be important simply to state that authority is a
positive social institution. The church preserves its revelation and
faith intact over the course of history not miraculously or without
historical means, but through ministries, offices, and structures of

---

28. I am indebted in this discussion to the essay of Joseph Komonchak, "Authority
and Magisterium," in *Vatican Authority and American Catholic Dissent: The Curran
Case and Its Consequences,* ed. by William W. May (New York: Crossroad, 1987),
103–14, who reflects on church authority from a Roman Catholic perspective.

29. Churches have a wide variety of different means for testing the competence of
ministers which range from simple recognition of charismatic authority to programs
of education and bureaucratic testing of the candidate.

discernment and interpretation that deal with the authenticity of ongoing Christian interpretation. The fundamental rationale for authority in the church, then, is entirely positive: various structures of authority are the vehicles for the church to retain its identity and integrity in the course of history.

Third, it helps to distinguish strictly religious authority from authority in disciplinary and political matters. Strictly religious authority engages the relationship people have in this case with God; it deals with matters that are transcendent. In the Christian church, the source and measure of this authority relate to Jesus Christ. Even the primary authority of the scriptures derives from Jesus Christ, because he provides the central and centering symbol that before all else unites the Christian imagination with God. The various witnesses to the Spirit of God must be tested against the scriptures that analogously function as a constitution for the church's belief because they continue to represent Jesus Christ to Christian consciousness.

Fourth, and this is the important point today, religious authority must in the end appeal to human freedom. The relation of human beings to God cannot be coerced; it must begin and end in freedom.[30] The ultimate authority in religious matters is God or the experience of God. Religious experience bears within itself its own self-authenticating authority. Thus religious freedom is increasingly being recognized as a human right. One cannot coerce or even argue anyone into authentic faith because relationship to God rests on a depth experience of transcendence that is ultimately inviolable.

These qualities of authority take on new significance for the churches at the present time in history. The situation of the whole church at the beginning of the twenty-first century offers new challenges for the clergy and the way they exercise authority. It also has a bearing on the authority of the whole church today vis-à-vis the world. More specifically, the phenomenon of increasing globalization and communication throughout the world throws a dramatically new emphasis on religious pluralism. Pluralism, always understood as differences interacting within some common field, affects the religions

---

30. The point is forcefully stated by Vatican II, *"Dignitatis Humanae:* Declaration on Religious Liberty," 1–2.

in relation to each other and the churches within the whole church. Still more pointedly, pluralism subtly relativizes, in the sense of de-absolutizes, the authority of the individual churches and the whole church in its commerce with other religions.[31] What are some of the constructive demands this situation places on the church?

More and more the actual pluralistic character of humankind is forcing a recognition that this is the natural condition of human existence in history. This recommends pluralism as not intrinsically bad, not something to be overcome, but a positive and potentially enriching condition of the human race. A positive conception of pluralism allows theologians to appreciate the variety that has been codified into the New Testament. Once differences are placed within a field of common conviction that allows them to interact in a potentially positive way, a new world of dialogue or noncompetitive conversation can also take place. For example, the ecumenical movement of the twentieth century moved from separation on the basis of difference toward unity: the movement drew energy from the premise of historical consciousness that many of the differences that divided churches were cultural phenomena that did not need to separate them. The more recent pluralist consciousness, by contrast, moves from unity to difference: it senses a substantial unity among Christians that allows differences to flourish. An affirmation of the substance of faith and the core of ecclesial existence allows different ecclesial traditions to retain their integral identity and authority.

The pluralist situation of today's world and an increasing pluralist consciousness affect the church and the churches in two ways. First, relative to the whole church, Christian theologians will think and write more self-consciously against the background of the religious pluralism of the whole world. It seems impossible in today's world to project a Christian imperialism that will absorb the whole world into itself. The Christian theologian must rather think about the Christian faith within a context of a pluralistic world of religious experiences that are vital and meaningful to whole populations. Second,

---

31. One might argue theologically that this should not be the case. But that seems short sighted. There are some positive aspects of globalization despite its many actual negativities. An ecclesiology from below cannot ignore the growing interdependence of people in the world but must interact with it.

the current situation suggests that Christian language will gradually become "dewesternized" in order to address other cultures, just as it changed during its first expansion into the Mediterranean basin. The church will also continue to deepen its conversation with other religions and be affected by them.

New demands are also being made on the Christian churches in their interactions with each other. It is more difficult, if not impossible, for one church to maintain its status as the one true church over against the other churches. In a pluralist situation such a claim appears incredible. The absolute character of the denominations is breaking down, even as the positive character and identity of each one is being enhanced. This simultaneous universalizing and particularizing dynamic is intrinsic to a globalized consciousness. On the one hand, there will be much more shifting or changing denominations on the part of Christians, while at the same time the specific character of a given church as providing a home and an identity will be cherished. If these two vectors and possibilities are held together so that they enhance each other, they can be read in a positive light. Should not Christians belong, worship, and act in a church where they feel at home? Across both of these movements the quality and exercise of religious authority has to become much more intentional in its appeal to human experience and freedom.

I now turn to another question that has to do with membership in the church: the distinction between a visible and invisible church.

VISIBLE AND INVISIBLE MEMBERSHIP IN THE CHURCH

A distinction between a visible and an invisible membership in the church has a long life in the history of ecclesiology. But it has not always meant the same thing. I will suggest a meaning that all the churches might accept relative to a specific issue. As the church begins a new millennium, it faces a new problem: how are Christians to understand the salvation offered in the church in relation to other vital religious traditions? For example, if we are willing to affirm that salvation is available to people outside the boundaries of the visible church, how should their relation to the visible church be conceived? Two responses to this question, or two conceptions of this relationship, are currently being debated within the Christian churches. They represent two primal conceptions about the church that are quite different. An understanding of the invisible church can help to mediate between them.

A Theological Understanding of the Invisible Church

What would it mean to talk about membership in a visible and invisible church? A good deal of controversy has revolved around this distinction. Some will suggest that the distinction be abandoned, but it "hangs around" by taking on new meanings in new and different contexts. I will outline several of these meanings and suggest a constructive theological usage that could be widely accepted and useful because it is simple and straightforward.

A first and classic meaning of an "invisible church" and thus an invisible membership can be found in the ecclesiology of Augustine. During the course of the fourth century, the church, newly legitimized in the empire, grew rapidly with conversions of convenience. The sociological constituency and the moral consistency of the church were altered considerably: a community of "saints" became much more obviously a mixed community of saints and sinners. Those who were baptized and received the sacraments were obviously enough members of the church, but only a relatively few, according to Augustine, were truly regenerated by God's grace and were united to God by a faith animated by divine love. The membership of this inner core of the saved was invisible because only God could know this inner dimension of faith.[32]

The conciliarist crisis and controversy in the late fourteenth and early fifteenth century brought a distinction into common usage that was quite different than that of Augustine, but bore a certain analogy. Two and then three popes, each with his different territorial loyalty, presided over the church. The situation made the following distinction virtually apparent: on the one hand, the church was divided institutionally and hierarchically; on the other hand, the great body

---

32. Augustine, *On Baptism, Against the Donatists, Nicene and Post-Nicene Fathers,* 4, ed. Philip Schaff (Peabody, Mass.: Henrickson Publishers, 1994), IV. 4. 5. See CCH, I, 226–28.

of Christians remained the same as they always were, united in the same faith in God through Jesus Christ. Thus a clear distinction obtained between the whole body of Christians united in one faith and the institutional structure that was supposed visibly to bind them together but in this case divided them.[33] The distinction in some measure deabsolutized the hierarchical structures in place by understanding them as being in service of the community of the faithful, and this allowed the actions that led to the restoration of the papacy to go forward.

The Reformers of the sixteenth century also used a distinction between the visible and the invisible church, but once again it took on new resonances from the particular historical context. The Reformers were reforming the church in various ways and depths. But for the most part the Reformers did not believe that the only true Christians or true churches were those defined by their own reforms. For example, Luther and Calvin defined the true church formally, that is, in terms of qualities that could be realized in many different churches. The true church existed were the gospel was preached and the sacraments were authentically administered. In this conception, the visible church referred to any given empirical church; usually the referent was the town, or city, or regional church. The meaning of the invisible church in this context varied: sometimes it referred to the communion of saints wherever it gathered united in one authentic faith around gospel and sacrament; sometimes it referred to the whole Christian movement united in one faith as distinct from the Roman institutional superstructure; sometime it referred to Augustine's inner core of those truly regenerated and united with God. By contrast, and thus reinforcing this meaning of the distinction, Roman ecclesiology strongly asserted that the church is a visible organization in history and that one cannot separate an invisible church from the empirical, hierarchical Roman Church.

All of these meanings of a visible and an invisible church are coherent in their contexts. The problem is that they do not travel well;

---

33. See Dietrich of Niem, "Ways of Uniting and Reforming the Church," in *Advocates of Reform*, ed. Matthew Spinka (Philadelphia: Westminster Press, 1953), 150–52. Also CCH, I, 380–81.

they carry historical baggage that clashes with elements of a new situation. What is needed is a theological distinction that is formal enough to transcend the particularities of history and yet preserves the dialectic between human and divine forces in the church.

Schleiermacher defines the terms of a distinction between the visible and invisible church that may be acceptable to all parties. He writes as follows: "Thus the *invisible* church is the totality of the effects of the Spirit as a connected whole; but these effects, as connected with those lingering influences of the collective life of universal sinfulness which are never absent from any life that has been taken possession of by the divine Spirit, constitute the *visible* church."[34] There is only one church and it is an empirical, historical phenomenon. But the Spirit of God released by Jesus the Christ is at work in this church, and the activity of God as Spirit sets up a tension between the drag of the sinfulness of the world within the church and the uplifting and divinizing effects of the Spirit. The term "invisible church" refers to all those effects, the sum total of them, which flow from God as Spirit. This preserves everything that was guarded by the distinction from Augustine onward. It underlines that the church can never be reduced to a human organization and never romanticized with a theological language that leaves the organization behind. This distinction of Schleiermacher goes a long way toward making sense of the visible and invisible dimensions of a single church.

A New Problem in Ecclesiology

The distinction between visible and invisible dimensions of the church arose in an intraecclesial discussion of membership in the church and the authenticity of church structures relative to the divine life within the community. A new problem in ecclesiology has to do with the relationship of the church and membership in the church to an encounter with God's salvation, either in this world or eschatologically. Other world religions are as vital as ever and in a new self-conscious way. How do these living religious traditions fit into the plan of salvation as conceived by Christians? Since the

---

34. CF, #148, 677.

time of Cyprian of Carthage the church proposed a teaching that the ordinary means of salvation was the church, so that there was no salvation outside the church. Despite the fact that the context of Cyprian's language does not support a universalized version of the axiom, and that qualifications continually circumscribed the proposition, it fairly accurately reflected Christian consciousness right up to the modern period. But the postmodern and globalized world, where other religions are becoming better known and appreciated by Christians, exerts considerable pressure on the doctrine of no salvation outside the church.[35] The roots of the theological problem go back to christology and are being discussed there. The problem also has a dimension of theodicy, for one cannot quite imagine how God would allow so many who are outside the church to live and die without an opportunity for salvation. But the issue also has direct implications for understanding the role of the church in history.

Various factors have made this particular problem come to the fore at this time. More and more historical consciousness has seeped down into general cultural consciousness. People expect different religions in different cultures. Many Christians have a certain curiosity about other forms of religion and are attracted to various practices of other religions. Fewer thinking Christians view the world's religions as devoid of God's grace and salvation. Pentecostal churches and the independent churches of Africa are inculturating Christianity in non-Western religious ways that are new and distinctive because of association with local religion. For a variety of reasons, therefore, the attitude of Christians toward other religions today is considerably more open than in the past. And this calls into question the absoluteness of the claim that no salvation exists outside the Christian church. The significance of such a development lies in the intimate relation of the nature and mission of the church to salvation, so that the issue engages a theological conception of the fundamental role of the church in human history.

---

35. In some ecclesiologies all who are saved are considered members of the church in some implicit manner or degree. A historical consciousness and a desire for straightforward language makes this "solution" theologically too easy and on the level of common sense confusing. I will say more about this in what follows.

Two Views of Membership in the Church

Openness to other religions on the part of Christians around the world carries with it changing understandings of the nature and role of the church in the world. One must continually accommodate new experiences in contemporary constructive theological understanding. A positive view of the role of other religions relative to the ultimate salvation offered by God entails a new understanding of the church compared to what prevailed prior to the modern period. Two distinct options can be singled out as representing two directions of thinking on this matter.

The first goes back to a christology that underlies a christocentric vision of the creation of the universe and of the salvation of humankind. God negotiated the salvation of all human beings in the event of Jesus Christ. This places Jesus Christ at the center of history in the metaphysical sense that all salvation, before and after his appearance in history, is constituted by that appearance, first as the promise of that salvation, and then as its actualization now in the present and in the ultimate future. This view is metaphysical because it proposes an understanding of a deep structure of reality subsisting below the level of historical events and transcending them as an overall divine plan. This view proposes that wherever salvation occurs, those who are saved are saved through Jesus Christ, that is, by the hidden efficacy of the life, death, and resurrection of Jesus. But this involves making all who are saved in some metaphysical way members of Christ's church, not the obvious, empirical church of history, but the anonymous, invisible, latent, and metaphysical church that corresponds with the boundaries of salvation itself. In this construction, the notion of an invisible church has been constructed to accommodate the maxim of no salvation outside the church. All those who are saved, no matter to what religion or situation in life they belong, are implicit members of the church, because they have been touched by "the effects of the Spirit." The influence of the Spirit is invisibly tied to Jesus Christ, in one way or another, as the mediator of this salvation.[36]

The second mode of thinking also has a christological provenance in a position often characterized as christological pluralism. In this

---

36. The connection of the Spirit of God with the historical appearance of Jesus Christ may be the subject of a variety of theological interpretations.

view, the methodological approach to the christological question pro-
ceeds from below, that is, giving due attention to the data of history
and integrating theological interpretation into the historical narrative.[37] This heuristic framework, for example, makes one hesitate
to say that someone who lived before Jesus Christ was saved by
Jesus Christ. The statement is too historically counterintuitive to
make sense on the hearing. By extension, the view that people who
lived before Jesus Christ are members of the Christian church also
seems paradoxical. It does not follow that this view cannot be explained metaphysically, but such language is speculative and yields
an explanation hardly convincing to many. By contrast, this second
view does not reach for a concept of the invisible church to make
Christians out of non-Christians, but is willing to say that God saves
non-Christians independently of Jesus Christ or in a way that is not
connected with Jesus by any perceivable historical causality. This too
is a metaphysical construct, but one closer to the historical data.

At the present time both of these conceptions, and perhaps others
as well, are held within the churches. Both of these positions can support a conception of the church as missionary, but the strategy and
tactics of mission may vary considerably. Both can be supported by
an "orthodox" christology, that is, one that is faithful to scripture and
the classical tradition of its interpretation. At the same time these
are considerably different understandings of the place of the church
in the situation in which it finds itself today, that is, in dialogue with
other vital religious traditions. But this difference may not be a difference that merits division among churches. It seems to be a difference
of views found in most mainline churches and about which churches
in communion with one another should continue to converse.

ECCLESIAL EXISTENCE

One cannot logically carve out space between being a member of the
Christian church and ecclesial existence because they are synonymous terms. Being a member draws up into itself the dimensions

---

37. This contrasts with a method "from above" that "begins" with doctrinal
conceptions and uses them to interpret the historical narrative.

of meaning that have been parceled out among these chapters. According to that division this existential account of being a member restricts the discussion to the topics engaged by this chapter: initiation, the faith world internalized by the church member, the egalitarian relations within the church, how the status and authority of ministers fit into this religious social existence, and the vision of the ultimate place of this community in the context of human existence itself.

Baptism initiates a person in a public, conscious way into a community that exists in an interactive relation with an accepting and loving God. In itself this initiation begs the question of whether such a relationship is available outside the community. The predominant view, that this initiation rite cannot and therefore should not be repeated, stems from the experience that formally entering into this relationship with God is decisive; one crosses a threshold into an ongoing relationship that lasts and cannot be broken even when a person fails to respond. The Christian has become attached to a God who is always accepting, forgiving, and loving. Baptism seals a relationship whose effects cannot be limited to the temporal moment of the event but formally introduces a person into a sphere of existence that conditions his or her being. It also constitutes ecclesial existence in a public way.

Faith constitutes and actualizes this relationship, and hence from several important perspectives faith explains the experience and meaning of the sacrament. From the perspective of the community that the individual joins, baptism is the prescribed rite of initiation that expresses the faith of the community. In this event the baptizing minister represents the community in welcoming a new member into the church. Infant baptism highlights the responsibility of the church as community for the nurture of the new member: this human being is an infant member of both the human and the faith communities. In the beginning the community holds within itself the faith as it does the means of life that together will sustain the growth of the child. Also from the perspective of the community one has to consider the content of the faith that is contained in the scriptures and summarized in the churches by confessions and creeds. That belief system plays a more important role in people's lives than can be detected in the particular events that mark their course. The large vision of faith operates like an inner compass that consistently points to the true north of authentic existence. Concrete decisions and particular beliefs do not usually exhaust its content or its comprehensive and integrating influence. All people live by some faith, and baptism initiates people into a community of faith. From the perspective of the individual and his or her personal faith, adult baptism best symbolizes the full cycle of gift and acceptance that constitutes the baptismal relationship with God. Infant baptism requires a later acceptance by faith to be existentially fruitful; that fruitfulness can be more dramatically symbolized in the adult ceremony.

Ecclesial existence urges conscious behavior that respects the gift of equality that is the result of God's gift of unmerited and infinite personal love. The equality mediated through the Christian community operates on a different plane than so-called natural equality or legal rights. God's love transcends all measure and raises up the lower to a common exalted status. The Christian community empowered by God's love provides the space where that new dignity and value of each human person can flourish. People are equal because they are so in the sight of God's loving eyes. But this equality does not eradicate inequality which remains as both the joy of particular individuals and the constant temptation of humankind to prejudice and self-promotion. When the Christian community follows the discriminating practices of a given culture that devalue groups or classes of people, it implicitly gives counter-witness to the object of its own faith. This is not an isolated temptation but the pervasive tendency of the human species. It requires constant surveillance and a kind of affirmative action to overcome it. The church needs consistent checks on whether the structure of its ministry dominates people or consistently raises them up.

The tendency toward group bias sometimes coexists with religious authoritarianism: the temptation to exercise control seems to be augmented by a feeling that one is acting with God's authority or, by some twisted logic, protecting it. Jesus and the gospels communicate suspicion of religious authority. In Jesus' portrayal of it, genuine religious authority serves; it does not reflect self-assertion; its authenticity appears in its humility before imperatives that have God as their source. It ultimately respects and appeals to freedom. As religious, this authority differs quite radically from the variety of different types of authority that govern life in society and that inevitably infiltrate into ecclesial existence. From the perspective of one who does not exercise this authority but is subject to it, the Christian view of authority liberates ecclesial existence from all authoritarianism, which by definition cannot come from God. For those who exercise authority, it requires close attention to the values of the gospel. Authority as sheer power over freedom will ultimately alienate Christians.

Authentic ecclesial existence cannot turn back into itself in the sense of devolving into a narrow ecclesiocentrism. The faith vision that sustains it bears universal relevance; its beliefs concern human existence itself. The many churches, however, house considerably different Christian beliefs about the world outside the church and its ultimate destiny. This point will return again in the consideration of the church-world relationship and how the church implements its mission to the world. But the new globalized situation of ecclesial existence has engendered a new sense of historicity and pluralism. And a new respect for the operation of God as Spirit in the whole world has allowed many Christians to look more positively on other religions and think of them in less competitive terms. An absolutely firm conviction of the truth of God revealed in Jesus Christ need not undermine the truth of other religions. Rather, Christians enter into dialogue with them because the truth they contain is inspired by God as Spirit.

The hard questions. The topic of church membership contains several disputed areas, and some of them are serious. One hard question has its roots in the two different conceptions of the church and of its ministry discussed in the last two chapters respectively. From there it reaches into the question of the status of the ordained minister relative to the other members. The one sets the minister apart within the community; the other defines the minister purely by function. Although the two conceptions are quite different, they can be bridged: the church at large can accommodate both views in a language simultaneously social and ontological that supports a real religious authority of the minister and at the same time renounces religious authoritarianism. But these two really different conceptions of what is going on in ordination and the status of the minister in the church will be tested in the following chapter that discusses the activities and the powers of the minister.

Another hard question has to do with the degree to which churches that hold different doctrines on substantial issues can enter into communion with each other. It is clear to all that many Christians in the same denominational church today, if they have not given up their faculty of critical judgment, will hold different beliefs about many issues. The same is true of churches. But on some relatively substantial issues one group of churches may declare a belief and practice that contradict the belief and practice of other churches. How should the churches handle deep differences?

Such is the case with the idea of the unrepeatability of baptism. BEM asserts that "Baptism is an unrepeatable act. Any practice which might be interpreted as 're-baptism' must be avoided" (BEM, B, 13). This provision met a good deal of opposition from those churches that "re-baptize." Some churches may simple call the unrepeatability of baptism into question (BEMresponses, I.80). Sometimes churches allow "re-baptism" as an act of personal care for believers who ask for it (BEMresponses, I.71; I.116). Faith and Order simply raises up as a problem that needs further discussion "the inability of some churches to recognize baptism performed by others, and the related practice of 're'-baptism" (NMC, 77 box). In other words, the practice of re-baptizing effectively denies the validity of the original baptizing church. Cyprian was faced with an analogous problem relative to the bishop of Rome. He believed that the value of unity was higher than that of a baptismal practice, and he remained in communion.

A final hard question has to do with the way the great majority of churches who celebrate the sacraments relate to those churches that eschew sacramental action altogether. For example, the Religious Society of Friends (Quakers) in Great Britain reject the necessity of baptism for salvation because they see "no necessary connection between this single event in a person's life and the experience of transformation by the Spirit. We cannot see that this rite should be used as the only way of becoming a member of the body of Christ." They regard fixation on particular sacramental forms as dulling the sense of God being present in all of creation and remain open to the mediation of God's grace through other religions. Grace cannot be restricted to particular forms, rites, or liturgies: "the reality of God's presence may be known in worship that retains none of the traditional elements that are central to the life of many churches" (BEMresponses, IV.219–21). The problem here is that these views do not quite supply positive reasons not to baptize, and, in fact, some churches supply other "sacramental" acts of initiation in place of baptism. The result is that, instead of interpreting baptism more broadly and acting in concert with the great majority of Christian churches, these churches erect a perhaps unnecessary obstacle to communion.

These and other hard questions remain. But they should not have the last word. In the conclusion to this work I will introduce the notion of partial communion that may capitalize on all that the churches share in common despite differences that up to now continue to divide.

Chapter 6

Activities of the Church

What do churches do? People who have been raised as Christians and continue to participate in church life largely take the answer to such a question for granted. But in places that are not predominantly Christian and increasingly in the Western world many have no idea whatsoever of what people in churches actually do. A description of the activities of the church helps advance an understanding of it.

The church as a whole, across individual churches and denominations, does many things that are common to all. While one might hesitate to say these actions are "the same," analogies bind them together in something more than a family resemblance. But these common practices, especially with respect to worship, also provide occasions for deep divisions. One reason for this lies in the intimate character of activities that relate one to God. Because of the personal and spiritual depth to which they appeal, language, style, form, and rhythm in liturgy all matter, and differences in the doctrine and performance of sacred actions become magnified. Describing and explaining the common patterns of worship in the Christian community thus becomes a delicate operation.

By stepping back and taking a wide view of the activities of the church, they easily fall into a division of two groups that correlate neatly with two aspects of the template I have used to organize an understanding of the church. I refer to two forms of ministerial activity in the church and the areas of church life to which they relate: the one pastoral and the other missionary. The distinction revolves around the direction or sphere of the activity that can loosely be designated as the internal life of the church (*ad intra*) and the world outside it (*ad extra*). Using sociological language, these different kinds of activity relate respectively to the maintenance and the mission of the church. This chapter will engage those common activities of the church that build up and continually nurture the internal life of the community, especially those intentionally meant to foster the relationship of its members to God and to one another. Chapter 7, which is dedicated to the relation of the church to the broader world in which it exists, will reflect on those activities that reach out into human society at large, the so-called "world."

The goal of this chapter, then, is easily stated and difficult to achieve. It seeks to characterize the internal life of the Christian church in terms of the activities that are common across the churches. After a brief section that locates this discussion more pointedly in relation to other phases of this ecclesiology, the chapter will focus on forms of worship. The next section deals with other activities that round out the picture of the social life of the church. I conclude the chapter with a description of ecclesial existence from the perspective of church activities.

PASTORAL ACTIVITY

Chapter 4 discussed, among other things, the relationship between church organization and ministry. It has been established by historical analysis that church organization grew out of communities with a charismatically based ministry by supplying more or less permanent offices that would guarantee the ministry needed for the well-being of the community.[1] Charismatic function leads to office; office supplies the function of ministry for the community. This chapter builds on the same relationship between community and office, but the perspective moves in the opposite direction. Our concern here is the way in which ministerial activity, in this chapter specifically pastoral activity, affects the whole life of the community. The analysis spontaneously moves back and forth between pastoral ministerial activity and the activities themselves that are led by ministers or pastors. A good way to begin this discussion of pastoral activity is by recalling some of the principles that emerged from the historical

---

1. See CCH, I, chapter 2.

and comparative analyses of the church in the first two volumes of *Christian Community in History* that were summarized in chapter 2.

A Teleological Relationship between Church Orders, Organization, and Ministries

Historical and comparative ecclesiology reveals that a consistent teleological relationship obtains between the offices of ministry, the organization of the church, the actual ministries that serve the body of the faithful in the church, and the practical needs that are served by all of these together. The organization of the church exists in order to provide for the pastoral care of the members of the church. Ecclesiology needs a strong statement of the functional relationship between office and ministry. Organization in the church and of the church cannot be an end in itself but exists for the community and its mission. Many churches conceive their church order as ontologically rooted in the will of God. It is quite important to understand that the insistence on the functionality of church office for ministry does not compete with such an understanding. The point being made here does not lie in any form of reductionism but in understanding the logic of church office. The New Testament quite practically insists that the criterion of ministry is the building up of the body of Christ.

The subject matter of this chapter are the activities of the church that define the inner social life of the people of God, the body of Christ, and the community of the Spirit, and the pastoral ministries that nurture that church life. The term "pastoral ministry" refers to ministerial activity that is directed toward building up the life of faith of the community. An ecclesiological discussion of pastoral ministry in any particular church would require a good number of distinctions and refinements of the concept.[2] But these distinctions exceed the limits of the quest for those elements of Christian pastoral ministry that are shared in common among the churches. It would be an exceptional church that did not possess a more or less stable

---

2. I have in mind, for example, such distinctions as these: between various offices, their responsibilities, and their relationships to each other; between full-time and part-time ministry; between professional and /or paid and volunteer ministry.

ministry dedicated to the maintenance, support, and nurture of the faith life of the community.[3]

The teleological and functional relationship of offices to ministry becomes most apparent on the level of the congregation or parish community. Existentially, the basic or primal unit of the church is the congregation. The assembly itself usually, but not always, defines the range and size of this unit.[4] The primary, in the sense of the most concrete, unit of the church revolves around the gathering of people for worship. In many churches and ecclesiologies this may not correspond with the juridically defined primal unit. But it provides a common imaginative frame of reference for this chapter and the next. This perspective flows from a historical, descriptive, and existential account of the church from below. In this view of things, "higher" forms of ecclesiastical structure, such as dioceses or synods, metropolitanates, presidencies, national churches, communions, and patriarchates, are viewed as being in service to the existential life of faith of the church ultimately in its congregational or parish communities. This perspective cuts across different juridical polities that hold congregations together in larger units. But it does not negate these various structures or minimize their authority relative to each church. The point is to keep the analysis within the range of what all the churches share in common.

The Correlation of Ministry and the Vitality of the Church

One of the goals of this chapter is to explore descriptively the effects of ministry on church life. In may seem obvious that there is a mutual relationship between the ministry of the church, its activities,

---

3. Distinguishing between pastoral and missionary activity and treating them separately does not entail any separation between them or minimizing either in relation to the other. These two forms of activity of the church are intimately related to each other, and the two distinguished kinds of ministry frequently imply each other. I will indicate later in the chapter why and how all pastoral activity should have a missionary dimension. Distinction here is in service of an analysis that will lead to an understanding of the unity of these two phases of church life in a clear, reflective, and integrated way.

4. The history of the church and of ecclesiology is filled with exceptions. For example, a parish may have outstations or mission chapels or dependent oratories. Basic ecclesial communities, house churches, small Christian communities and so on can be constituent elements of a basic ecclesial unit. The point here transcends juridical definitions of a basic unit of the church and reaches for an existential concept that readily admits variations.

and the vitality of church life. But this may be obscured by the fact that ministry is frequently analyzed in terms of power. The ecclesiology of John Zizioulas provides some clarification and help in this area. Although Zizioulas has a strong sense of orders in the church, he describes them in terms of relationships that are both functional and ontological, not in terms of power and authority, but in terms of ontological "place" and function.[5] This opens up a way to appreciate the relationships of those who hold ministerial positions in the church in existential as distinct from juridical terms.

A few foundational principles help to set the context for the rest of the chapter. One is that the vital activity of the church is directly proportional to the leadership it receives, in this case, the leadership of pastoral ministry. In other words, one cannot simply wish that the quality of church life were higher. It depends directly upon the quality of the leadership and ministry that animates church life. To echo an earlier maxim: where ministers are competent and dynamic, these qualities will affect the church; where churches are alive, they will supply charismatic ministers.

Another generalization about pastoral ministry might be formulated in this way: the actual way in which ministers and pastors relate to their communities varies considerably. There is no single pattern or form of the delivery system by which ministry is carried out. Churches have different polities, and within them an ethos, and within it styles, and within them personalities. One major variation slides along an axis between a *ministerium* dominated by clergy and a *ministerium* that is appropriated congregationally by the members of the church at large or the laity.[6] In some churches the polity is set up in such a way that believers appear to be clients of the clergy, in the sense of passive recipients of the gifts from God offered by the church through the hands of ministers. Other churches, especially those with a congregational polity, may be more participatory in ministry and decision making. These structural differences will

---

5. CCH, II, 445–50. See supra, 172–73.

6. I use the Latin word *ministerium* to symbolize "ministry" because of the significant variations in the structures and offices of ministry within the churches. *Ministerium* captures the formal and abstract character of the symbol as it is being used here to encompass such actual differences.

have a major influence on the life of the community. So, too, with the church's symbiotic relationship with society and culture. When a polity or ministerial pattern loses touch with a culture or, inversely, becomes co-opted by society, it will show in the quality of the life and membership of the church.

The goal of ministry is to create, lead, and nourish a community in its relation to God in such a way that it internalizes into its corporate climate an instinct for mutual care. The whole community is the object of ministry, not just in its individual members, but also as a community. Even in more clerically oriented churches the object of ministry is never the subjection of the laity but the animation of the laity in such a way that the whole church becomes a community of mutual support in which everyone finds his or her home and identity.

The goal of ministry in the church might also be characterized as aiming to make the church a spiritual and in some measure social safety net for life on the high wire. On the spiritual level, the church provides its members with a system of symbols with which to formulate a conception of the source, nature, and destiny of human existence itself. One cannot readily grapple with such questions alone. The metaphor of a spiritual safety net surely comes up short, but at least it suggests a resource that is there and operative whether or not one is conscious of it. This safety net is infinitely expandable. It ranges from the ability of the community to be on hand as a resource to help meet personal and family crises on a deep spiritual level. It extends to the everyday and weekly services that mediate the community's dialogue with God. It reaches further in sustaining a set of meanings that locate human existence in the sphere of being itself and providing a vision of ultimate destiny. It would not be accurate to characterize this safety net as a comforting womb. It functions rather as a platform that grounds human life and supplies the premises for a freedom freed for active, creative engagement in society.[7]

---

7. Jürgen Moltmann warns against the way modernity has made three functions of the church, namely, protecting the individual, providing interpersonal community, and being an anchor within changing society, into possible negativities by supporting privatization and withdrawal from social engagement. His caution is something that

The idea of a social safety net is less obvious because the relationships between the church and any given society vary infinitely. The church may perform functions in one society that are carried out by the state in another society. This relationship cannot be defined generally and is open to continual flux. But the church has traditionally been attentive to those who live at the margins of life itself and usually has ministries and ministers that exercise that role. The idea will be discussed further later in this chapter and in the next.

In sum, a direct and proportional relationship obtains between the activities of the church and the ministerial leadership of the church. The organizational pattern by which ministry is structured and the quality of the ministry determine in large measure the actual character and quality of the church.

The Pastoral Agent

If ministry is a deciding factor in the character of church life, it must be added that the candidates who are ordained into ministry have a major influence on the quality of that ministry. *Baptism, Eucharist and Ministry* provides a collective wisdom on ordination and the conditions for it.

The act of ordination by the church is a visible testimony to the action of God in the calling and missioning of ministers. Ordination "attests the bond of the church with Jesus Christ and the apostolic witness, recalling that it is the risen Lord who is the true ordainer and bestows the gift" (BEM, "Ministry," 39). Remember the definition of ordained ministry cited in the last chapter: "Properly speaking, then, ordination denotes an action by God and the community by which the ordained are strengthened by the Spirit for their task and are upheld by the acknowledgment and prayers of the congregation" (BEM, "Ministry," 40).

Given the differences of polity and denominational style among the churches, not to mention theological interpretations of the Christian life, one may expect considerable variety in the profiles of candidates for ordination. But BEM has formulated three conditions

all churches should consider. See *Theology of Hope* (Minneapolis: Fortress Press, 1993), 311–24. The following chapter will provide antidotes to such tendencies.

for the selection of candidates that would find wide agreement among the churches. They are foundational.

The first has to do with personal conviction and a sense of being called to ecclesial ministry: the candidate should have "a personal awareness of a call from the Lord to dedicate oneself to the ordained ministry" (BEM, "Ministry," 45).

Second, this call should "be authenticated by the church's recognition of the gifts and graces of the particular person, both natural and spiritually given, needed for the ministry to be performed" (BEM, "Ministry," 45).

The third condition for the ordination of candidates has to do with training for ministry. In the early church competence was measured more by charism than by formal, directed education and training. In fact, across the history of the church, training for ministry has varied considerably and ordination has not always required formal or school education. But in a world where education is more prevalent, the tendency of the church is to move toward an educated *ministerium*. This usually entails formal training; education is a value. "Candidates for the ordained ministry need appropriate preparation through study of scripture and theology, prayer and spirituality, and through acquaintance with the social and human realities of the contemporary world. . . . The period of training will be one in which the candidate's call is tested, fostered and confirmed, or its understanding modified" (BEM, "Ministry," 46). The church has to oversee the competence of its ministry.

As general as they are, these norms, if they were consciously applied, would go a considerable distance toward insuring a certain quality of ecclesial activity in a pluralist way that corresponded with the different ways of being church in the various traditions. The ideal minister is one who, with competence, virtue, and responsibility, is centered on service to the community. I turn now to the activities the leader leads.

WORSHIP

The church is a religious community. Religious faith holds it together, and Christian faith in God is mediated by Jesus Christ. The principal activities of the church, then, will be religious activities, even though church activities extend much further. We begin with some general principles regarding Christian worship before narrowing the focus to preaching and the Lord's Supper.

General Principles

It is important to recognize that the center of gravity of the Christian church lies in assembly for worship. This provides the very ground of the church's being: it continues to exist on the basis of its existential communion with God on a formal, public, communitarian level. This does not mean that Christians, formally as Christians, do not do many other public things together. But it does mean that worship in the name of Jesus Christ continually lies at the foundation and at the center of the life of the church.

The church as a community provides an existential context in which its members as individuals personally pray to God in innumerable practices of devotion. But Richard Hooker emphasized the role that the church has in providing public forms of worship for the church as a body. These standardized public practices draw the passivity of individuals into recognized patterns of expression; they strengthen the weakness of the individual's devotion at any given time with the enthusiasm of the community. He also pointed out that the church has two central functions in history: the one is to preserve and give witness to the word of God revealed in Jesus Christ and contained in the scriptures, the other is to channel back to God the human response of gratitude and prayer. The main way in which these two functions are carried forward occurs in the public worship of the church.[8]

In several respects the principles for prayer of John Smyth were diametrically opposed to those of Hooker on this point. Smyth stressed the authenticity of prayer measured by its spontaneity enlivened by the Holy Spirit. This led to a certain distrust of objective forms as encouraging passivity.[9] This stress on active engagement in the forms of

---

8. CCH, II, 193–94.
9. CCH, II, 256.

worship lives on today with decided emphasis in pentecostal communities.[10] These two traditions, then, have adopted different expressive styles of worship, each with a coherent theology behind it and clear ties to the apostolic witness of scripture. One need not discount the other. The two "systems" seem rather to reflect different styles of worship that can readily help differentiate different churches for different people.

Regarding the ritual forms of public worship, the history of ecclesiology shows a remarkable stability in the patterns of worship. This is an area that is deeply influenced by historical factors; language, culture, and sets of meaningful symbols have a strong impact on how people respond to God. But despite the diversity of the conditions of the Christian church across time and culture, it has preserved a two-fold dimension in its gatherings for worship: on the one hand, the community listens to and interprets the word of God in the scriptures; on the other hand, it celebrates the eucharist or Lord's Supper. Most often these two ways of formally and explicitly actualizing the relationship of the community with God are intertwined. So basic are these patterns of responding to God that the reformers tended to build their primal understanding of the true church around them. "Wherever we see the Word of God purely preached and heard, and the sacraments administered according to Christ's institution, there, it is not to be doubted, a church of God exists."[11]

Before taking up explicitly a theology of the word and the eucharist, it will be useful to lay out some more or less commonly accepted principles regarding the sacraments. A broad sacramental theology can provide principles for overcoming dichotomous conceptions of word-centered and sacrament-centered spiritualities. I call attention to three ideas that would foster an approach toward a common understanding.

First, the definition of a sacrament always involves a two-fold dimension to its nature and functioning. A sacrament is an external action, or sign, or event, or thing that stands for, mediates, symbolizes, or actualizes a spiritual or transcendent reality. The many

---

10. CCH, II, 472–75.
11. Calvin, Institutes, 4, 1, 9.

definitions of sacraments illustrate the pattern. A sacrament is an external sign of an invisible grace. The outward actions or ritual events and their elements are used to mediate or sign forth something real that transpires between God and the person and the community of faith. This foundational structure provides material and opportunity for rich theological reflection using a variety of methods and frames of reference. But these analyses usually presuppose and work within this matrix of symbolic mediation.[12]

Another principle builds on the first: because sacraments entail a dual structure of external physical event and internal spiritual meaning and effect, sacraments always require or entail the word of God as the designator of that meaning. Word and sacrament belong together. The mutual entailment of word and sacrament in Christian life and church practice means that, when a sacramental ritual is posited, the understanding of what is happening in the action is drawn from scripture. The word of God in scripture interprets and explains what is going on in the ritual event. From apostolic times onward one sees this double dimension in the celebration of the eucharistic meal: the banquet of the Lord involved reading the scriptures and remembering the tradition. One can scarcely imagine a Christian ritual or sacramental action that is not accompanied implicitly or explicitly by a scriptural reading that defines the context of the action itself and ultimately its meaning.

A third principle that enjoys common acceptance among the churches concerns the objectivity of the sacrament analogous to the way this was formulated by Augustine. This means that the efficacy of the sacrament is due to God's promise and action in the sacrament and does not depend on virtue of the minister. This has to be understood in a way that does not reduce the sacraments to some form of supernatural "magical" power contained in a formula or action. But it makes no sense and opens up the possibility of far worse abuses

---

12. This first principle is so elementary that it may be applied to preaching as well as sacramental activity. The act of publicly reading the scriptures or of preaching about their content is a physical event. Although varying degrees of importance are assigned to the action of preaching itself, most theologies of preaching would recognize that it is the internal Word of God or the Holy Spirit who is responsible for the enlightenment and inner conversion of the person preached to.

to maintain that the minister of the sacrament in any way controls God's grace.[13]

These principles of a general sacramental theology help define a common framework for situating a ministry of word and sacrament. Their recognition would open up a rather large area of mutual understanding and positive appreciation.

Gathering around the Word of God

What did the first Christians who formed a community that gradually grew into a church do when they came together? "If (as seems likely) the early Christian assembly was influenced by the practice of Jewish synagogues, we can assume that there were readings from scripture (the Old Testament in its Greek version), some reflection or homily, and prayers of petition (at least the Lord's Prayer)."[14] From the beginning, before specifically Christian scriptures were written, the content of Jewish scripture nurtured the self-understanding of Jesus and his followers. The emergent church grew in its understanding of Jesus Christ and of itself by interpreting Jewish scriptures. Christian writings were gradually added to the mix of the privileged texts by which the self-constituting church defined itself and formed for itself a classic expression of its original and originating faith. From a theological perspective, this development followed the revelation of God in Jesus and was led by the Spirit. The community consistently testified to its experience of the primacy of grace in these historical developments. Assembling together in faith and assembling around the scriptures are, with some exceptions, synonymous phrases; the church was founded and continues to exist by engaging and responding to scripture that, as the word of God, interiorly illumines.

Christians are used to hearing the couplet "word and sacrament." The phrase often contains a connotation of an implicit polarity or tension between a word-centered and a sacrament-centered Chris-

---

13. CCH, I, 229–31.
14. Daniel J. Harrington, *The Church according to the New Testament: What the Wisdom and Witness of Early Christianity Teach Us Today* (Chicago: Sheed & Ward, 2001), 51.

tian spirituality. It is possible to create such a contrast, but it can never amount to an antithesis. In fact, as I just indicated, a sophisticated theology of the word bears a close structural analogy to a sacramental theology. Words, whether they be oral or written, are sensible symbols that mediate meaning. In a theology of the preached word or the read word, these words communicate the Word of God or God's grace. The external words, that is, the human words, become the mediator or symbol or sacrament of the inner communication of God to the human person. Surely there is a difference between a conceptual symbol such as a human word and a material object such as bread or water. And these differences at such a primal level give rise to different textures in the forms of communication upon which corporate spiritualities are built. But this should not distract from the common elemental way in which faith is communicated, interpreted, internalized, and articulated within a community. The Word of God has as one of its foundational mediums of communication the words of scripture. These words become the audible and verbal sacraments of God and of Jesus Christ, even as sacraments are visible and tangible "words" of Jesus Christ and God.

A variety of practices across the many churches focus upon scripture as the central medium of its worship of God or provide an essential component of a differentiated worship service. Perhaps the central mechanism of Christian self-understanding consists in the dual practice of reading the scripture and interpreting it in homily or commentary. That dialogue or interchange — of God's word addressed to the Christian community and the human word of appropriation, application, and response — constitutes the Christian community or church. The church moves through history as a community that continually grounds itself by being in dialogue with God. The multifaceted character of this dialogue can be detected in the various genres of the word of God. When the community reads the history of Israel and the nascent church, it defines itself by remembering its history. When it reads the psalms, the word of God becomes the words of the prayer of the community in response to God's grace. Reading the gospel stories mediates Jesus as the revelatory parable of God. Reading the scriptures, in public and in private, supplies the Christian community, the whole great church, with a common language by which members can communicate with each other across time and cultures.

The Eucharist

In the context of the general principles that analogously govern both the preaching and sacramental activity of the church, we turn to the sacrament of the eucharist or Lord's Supper. Baptism and the eucharist are the two sacraments that are almost universally recognized among the churches. The ecumenical representation of the eucharist by Faith and Order's *Baptism, Eucharist and Ministry* proposes a common apostolic understanding of the sacrament in terms of its origin, its theological interpretation, and certain practical considerations of its celebration.

Origin. BEM connects the Lord's Supper to the meals Jesus had with his disciples. It describes the historical and theological origin of the sacrament in the testimony of Paul to the tradition and, before that, in the reconstruction of its association with the meals of Jesus during his lifetime and before his passion. "The meals which Jesus is recorded as sharing during his earthly ministry proclaim and enact the nearness of the Kingdom. . . . In his last meal, the fellowship of the Kingdom was connected with the imminence of Jesus' suffering. After his resurrection, the Lord made his presence known to his disciples in the breaking of the bread. Thus the eucharist continues these meals of Jesus during his earthly life and after his resurrection, always as a sign of the Kingdom. . . . Its celebration continues as the central act of the church's worship" (BEM, "Eucharist," 1).[15]

Theology. BEM's theology of the eucharist stays close to the New Testament in order to keep the interpretation within the bounds of the apostolic tradition. It begins with a definition of the eucharist as follows: "The eucharist is essentially the sacrament of the gift which God makes to us in Christ through the power of the Holy Spirit. Every Christian receives this gift of salvation through communion in the body and blood of Christ. In the eucharistic meal, in the eating and drinking of the bread and wine, Christ grants communion with

---

15. Throughout this section on the eucharist the references in the text are to the paragraph numbers of BEM, "Eucharist."

himself. God himself acts, giving life to the body of Christ and renewing each member" (2). Like baptism, the eucharist is interpreted in several different ways in the New Testament: it is a ritual of thanksgiving to God, a memorial or *anamnesis* of Jesus, constituted by an invocation of the Spirit (*epiklesis*), constituting a communion of the faithful among themselves, and as a meal symbolizing the kingdom of God.

Eucharist as thanksgiving. It is a rite of thanksgiving as in the prayer of blessing at meals. "The eucharist, which always includes both word and sacrament, is a proclamation and a celebration of the work of God. It is the great thanksgiving to the Father for everything accomplished in creation, redemption and sanctification, for everything accomplished by God now in the church and in the world in spite of the sins of human beings, for everything that God will accomplish in bringing the Kingdom to fulfillment. Thus the eucharist is the benediction (*berakah*) by which the church expresses its thankfulness for all God's benefits" (3).

Eucharist as anamnesis *or memorial of Christ.* "The eucharist is the memorial of the crucified and risen Christ, i.e., the living and effective sign of his sacrifice, accomplished once and for all on the cross and still operative on behalf of all humankind. The biblical idea of memorial as applied to the eucharist refers to this present efficacy of God's work when it is celebrated by God's people in a liturgy" (5). Memory attaches the community to the ministry of Jesus and projects it forward into the final kingdom (6). *Anamnesis* both remembers and proclaims the efficacy of Christ in the present (7), especially Christ's unique sacrifice and the Pascal mystery (8). "Since the *anamnesis* of Christ is the very content of the preached Word as it is of the eucharistic meal, each reinforces the other. The celebration of the eucharist properly includes the proclamation of the Word" (12).

BEM also underlines the doctrine of real presence, while refraining from theological constructs that give the appearance of an explanation. "The words and acts of Christ at the institution of the eucharist stand at the heart of the celebration; the eucharistic meal is the sacrament of the body and blood of Christ, the sacrament of his real presence." (13). I will return to this common faith as an area of difference and discussion further on.

Eucharist as invocation of the Spirit. BEM carefully includes among the interpretations of the eucharist one that stems from a broad, trinitarian perspective on the economy of salvation. The Father is "the primary origin and final fulfillment of the eucharistic event. The incarnate Son of God by and in whom it is accomplished is its living center. The Holy Spirit is the immeasurable strength of love which makes it possible and continues to make it effective" (14).[16] From this perspective, the invocation of the Spirit or *epiklesis* receives attention because the "Spirit makes the crucified and risen Christ really present to us in the eucharistic meal" (14). "It is in virtue of the living word of Christ and by the power of the Holy Spirit that the bread and wine become the sacramental signs of Christ's body and blood" (15). Thus the "whole action of the eucharist has an *'epikletic'* character because it depends upon the work of the Holy Spirit" (16).

Eucharist as communion of the faithful. This aspect of the eucharist appears in virtually all ecclesiologies, and it is multifaceted. The eucharist is a bond that holds the whole church together. "The eucharistic communion with Christ who nourishes the life of the church is at the same time communion within the body of Christ which is the church. The sharing in one bread and the common cup in a given place demonstrates and effects the oneness of the sharers with Christ and with their fellow sharers in all times and places" (19).

The eucharist also furnishes theological grounds for the whole church being present in the local assembly. A given congregation is part of the whole church. At the same time, all that being church substantially means and entails subsists within a given local church. "It is in the eucharist that the community of God's people is fully manifested. Eucharistic celebrations always have to do with the whole church, and the whole church is involved in each local eucharistic celebration" (19).

This bonding of people together brings with it social-ethical responsibilities and implicit requirements for reconciliation. "The

16. This trinitarian perspective is drawn out further in these words: "The bond between the eucharistic celebration and the mystery of the Triune God reveals the role of the Holy Spirit as that of the One who makes the historical words of Jesus present and alive" (14). Readers familiar with the history of ecclesiology will recognize in these phrases accents analogous to those of other theologians of the Spirit such as John Calvin and John Zizioulas.

eucharistic celebration demands reconciliation and sharing among all those regarded as brothers and sisters in the one family of God and is a constant challenge in the search for appropriate relationships in social, economic and political life" (20). Eucharistic practice within the church community sets up a bond of solidarity in love as the context of human existence. Thus Christian life is subject to a "continual judgment by the persistence of unjust relationships of all kinds in our society" (20). "As participants in the eucharist, therefore, we prove inconsistent if we are not actively participating in this ongoing restoration of the world's situation and the human condition" (20).

Eucharist as meal of the kingdom. The eucharist is a sign of the final banquet, the goal of human existence. "The eucharist opens up the vision of the divine rule which has been promised as the final renewal of creation, and is a foretaste of it. . . . The eucharist is the feast at which the church gives thanks to God for these signs and joyfully celebrates and anticipates the coming of the Kingdom in Christ" (22). This dimension of the eschatological future also carries an ethical imperative; it functions as a "utopia" that allows us to judge the way things should be in God's plan for and rule of the world. The values that are intrinsic to the vision of life revealed in the ministry of Jesus become the ethical ideals of the church. For example, as Jesus addressed publicans and sinners and had table-fellowship with them during his earthly ministry, so Christians are called to solidarity with the marginalized (24).

The mission of the church in human history thus finds explicit grounding and continual nourishment in the eucharistic practice of the Lord's Supper. "The very celebration of the eucharist is an instance of the church's participation in God's mission to the world. This participation takes everyday form in the proclamation of the gospel, service of the neighbor, and faithful presence in the world" (25).

Celebration of the Eucharist. Churches can share New Testament theologies of the eucharist and still be quite distant in their present-day understanding and practice. In fact, theology of the eucharist has proven to be one of the most divisive issues in the church. Various reasons account for this. For example, the suppositions about religious epistemology and theological language and the methods of theological reasoning may vary considerably among theologians and implicitly among churches. These issues are indeed fundamental, and they have often become hardened presuppositions by the time the conversation reaches the topic of the eucharist. They can make all the difference in the way shared propositions are construed. Eucharist practice in many churches goes to the very heart of Christian existence and cannot be treated in a thoroughly objective and dispassionate way. In what follows I follow the lead of BEM in bringing forward several areas in which serious differences separate various churches and therefore need attention in a synthetic comparative theology of the eucharist.

The many churches have different orders of liturgical service of the Lord's Supper or eucharist. Some of the churches may consider the differences incidental and unimportant, while others consider certain elements of the essence of the sacrament. Is there a norm that may in some measure set a standard for the celebration of the eucharist? BEM indicates that the "liturgical reform movement has brought the churches closer together in the manner of celebrating the Lord's Supper" (28). Wisdom dictates going back toward the origins of the church in seeking a less developed point of departure for ordering the eucharist in a way that antedates disputes. This earlier starting point could function as a norm by providing an embryonic form that might be read as open to different practices. BEM suggests a skeletal order of the eucharistic liturgy that is quite open to many variations. It presents the eucharistic liturgy as "essentially a single whole, consisting historically of the following elements in varying sequence and of diverse importance" (27) and then lists the elements of a relatively early form of eucharistic ceremony.

The question of the real or true presence of Christ in the sacrament has been a typical area in which theologians and churches have been in conflict. BEM proposes a common but not universal belief in this doctrine: "The church confesses Christ's real, living and active presence in the eucharist. While Christ's real presence in the eucharist does not depend on the faith of the individual, all agree that to discern the body and blood of Christ, faith is required" (13).

Another area closely related to the eucharist that will consistently need attention and careful language in the relationships between the churches concerns public ministry and who can preside at a genuine eucharistic ceremony. In many churches this question is deeply embedded in the question of ordination: what is going on theologically in the ordination of ministers? This question is frequently attached to episcopal succession, which in turn may be tied to a physicalist understanding of both succession and the presence of Christ in the sacrament. Conceptions such as these and their rivals can be quite deeply engrained in the language of a tradition and hence the imagination; such ideas cannot easily be transcended. There will always be need for dialogue and education within the churches on these points.

This raises yet another issue that lies deeply buried in fundamental religious attitudes: Does eucharistic practice presuppose a commonly shared theological understanding before it can be celebrated in communion across denominational boundaries? Or does eucharistic practice bind Christians together in a common faith in Christ and in a relationship of love that carries and sustains the different theological reflections on what is going on in this sacrament before complete agreement is reached? Because this is not just a theoretical but also a practical issue, it does not yield an easy answer.[17] But it also can be the occasion for intellectual hubris and hypocrisy on the part of churches. Surely historical consciousness and pluralism among the Christian churches have taught us that no single church's theological language about the eucharist "controls" the mystery of how Christ is present in the community's practice of the sacrament. And surely the common confession that this is a divine action and not a human contrivance, that God in Jesus Christ takes the initiative in the eucharist and not the minister, should render the churches more compliant to Christ's commandment of unity in love.[18] Much

---

17. An example of how theology and practice interpenetrate each other is found in the way ministers treat the eucharistic elements. For example, in the Roman Catholic Church, after a eucharistic celebration the consecrated elements are preserved in the tabernacle; in other churches they are not. "The way in which the elements are treated requires special attention" (32).

18. BEM's testimony on this point is penetrating: "In the celebration of the eucharist, Christ gathers, teaches and nourishes the church. It is Christ who invites to the meal and who presides at it. He is the shepherd who leads the people of God, the

is at stake on both sides of these alternative attitudes toward eucharistic celebration, and leaders of the churches cannot hide behind caution. The World Council of Churches clearly relays the challenge that comes from the gospel message to the churches: Christ's call to unity, to communion in his name, is not conditional upon theology; theology is conditioned by it.[19]

BEM urges frequent, that is, weekly eucharistic services. It also acknowledges and encourages a certain amount of pluralism in the way these eucharistic ceremonies are practiced. It explicitly recognizes that "a certain liturgical diversity compatible with our common eucharistic faith is recognized as a healthy and enriching fact. The affirmation of a common eucharistic faith does not imply uniformity in either liturgy or practice" (28).

Finally, a balanced attitude toward the liturgical behavior of the church within the context of the many churches would at least follow these three rules. First, the many churches should protect the shared commonalities of baptism and assembly around word and eucharist which together make up an almost universal pattern of Christian worship. Second, churches should view positively the impulses of local churches to develop local forms of worship, rituals, and ceremonies that help define the particular tradition of a group of churches. This principle can be applied denominationally, regionally, or culturally. Third, the concern for communion, which extends mutual recognition among the churches in principle, should also stimulate critical assessments of the appropriateness of patterns of worship. The first principle should allow the third: communion in Christ in word and sacrament should allow churches to remain in communion and critically discuss important issues.[20]

---

prophet who announces the Word of God, the priest who celebrates the mystery of God. In most churches, this presidency is signified by an ordained minister. The one who presides at the eucharistic celebration in the name of Christ makes clear that the rite is not the assemblies' own creation or possession; the eucharist is received as a gift from Christ living in his church. The minister of the eucharist is the ambassador who represents the divine initiative and expresses the connection of the local community with other local communities in the universal church" (29).

19. See CCH, II, 380.

20. These three principles, which call for communion within differences, depend on a religious and theological discernment about the status and importance of things according to the principle that is called by some a "hierarchy of truths" and others

Other Sacraments and Devotions

Each church possesses an array of prayerful ministrations to other facets of human existence. Whether or not the activity formally uses scriptural texts, or is called a sacrament in a technical sense, prayer and ritual practice are occasioned by and address a wide variety of human situations across the churches. Churches attend to stages in human development: childbirth, adolescence, creative adulthood, sickness, old age, death. Churches minister to many of the groups and the memberships in them that structure human existence: family, parents and children, youth, professional associations, the poor and marginalized. Churches are places where people find forgiveness, reconciliation, blessing, healing of the spirit, healing of the body, spiritual counseling, and exorcism.[21] These "spiritual" activities are delivered in ways that are Catholic and Orthodox, evangelical and pentecostal, Anglican and Protestant. While they have much more in common than is generally acknowledged, the point is that the differences in the style and interpretation of these activities are not a negative but a positive feature within the larger church.

These differences in the devotional life of Christians are in the process of multiplying. The Christian church continues to become non-Western at a rapid rate. Just as the church inculturated itself in the Greek cultural world, and in a parallel fashion in the Roman Empire of the West, so too the church will have to shed its Western garb and take on the cultural forms of various Asian and African cultures if it is to thrive there. In fact, the young churches possess a strong, self-conscious, and active desire for inculturation. But this entails the expression of faith in new languages, and the ministering to Christian life and practice in new ways. And this will inevitably stimulate discussion, controversy, and threats of new divisions within the church. Historical consciousness, together with a strong sense that

the principle of adiaphora. For example, to break the ecclesial bond of communion in Christian faith over matters of sexuality or the ordination of women mistakenly raises these last two issues to the level of the importance of God's revelatory and sacramental presence to human life. This is a fundamental mistake.

21. It is interesting to note and to compare how churches with such different styles of worship and spirituality as Roman Catholics and pentecostals share practices of exorcism and speaking in tongues. Boundaries between denominations are more porous than frequently imagined.

diversity is not necessarily bad, and that pluralism understood as difference within a larger framework of unity can be enriching, may help foster the trust that a common faith under the influence of a common Spirit will prevail. In any case, these problems should never be an occasion for breaking off conversation and mutual recognition.

NURTURING THE WHOLE LIFE OF MEMBERS

Being a member of the church influences the whole life of the people who belong. It will be useful to preface this discussion with the realistic fact that various cultures and societies encourage different "levels" of commitment to the church as an organization. This is most clearly reflected in the amount of time dedicated to exercises of formal participation in church activities. Memberships and the responsibilities that go with them usually multiply with the development and complexification of society. Nevertheless, despite that correlation, membership in the church engages the whole person at deep levels of existence: in the fundamental worldview that orders reality, in the system of values that shapes responsible decisions, in the sets of behaviors that define an actual personality. Within these spheres members participate in the church across a spectrum that ranges from activity to passivity. At one end, some members are highly engaged practitioners; at the other end, some members are content to be occasional recipients of what the church provides. But across differences in degrees of participation, all share in some measure a common Christian life of community. What follows divides the way the church nurtures the whole life of its members into three dimensions of this social support. The first deals with the ideological side of Christian faith, the second with the axiological dimension of human life, and the third with aspects of the social safety net to which the church contributes according to its means.

A Community of Meaning

The church is a community that shares on its deepest levels a common vision of the source, the meaning, and the destiny of human existence. No one doubts that this single common vision becomes refracted in innumerably different ways through the churches, the congregations within the churches, and various segments of the congregations. But within and despite the differences lies a conception of ultimate reality, of the relationship of God to the world and to human beings, and of the responsible relationship that human existence bears toward God. The whole phylum of Christians shares this.[22]

This common vision is codified for all Christians in the Bible, especially the New Testament. All Christians share a common biblical language; the church is a linguistic community. Christians together possess the Bible's innumerable points of reference, its variety of genres and modes of communication, its history, its stories, its prayers, its teachings, its wisdom, its letters, its challenges and reprimands, its encouragements, in prophetic harangue, in lament, in joyous song.

The church as a community teaches; it is a school. It teaches all its members young and old all the time. It introduces its children into the community of meaning through the family, the congregation, informally and in its gatherings and celebrations, in its catechisms, Sunday schools, and sermons. It teaches adult initiates at a deeper level the language and vision of the community into which they are being baptized. The church runs or promotes schools to explore at a more technical and critical level the correlations between the expressions of the common faith and the current understanding of the world mediated by other disciplines. The church simultaneously uses a language of devotion or naïve faith and a language of mediation between faith and the various exercises of human reason in which its members also participate.

A social-psychological account of the role of ideology and meaning for a community would show that the church plays a potentially major role in the lives of its members. At the same time, a theological analysis of what is going on in this social transaction transforms it into a social mediation between God and human existence. The

---

22. James M. Gustafson, in *Treasure in Earthen Vessels: The Church as a Human Community* (New York: Harper and Brothers, 1961), analyzes the church as a natural community from a variety of perspectives: as a political community, a community of language, a community of interpretation, a community of memory and understanding, a community of belief and action. Each of these categories opens up ways in which the church helps sustain the existence of its members.

consistent theological conception of the role of the church across the history of ecclesiology maintains that the church, animated by the Spirit, plays the role in history that Jesus, now ascended and no longer physically among us, acted out in his ministry. This role is performed not simply by the church as institution, as hierarchy, as clergy, but as a whole community of meaning. This meaning is carried in the community, by the community, for the community. It comes from God, and it is for the human community. The community should not be understood abstractly here in such a way that it could exist without institution or leadership. Far from it. For when the church as institution fails to live up to the very message it bears, it loses its authority and gradually its members. Meaning ultimately has to be carried in the organized lives of members.

A Community of Values

The church is a community of shared values. This conception does not conflict with the observation that the Christian community unites within its boundaries groups whose values seem to be very much at odds. As in the case of basic ideas, fundamental values do not go uninterpreted and, when they are applied to different cases, one can be sure of no universal consensus. Despite this fact, in the face of it, Christians share a whole world of value in common. They relate to one mediator of God, Jesus Christ, whom Paul placed at the head of a new race. His teaching and his person display a whole range of basic moral attitudes that no Christian would deny, no matter the differences of their interpretations, applications, and behaviors. One can appeal to a whole host of presuppositions at the start of a discussion or reasoning process: the dignity and sanctity of an individual human life, the equality of human beings within the framework of the love of the creator God, human freedom and its accountability before God, the commandment to love the neighbor, and even one's enemy.

The church is a community that teaches moral values. It instructs. It reinforces values in its families, its schools, and its social action teams. The church has many ways of teaching. The church teaches by instruction as it communicates to its members the commandments that were given to it by its parent, Israel. The church has so taught from the beginning, in household codes, in medieval catechisms, in families, in Christian schools throughout the world. The church teaches by socialization; it strives to draw people into a community that exemplifies in various subgroups a moral response to various issues. It promotes the ideals of a virtuous life in its saints. As William James insisted, the saints are those who communicate to us by making actual in history levels of virtue we would not have thought possible without them.[23] The church also promotes a moral life by positive encouragement and by the injunction of behaviors that would prove ruinous to the individual and community. The church has to assume public responsibility for its public behavior, and so it has through the ages with its inquisitions, consistories, excommunications, and bans. Each has to be read in its unique context to be judged too extreme. But despite that judgment, it reflects a church trying to assume responsibility for this aspect of its mission. Where this happens one will observe a variety of mechanisms for inculcating and maintaining an atmosphere of moral integrity within the community.

Perhaps more important for the church today than being a moral teacher is its call to be a community of moral discernment. No matter how stable the values, ethics has to play out in ever-new historical situations. And never before in the history of the human race has there been such a corporate sense of rapid change than in these latest times. Everything is moving faster: travel, communication, expansion of knowledge. The community is constantly bombarded with novelty as more cultures directly interact, science makes new discoveries, technologies make new things possible, and machines make human beings stronger. What was usurious yesterday is virtue today; what was once politically incorrect may be criminal now. Responsible Christians today have to enter into dialogue with the world outside itself, and the community takes up this task in the name of and on behalf of its members. By a division of labor, a cadre of its members enter into dialogue with various sectors of the world, the sciences, the medical world, the world of politics and statecraft,

---

23. William James, *The Varieties of Religious Experience* (London: Collins, 1971), 347.

the world of economic policy and practice, the world of social practice and the lack of it. The complexity of the interchange between these specialized worlds and the world of Christian values requires professional expertise. Moreover, the members of these groups and the communities at large converse and debate among themselves. Increasingly, this conversation reaches across cultures as the young churches of non-Western cultures become stronger. This moral discourse is ongoing and without it the church would lose touch with reality. Moreover, societies themselves need this kind of reflection because corporate human existence cannot move forward responsibly in its absence. Such reflection is right at home within the church. The church, together with other religions, should be able to propose to secular governments and societies humane values, such as concern for the poor, which would help direct political decision making.

A Community of Mutual Support

The church is a community of mutual support. This becomes actual at a variety of levels, but one can distinguish between the spiritual and the material spheres of mutual interaction. Ministers are ordained primarily to address the "spiritual life" of the community.[24] Besides the formal roles of leading the community in worship, prayer, and other pious devotions, the ordained member addresses the spiritual problems of individuals through counseling and spiritual direction. Other members of the community, deemed competent by charism or training in an office of ministry, may in effect be delegated by the community to address a wide range of spiritual dilemmas, from medical-moral problems to personal spiritual crises. In Luther's conception of the priesthood of all the faithful, each member of the community individually has the right and power to pray for the other members of the community. In times of crisis, such ministrations can be of enormous comfort.

---

24. I place "spiritual life" in quotation marks because the sphere of the spiritual is contested. The main enemy here is a "dualism," itself a contested category, that would drain everyday physical action in society of spiritual and religious value. Even the word "primarily" in this statement is deliberately vague. I will not enter this conversation at this point, but it is important to be attentive to these issues.

The church frequently sets up agencies to provide material or social assistance to members of the community who are in need. Earlier I used the image of a safety net to characterize how the church could and often does respond to those members of the community who are in need. These needs can be far ranging and addressed in a variety of different ways. For example, offices may be set up within the small community or congregation to attend to specific issues. But churches with larger organizational polities may create agencies with a wider scope and greater resources at the diocesan, synodal, regional, or national levels. The larger the network of intercommunion, the greater the chance that resources for a given crisis will be available within the community itself.

Churches across the board create agencies of all sizes to respond to all manner of social problems within the community. Sometimes churches channel social concern through the social agencies of the secular community. Frequently in the course of history, where society is less friendly to the Christian church, the church has created a parallel set of social agencies to nurture its members. Thus one finds educational and heath care systems, hostels and homes for the battered, indigent, or neglected. Sometimes other support groups for professionals are created in the tradition of the guilds and the confraternities of the late medieval and early modern periods.

It should be clear within the Christian community that the line separating spiritual and material support is not as clear as the concepts themselves may appear. The dynamics of love of God and love of neighbor, although formally distinct in their objects, entail each other, cannot be separated, and practically overlap. It may seem a distant journey from belief in Jesus Christ as redeemer to agencies of social service, but they are interwoven.[25]

Maintenance and Mission

The distinction between maintenance and mission employed at the head of this chapter is sociological and refers respectively to the task

---

25. This account of a community of mutual support approaches the many issues contained in the relation of the church to society and the prophetic, liberating role of the church in it. I have reserved those topics for the next chapter.

of sustaining an organization by care for its structure and its members and the task of carrying out the goals of the organization.[26] The distinction roughly indicates the two directions in which the church faces, inside itself and outside itself. These two directions correspond loosely to two directions of ministry, pastoral and missionary, that mutually entail each other. There can be no church mission without a stable church to pursue it; no authentic church without a sense and practice of mission. The point of introducing this distinction and polarity late in this chapter is to underline how the distinctive identity of the churches animated by pastoral activity has to be held in tension with the imperatives of the universal mission of the whole church. Pastoral activity cannot be considered independently of the church's mission.

H. Richard Niebuhr, writing within the context of the ecumenical movement, analyzed the churches to show the degree to which the individual identities of the denominations were determined by social and cultural factors.[27] He included many factors in a wide net of "social sources": language, culture, nation, race, ethnic belonging, geographical location, economic class. People spontaneously gravitate to homogeneous groups. And the glue that holds churches together and distinguishes them from other churches lies much more deeply in these social and historical dimensions of the church than in distinctive doctrines or beliefs. This is not to deny beliefs their important role in the self-differentiation of a particular church. But Niebuhr reminds the reader of the degree to which social factors also have an influence on theological reasoning and resultant doctrinal formulation. There is no ideal church; every individual church is rooted in history, has particular interests and biases, and involves some compromise with the world.[28]

The significance of this analysis lies in the relevance of the social dimensions of the church for its identity and mission. These social factors largely determine the specific identity of a particular church. Christianity has to take on the particularities of a people in order to

---

26. The distinction was introduced earlier; see supra, 103.
27. H. Richard Niebuhr, *The Social Sources of Denominationalism* (New York: World Publishing, A Meridian Book, 1957, original 1929).
28. Ibid., 3–6.

communicate with them and become an integral part of their lives. One of the main problems of the twenty-first century will surely be the inculturation of the church into the many social particularities of non-Western developing nations and cultures. But these worldly factors would become negative if they overshadowed the transcendent source of Christian identity. In Niebuhr's view, every attempt at making Christianity a concrete reality in history involves a certain compromise of the New Testament ideal, especially when distinctiveness yields to divisions. The ideal is clearly stated: unity, solidarity, equality; no Jew and Greek, no male and female, no slave and free, no division by social class or race, but unity in Christ. Division among the churches does not come from God, but from the human, the historical, the social factors that overpower what Schleiermacher called the effects of the Spirit in the church as mediated by Jesus Christ.

The social determinants of each church's particularity also become negative when they endanger the mission of the church in history. When attention to maintenance crowds out the mission of the church in history, or so undermines the unity of the whole church that its mission is blunted, then clear steps have to be taken to reverse this distortion. This formulation of the problem leads to recalling that pastoral activity aimed at building up and nurturing the inner life of the community should always entail concern for mission.

The issue can be formulated in terms of a tension. On the one hand, the church is a community that needs pastoral ministry to nurture its distinctive identity. On the other hand, the church conceives itself as sent by God to the world to communicate the message it received from God as mediated by Jesus Christ in the Spirit. The authentic communication of this message to the world entails the church being a force for transformation in history. More specifically, this transforming power moves in the direction of religious, personal, and social liberation and reconciliation. If the positive dynamic tension between maintenance and mission is broken, pastoral activity itself becomes ambiguous. Niebuhr puts it more strongly: denominationalism becomes bankrupt when it undermines the mission of the church. The fragmentation of the churches and the lack of communion among them frequently indicate a subordination of the mission of the church to the expediency of sectarian identities.[29] The self-transcendence and the mission of the church are sacrificed to denominational identity and maintenance of social differentiations. When a church becomes preoccupied with nation, class, race, territory, ethnic group, or itself as a self-enclosed community, it weakens its power for meeting captivity with liberation and estrangement with reconciliation.

The resolution of this problem, when it exists, lies in recognition of the tension between maintenance and mission, between energy concentrated in pastoral and missionary activities. Recognition means oversight and attention to these dimensions, each of which cannot succeed without the other. Pastoral activity has to bear a missionary sensibility; missionary activity has to keep its roots in the soil of community. This can be provided by policies that contain at least the following two components.

First, churches should be able to distinguish the factors that Niebuhr called the social sources of denominationalism, recognize them as such, and refuse to allow them to be divisive of the larger church. The churches must become part of the lives of their constituents and this requires inculturation. But one must be clear that compromise with a particular culture, ethos, and social ethic risks abandoning the more universal role of transformation and reconciliation between groups who are alienated. Churches have to be mindful of a distinction between the essential transcendent principles of the gospel and the particularities of identity.

Second, the distinction between the historical particular and that which is transcendent in the church applies to doctrine as well. The churches have to recognize the social dimension of Christian theology and doctrine and not let churches be divided on the basis of historically conditioned formulas. Historically conditioned formulas are precisely the occasions for churches to discover their present-day meaning in dialogue with each other in a way that is responsive to the present-day world. Clinging to past formulas helps to provide each community with its identity through continuity with its originating

---

29. Ibid., 269–75.

genius. But the transcendent element in that identity opens the tradition up to analogous transcendent dimensions of the other church traditions. For example, few of the old battles of the Reformation in the languages in which they were fought have any relevance to the transformed world in which we live today. The church as teacher should attend to the dialectic between substance and form, between transcendent meaning and finite language.[30] The transcendent dimension of the church, the communication from God, through Jesus Christ in the power of the Spirit, drives each church into the arms of the other churches and outward in a common mission to the world.

ECCLESIAL EXISTENCE

The topic of the activities of the church provides the closest and most concrete entrée into ecclesial existence. Those who participate in the range of church activities know what ecclesial existence entails. Although the goal of this work still prevents me from describing Christian life as it unfolds in any particular denomination, readers from the particular churches should be able to identify with this slice of ecclesial existence in the concrete terms of their own churches. The effectiveness of the analogy between particular church practice and this abstract account should bear striking witness to the deep level of common ecclesial existence shared across the churches.

I have divided the portrait into two distinct but overlapping aspects of ecclesial existence that mutually affect each other, a range of activities that are liturgical and those that nurture the community. The next chapter adds a third dimension to these two, namely, the activities that engage the world.

Liturgical Existence

I begin with those activities that most directly manifest people's relationship to God, that is, liturgical activity that shapes in turn a liturgical existence. Ecclesial existence normally entails assembly for worship of God. In some traditions assembling on Sunday is "doing

---

30. Both the World Council of Churches in its official documents and Vatican II have made this principle explicit: the content of faith exceeds what doctrine can express in formulas. See CHH, II, 380, 398, 423.

church." Perhaps the most universal activity of the church consists in gathering to listen and respond to the word of God. Such a gathering, inherited from Judaism, appeared in the very beginning of the Christian movement and helped to define it. People assembling in the synagogue in the first century, the gathering of Christians described by Justin around 150 CE, and congregations around the world today are doing the same thing. The basic action of listening to the scripture, commenting on it, and internalizing it provides form to Christian life. So fundamental is this pattern of behavior that one could say the church is the community that reads the scriptures together, or the place where the scriptures are read, or the community constituted by the scriptures. Christian ecclesial existence shares a self-defining symbolic language.

Gathering together to listen to God's word presupposes and actualizes God's self-revealing presence to the community in and through Jesus Christ and the scriptures. This community event is founded upon God's scriptural promise to humankind. The response to this interruption of God into human lives in and by God's word can only be faith and gratitude. Ecclesial existence, in every church, responds to being summoned by the word of God to an always deeper faith and hope in God's promise, and a love of God and neighbor that is informed by gratitude. A Christian account of what it means to be saved will reflect this deep dimension of ecclesial existence.

A second form or mode of assembly consists in gathering for the Christian meal, the Lord's Supper or eucharist. This form is often united with the first, but in many denominations the two services are separable. Because the Lord's Supper has become so stylized and ritualized over centuries, many Christians may find it difficult to discern from the surface the source and developmental lineage of this sacrament. It too goes back to Jesus, his interactions with his disciples, and the meals they took together. Present-day ritualized meals do not resemble visually or physically the way the Lord's Supper was embedded in the ordinary and extraordinary meals of the earliest Christians. Studies of the significance of meals in the formation of the church, in Jewish and Greek and Roman culture, help release new meanings encoded in this particular form of encounter with Jesus Christ. These roots need to be recalled lest the different developments of this common practice be allowed to obscure what Christians share within all the variations. Ecclesial existence entails a communion of church members with Jesus Christ and among themselves "in Christ" that is actualized in eucharistic liturgy.[31]

The common practice of participation in the Lord's Supper or eucharist has taken on so many different forms that those accustomed to one church tradition may hesitate to recognize the service in another church as the same eucharist. Yet a moment's reflection on any eucharistic service should reveal that it involves membership and participation in a community of Christians, that the bond of unity of that community is Jesus Christ, and that that bond becomes real and actual in the celebration itself. Ecclesial existence expresses itself formally in the Lord's Supper; the practice is ecclesial existence in act. This community activity also constitutes a continuity between Christians today and the disciples of Jesus, and between all Christians yesterday and today, living and dead. Awareness of this deep, shared metaphysical reality cannot but summon impulses toward solidarity and even love of others in Christ. Some level of consciousness of what goes on or, better, of what is effected in the symbolism of this sacrament correlates with the image of the church as "the body of Christ." This image itself may or may not be effective today. But it raises up a dimension of ecclesial existence that is real and thus potentially shared across the churches, from the studied informality of Pentecostalism to the formal liturgical practices of Eastern Orthodoxy. Ecclesial existence is common life in Christ, and it is actualized in eucharist.[32]

---

31. Because the eucharist is so profound and intimate a sacrament it has consistently been a source of division. Even the reactions to BEM frequently did not transcend differences and attend to the unifying power of this sacrament: churches often insisted on dimensions that were different from the way they did things despite the formal request to fix attention on the unifying power of Jesus Christ and the Spirit. See Max Thurian, ed., *Churches Respond to BEM*, I-VI (Geneva: WCC, 1986–88).

32. Ecclesial existence in every specific local or denominational configuration will be defined by many other corporate religious ceremonies and practices. Ecclesial existence includes hundreds of different prayer forms and devotional practices which have become indigenous to particular churches. In defining a particular church these local forms also have a potential for dividing them. This fact highlights the need to underline the foundational and essential character of the "sacramental" forms that define common ecclesial existence.

Beyond these two patterns of worship Christians come together for a wide variety of other forms of prayer and worship. Catholics have other sacraments beyond baptism and eucharist. Other churches celebrate weddings, the forgiveness of sins, and funerals without designating these events as sacraments, but the events intend a mediation of God's grace and constitute a factor in ecclesial existence. Churches gather for all sorts of reasons that commemorate events in the community or recall constitutive anniversaries of the church's tradition.[33] The Christian life of prayer and worship always involves a host of rituals and ceremonies that are potentially sacramental. It is most important simply to take cognizance of the way the character and identity of a Christian existence take shape through local ways of doing things, either the universally recognized sacraments or the rituals and sometimes informal ceremonies that fill out the particular social life of each congregation and parish. The many concrete patterns of participation by the people in the parish church more than anything else determine the existential and actual historical identity of ecclesial existence.

Communitarian Existence

The activities of the church beyond the circle of explicitly religious actions push the experiences of meaning and value into the wider secular sphere. The many church activities that nurture the mind, that promote values and ultimately a community of love, and that enable a community to respond to particular needs and crises leave a strong imprint on ecclesial existence.

How churches help shape the minds of church members goes beyond telling. Churches wield a powerful influence and not all of it has been positive. But at its best, the many vehicles of education and intellectual formation by the church have opened the human spirit to a recognition of the depth and the height of humanity and of material reality itself. Ecclesial existence, schooled in spiritual apperception, can recognize the religious dimensions of created reality

---

33. A cogent line of sacramental theology resists limiting the sacraments to two or to seven or to another number of public liturgical events because it tends to set up blinders to the potential encounter with God's grace in so many facets of life. The whole world is potentially sacramental.

and the transcendent constitution of the human spirit. Ecclesial existence is religious, formed in faith and hope, and oriented toward an eschatological dimension that is finally real.

The church from its very beginnings as reflected in the New Testament period was quite concerned about the moral values of its members. The church understands itself as a body of people who are governed by standards of behavior that in one way or another correlate with God's will for human existence itself. Jesus preached the rule of God, and Christians pray: "Thy will be done on earth." Ecclesial existence cherishes basic values that should engender fundamental moral responses to critical areas of life: personal care, responsibility to others, ideas of justice and equality, in areas of society and in personal relations, in matters of family, sexuality, and gender. Ecclesial existence thus entails moral discernment as an intrinsic reflective trait of the way one lives. The possible negative consequence that moral concern may create an obsessive feeling of guilt really runs counter to the Christian mediation of the mercy and reconciling forgiveness of God in baptism. Rather, ecclesial existence should embody a quiet moral concern that patiently discerns with the community a proper response to new problems.

A third form of activity falls within the broad category of community support. From the beginning the church responded to ordinary needs that individual Christians or Christian families or groups could not handle on their own. Church organizations or agencies respond to all sorts of practical spiritual and material needs of the community: individual needs and requirements of sociality and community. The church has always tried to be responsive to the needs of the poor or those who are otherwise marginalized. This spontaneous activity on the part of the church engenders a spirit of attention to the needs of others and, reciprocally, a feeling or sense of confidence that the community will support one when the vital needs of life itself are threatened by sickness or poverty. Ecclesial existence at its highest communitarian level would feel the support of the church community as analogous to family support. That kind of solidarity, however, seems possible only within the context of the basic ecclesial unit of the local community.

A hard question. Perhaps the hardest question of all concerning ecclesial existence is why Christians do not allow Jesus Christ to unite them around the eucharistic table. One reason this is such a hard question to answer lies in the inability of churches, or church leaders, to really hear or ask the question. It is an accusation. The frequent response, that celebration of the Lord's Supper presupposes unity rather than creates it, appears to be little more than implicit corporate Pelagianism. There is only one single response: only sin prevents the eucharist from uniting Christians in a common memory of Jesus Christ. Where exactly the sinful responsibility lies is subject to various analyses, but the question should certainly lie heavily on the consciences of the leaders of the churches. Members of the churches seem to be much more open to intercommunion.

Chapter 7

Church in Relation to the World

The relation of the church to its environment, that is, the world in which it exists, does more to determine its character than most people recognize. Distance is required to see it. In fact, it would be hard to overestimate the importance of this aspect of the church's existence in the formation of an ecclesiology. The interaction between the church and the world, when the world is understood broadly to refer to history and society, is the single main force of change and development of the church. The history of ecclesiology demonstrates how the church's symbiotic relationship with its successive historical milieux consistently and irresistibly changes the church. The church always exists somewhere; it interacts with the world around it; even the church that tried to "escape" from the world would be withdrawing from one world and entering a new particular situation in space and time. The church really cannot be understood apart from the world in which it participates. The church's nature may be defined abstractly in a way that seems to remain essentially the same on a formal level. But the concrete, historical, and real church never ceases to rearrange itself in and through its interchange with the world. And the rapidity and comprehensive character of that change in our times are unprecedented.

The consideration of the church in relation to the world elicits a specific point of view that can be illustrated by the distinction between pastoral and missionary activity. As these two terms were explained earlier, the one, pastoral activity, embraces various activities and ministries that nurture and maintain the church as a community. The direction of this activity is turned inward and focused on the internal life of the church. Missionary activity, by contrast, is directed outward toward nonchurch or world. This shift of attention can be quite expansive in its affects on how the church is understood. I will say more further on about how a consideration of the missionary nature of the church turns understanding of the church "inside-out."

The discussion of the church in relation to the world that follows is divided into four parts. The first takes up a way of understanding "the world" that is consistent with scripture and understandable in the present context of globalization and rapid change. I will propose a multilayered conception of "the world" that still remains simple and straightforward. The second part dwells on the notions of "mission" and "missionary activity" because they too have encountered problems in the world in which we live today. The third will propose some fundamental principles that arise from the conjunction of a "world" and a "missionary church" that is sent to it. The idea of dialogue brings together church and world in an interactive relationship that need not be conflictive and should be constructive. I will close the chapter with an account of ecclesial existence from this particular vantage point.

THE WORLD

Many accounts of the relation of the church to the world rest on an assumption that the category "the world" is intuitively understood by all in more or less the same way. But "the world" in the New Testament has layers of meaning that range in value from the positive to the neutral to the negative. On the one hand, the world was so loved by God according to John that God sent the Son to it for its salvation. On the other hand, the world was so blind that it refused to recognize the light (John 1:1–18). On the one hand, the world is the neutral sphere created by God in which human life unfolds. "And God saw everything that God had made, and behold, it was very good" (Gen 1:31). On the other hand, "this world" is deeply seared by sin and stands resistant to the initiative of God's grace and salvation.

If there is to be an intelligent discussion of the relation of the church to the world, it will have to be prefaced by a prior attempt to define what is meant by the term "world." But that term is appreciated differently in different ecclesial traditions. This discussion, therefore, is not aimed at establishing a standardized view of how

Christians should relate to the world. On the contrary, I propose that different churches will relate to the world in different ways. But it seems essential to at least sort out a range of meanings and connotations of the term that can be inclusive and accommodating to different ecclesial traditions. Such pluralism corresponds with the witness of the scriptures.

The Referents and Meanings of "the World"

As societies develop in terms of expanding knowledge, more sophisticated technology, and more varied social relationships, spheres of behavior that were once lumped together become differentiated and even compartmentalized. One such sphere is that of religion. One can chart the history of the development of modernity in the Western world in terms of a growing distinction between and sometimes separation of the spheres of religion and secular life. This in turn complicates the theological language that already presupposes some sort of distinction between church and world. In what follows I describe in material terms distinct referents of the term "world." But "the world" is also a theological category, and this adds a formal theological layer to its meaning. Without claiming to exhaust the possible referential meanings of the idea of the world, three distinct spheres readily come to mind. "The world" refers to society, to government, and to culture.

The idea of the world frequently refers to temporal society, the world of everyday historical life. Both aspects, society and time, contribute to the idea. Everyday life is intrinsically social, despite the individualisms of developed societies. Beginning with language itself, which is a social construct, social relationships between the self and others structure and actually constitute human existence. Included in this realm are the many public agencies that make up human life in common. Systems of education, business, commerce, and communal celebration provide standards for human understanding and behavior. And this ongoing, socially structured relationship of each person to society extends through time. Frequently enough in a religious context the limitations of time are contrasted with the eternal sphere of God or the absolute and eschatologically open human future.

The church came to be in society and has always existed in society. Even when a church seeks in various ways to understand itself over against society, these stances constitute a relation to society. But increasingly in the modern period, as defined by developments in the West, society grew away from an earlier symbiotic relationship it had with the church into a more autonomous sphere. Frequently, temporal or secular society stands over against the church and the religious realm. Secular society represents autonomous knowledge based on "scientific" evidence or "objective" reason in contrast to the religious authority claimed by the churches. Societies that have become urbanized and pluralistic frequently offer a sphere of law and social regulation distinct from the religious norms of a particular church. In this respect, then, the notion of the world can refer to the public sphere of society that lies outside the church and is autonomous relative to the church. But at the same time the church inescapably exists within its confines. And society continues to provide standards of knowing, valuing, and acting that may or may not be at odds with the church. Thus the church cannot avoid this relationship and usually attends to it carefully.

It is useful and important to distinguish between society and government or state. From its beginnings in the period of the formation of the New Testament the church has been conscious of its relationship to civil authority and government. The influence of state or nation or civil authority includes various institutions of government and law. Normally the church finds itself within the scope of the external rule of a given state or government. Church members live within the jurisdiction of two authorities or sets of laws, the one divine and the other human. Theoretically, from the church's perspective, these religious and secular regimes should be harmonious. In practice, some degree of tension inevitably obtains between these two claims on the allegiance of citizens who are members of the church. This tension can be traced on the macro level in theologians like Tertullian in the patristic period and in popes and bishops in the Middle Ages. On the micro level of individuals and congregations the tension is constant across the whole history of the church.[1]

---

1. Since the fourth century the greatest part of the history of the relation of the church to government presupposed knowledge and acceptance of the church in principle. As the church grows in non-Christian cultures or nations new dynamics

The church also relates to a culture that is outside itself, larger than the church, and more or less autonomous in relation to the church. By culture I refer broadly to the commonly shared ideas and values of a people that are embedded in language and patterns of behavior, that are prior to each individual, into which individuals are socialized. "More or less" autonomous from the church means that the church may succeed in so insinuating itself into a people's culture that it contributes to the deep structure of its ideas and values. For example, Christianity has become so inculturated in some Western cultures that at certain points it becomes difficult to distinguish between what is essentially Christian as distinct from its Western formulation and congruous patterns of behavior.[2] The counterpart of this historical situation is the problem of the church becoming "inculturated" in non-Western cultures so that it may truly communicate with non-Western Christians and become deeply internalized in people's lives rather than alienating. The church is called to become so inculturated but without losing its identity. This programmatic imperative forms part of a consistent church-world tension involving many practical challenges to communion. So it was in the first transition to Greek and Roman culture from the Semitic East; so it will always be.

The relation of the church to cultures frequently includes its relation to other religions that may have close symbiotic relationships to indigenous cultures.[3] Here the issue becomes far more complicated by the theological self-understandings of the church and its theological appraisal of other religions. This aspect of the church-world relationship has become a major issue occupying the church today.

I have referred to these three systems of meaning and behavior, the social, the governmental, and the cultural, as existing "outside"

will take over. The history of the Russian Orthodox Church in the twentieth century provides a dramatic example of this.

2. This discussion is overly simplified by reference to a single culture. Globalization has helped us realize that culture, as deep as it is, continually shifts and is pluralistic. The large cities of the world, where culture changes most rapidly, provide a metaphor for the world. It is harder to make cultural generalizations because so many individuations and exceptions exist within it.

3. Locating the issue of the relationship of the church to other religions under the umbrella of the church-culture relationship should not be read as a reductionist interpretation of the world's religions.

the church in order to emphasize their autonomy. But on the more practical level of actual life they are also inside the church. The members of the church are members of society, citizens, who bear a cultural identity. They carry these worldly determinants of their being into the church so that they become elements of the body of Christ. The relation of the church to the world does not unfold in a give-and-take transaction between two separable commodities. The relationship subsists in ideas, convictions, and expectations of behavior that make up human subjects and the communities they form. The tension between the church and the world unfolds within the lives of the members of the church who live in these two spheres.

Moreover and perhaps most importantly, this tension between mutually affecting influences involves a deep theological interpretation with important implications. From the beginning, as mentioned at the outset of this discussion, the symbol of the "world" carries a theological weight that is heavy. Because of their very autonomy, the systems of the world have gained an association with sin. Indeed, the world is frequently understood as the primal root of sin, and it stands over against the kingdom of God as the kingdom of Satan. Each area, in its autonomy, threatens the primal relationship of the Christian to God. Each area in itself provides temptation to primal sin: to pride instead of humility before God, to power instead of submission to God, to egoism instead of self-transcendence in relation to God and neighbor, to pleasure and self-indulgence instead of commitment to God's values in history. Thus is reality divided into the kingdoms of light and darkness that correspond with the warring factions of the divided self described by Paul. Sin has become a personified force in history. The various autonomies of the world have become the agencies of temptation drawing people away from their correct relationships to God and fellow human beings. Augustine depicted this contest as unfolding within the subjectivity of each person.[4] But on a grander historical scale, the two trajectories of self-transcendence and

---

4. It would be fitting to develop a theology of personal and social sin at this point. While this is appropriate, it would far exceed the limits of this work. But it is rather important to see the correlations here between these symbolic interpretations of the world and the drama of sin and grace that so deeply marks the interpretation of the Christian message.

sin in his view had their social historical agents in church and empire. This symbolism is so thoroughly engrained in the church that
theological reconstruction will have greater success working with it
than against it wherever possible.

Dynamic Reciprocity between Church and World

The relationship between the church and the world is dynamic, involving a reciprocal or mutual determination of each by the other, and
this results in constant change. The previous section underscored the
ambivalent character of this relationship: the world from various an-
gles appears as good or as a source of temptation. The relationship
is thus inherently unstable. But within this constant interaction two
principles can be set out that establish a framework for understanding and discussing the church-world relationship in a positive and
constructive fashion.

The first of the four orienting principles outlined in chapter 2
states that the church is constituted by or exists in a double relationship: it is related to God and to the world. The relationship to
the world has just been characterized: the church is an organization
in history that by and large obeys the laws of any social organization.
But this organization cannot be reduced to or fully understood by its
social-historical genesis and constitution. As perceived by the faith
of its members, the church takes up where Jesus left off and is thus
understood as coming into being by the will and in the power of God.
All this was explained in the chapter on the nature and mission of
the church.

What commands attention at this point of the discussion of the
relation of church to the world is the way these relationships interact.
This interaction can be formulated in two corollaries flowing from
the double relationship of the church to God and the world. One says
that the church's relationship to the world should be understood in
the light of its relationship to God; another says that the relationship
of the church to God is conditioned by its relationship to the world.

The first corollary, that the church's relationship to the world
should be construed in terms of its relationship to God, sets the
church apart from other secular organizations or institutions. Its relationship to God distinguishes the church as a religious organization

from other social institutions. The church is a voluntary society or assembly based on the faith of its members that God as Spirit has empowered the church in the wake of the ministry of Jesus Christ, Son of God and Messiah. This constitutive principle, which transcends social determinations and can only be recognized in faith, determines how the church relates to the world. Surely the beliefs of the community can be rendered public so that outsiders can in some measure appreciate the rationale of the church's behavior. But the truth of the church's stance in history cannot be fully rationalized or appreciated apart from the internalized commitment of faith itself. The wellspring of the church's relationship to human history and society ultimately flows from the internal and corporate conviction of God being at work in this project.

The second corollary is equally important: the way the church relates to God is conditioned by the world. For naïve believers within the churches this may seem less obvious than the first corollary. But the whole history of the church and its ecclesiology demonstrates the degree to which the church is conditioned at each stage of its historical journey by the place and social-political conditions of the world in which it exists at any given time. The pluralism of different forms that the church has assumed over time can only be matched by the differences in polity, worship, and ethos that prevail across societies and cultures today. A conservative reaction to this pluralism says that pluralism presupposes some common ground and should not be allowed to compromise the idea that some ecclesial forms are more faithful to Christian origins and more successful in holding the church together than others. This is true. And so is the progressive insight that those churches that dogmatically claim to possess the only true way without serious conversation with other churches are probably reflecting sectarian bias. These two corollaries are the product of historical consciousness and, taken together, explain the dynamic interactive relationship between the church and the world.

The explanation of the dynamic character of the relation between church and world leads to the second principle for understanding this ecclesial relationship. This principle can be stated simply and sharply: there is no single correct relationship of the church to the world; rather, the church properly relates to the world in different ways. No a priori character defines what the relationship of the church to the world should be. On the contrary, all sorts of different corporate attitudes may be appropriate for the church's attitude to the world at any given time.[5]

The grounds for this principle have already appeared in the discussion. The church relates to the world in different ways because of the differences that characterize human societies and cultures. The church relates to the society, government, and culture that are in place; but these differ in great measure across history and throughout the world. General principles defining how the church should relate to all societies and cultures would be so obvious as to be practically worthless.

But it is also the case that the church and the churches may relate to the same world, the same society, political regime, and culture in different ways that may be legitimate. This flows from the inherent ambivalence of social realities. Some aspects of the world are good and provide opportunities for the church to materialize certain values and potentialities. Other aspects of the same world may plainly contradict the Christian message. The multiple aspects of social reality prevent the church and the churches from adopting a monolithic or invariant attitude toward the world.

Few theologians have demonstrated this thesis more clearly than H. Richard Niebuhr.[6] Niebuhr constructed types of ecclesial attitudes of the church to the world, all of which have scriptural and theological warrant, as well as examples from the history of the church and ecclesiology. Some churches either stand against the world or are deeply suspicious of it. Other churches either accommodate themselves to the world or in some degree build on its structures. Still other churches in various ways take up the mission of entering into and transforming the world. Individual churches may incorporate any one of these attitudes for various reasons at a given time and place;

---

5. This principle does not call Christian social ethics into question but underlines its importance. The point is not that it makes no difference how the church relates to the world, but that the proper relationship requires reflection and deliberation, not that all are right or equally appropriate, but that there may be several correct relationships that need not compete.

6. Specifically in H. Richard Niebuhr, *Christ and Culture* (New York: Harper & Row, 1951).

larger churches may exhibit factions within themselves dedicated to one or another of these tendencies.

In sum, the relationship of the church to the world is intrinsically variable and pluralistic, but some relationship to the world is inescapable. And the quality of this relationship is perhaps the most determinative of the particular character of a given church. Few principles for understanding why the churches have to be open to and in dialogue with one another are more important on a practical level than these.

MISSIONARY CHURCH

Chapter 3 offered an interpretation of the nature and mission of the church. There the term "mission" carried a fundamental theological meaning. It was correlated with the category of the purpose of an organization as that is understood in sociology. But it was defined from a theological perspective that specified the nature of the Christian church in a theological way. The church is ultimately grounded in the will of God; it provides a historical agency for God's dialogue with humanity that was begun with Israel and further specified in the event of Jesus Christ. The purpose or mission of the church is to be the sign and vehicle for God's outreach to the world as that is revealed in Jesus Christ. Evangelical churches and those churches fashioned by a more dogmatic imagination may spontaneously appeal to different warrants in order to ground the mission of the church, the one relying on the missionary mandate in Matthew's Gospel, the other turning to propositions defining the trinitarian sweep of God's economy of salvation. But both traditions agree that God's mission is prior to the church and that the imperative to mission constitutes the church. God's mission has a church, and therefore church is essentially missionary by its nature.

With this theological understanding in the background, this chapter and more pointedly this section shifts attention to the practical meaning of missionary activity. At no time in the history of the church has the very idea of missionary activity become more problematic. In order to understand these problems, I will first characterize in broad strokes the practical outreach of the church to the world and then attend to the problems such activity is encountering. This will raise the question to be addressed in the next section of the chapter.

The Practical Meaning of Missionary Activity

In practice, the meaning of missionary activity has been narrowed down considerably and tends to be equated in the popular imagination with "foreign missions." Missionary activity refers to the ministry of missionaries, those who are sent from their home church to other lands to plant or assist the growth of the church in other places. The history of the church supports this common understanding. From a certain perspective, the Christian church's foundation depended upon the earliest mission to the gentiles. If there were no opening up of the preaching of the Jesus movement to the gentiles, by definition the Christian church would never have evolved, but would have remained a particular segment along with others of Judaism.

The history of Christianity can be written in terms of this missionary activity. The church spread to the East as well as the West, but gained a foothold in Greek culture and the Roman Empire. Various periods of the Eastern and Western churches generated great expansions through missionary movements. Beneath this dynamic outreach of the church beyond its established borders lies the conviction that the revelation it has received through Jesus Christ and in his person has universal relevance. The revelation has its source in the one God of power and might, creator of the universe and of human history, and it assures all humanity of God's outreach of love, care, accompaniment, and final salvation. This salvation is not for a few or a designated group. Rather, just as the one God is the creator and source of all, so too is God the end and goal of all. God is universal savior, and God's salvation is the appointed destiny of creation itself and all human beings in it.

The universal relevance of God's message of salvation in Jesus Christ is short-circuited when it is narrowed down to refer exclusively to the eschatological goal of human existence, the final destiny of humankind. Since God is the intelligent and personal creator of heaven and earth, it is reasonable to assign to God's intention whatever intelligible design can be discerned in the evolution of human life in history. The patterns of order in nature and the arrangements of society that foster the common good are spontaneously assigned a place in God's benevolent and gracious will. This was the deep conviction of Israel; this was the implication of the conviction about God's kingly rule. And this formed the controlling center and kernel of Jesus' preaching of the kingdom and rule of God. Jesus' ministry revolved around the centering assurance that the will of God should be done, and ultimately will be done, on earth as it is in heaven. But this means that the relevance of Jesus' message about God's kingdom does not merely extend forward toward everlasting life; it also extends laterally and spreads through the whole domain of human living into society, nation, and culture.

Up until the modern period, the church spontaneously reached into the whole range of social activities in regions where it became established.[7] Only with the modern period were the lines between differentiated spheres of authority and expertise drawn so clearly that they did not intersect. But this differentiation has in turn affected the way people generally conceive the role of the church in society, nation, and a globalized world. These realms are sometimes considered outside the church and even beyond its legitimate concern. The extension of the church's influence into the common life of modern society appears much more readily today as a kind of missionary activity, a reach beyond its own borders or boundaries. And this raises a number of serious problems that for many, both inside and outside the church, call missionary activity into question today.

Problems Associated with Missionary Activity

Developments in the course of the late modern or postmodern period, particularly during the twentieth century, have led to a calling into question of the whole idea of missionary activity. Three factors of the current situation, without being exhaustive, can be raised up as contributing to the problematization of missions: globalization, historical consciousness, and pluralist consciousness.

---

7. I use the word "established" in a common, nontechnical sense and not to refer to a church recognized by law.

Globalization, the process by which the world is shrinking and nations and cultures become ever more interdependent, forces specific groups of people to take note of other nations and cultures. The international rubbing of shoulders across great distances has a universalizing and a particularizing effect. The common international standards of communication and commerce that are being constructed threaten local cultural values and encourage them to become more entrenched. Because Western nations hold such power, globalization carries a Western bias. For example, though the majority of Christians now live in the developing world, the church still remains associated with Western culture and is often resisted on those grounds alone.

Historical consciousness, once part of the subculture of academics and intellectuals, has trickled down. An awareness of how particular location and culture influence thought patterns, ideas, and behaviors of people may almost be taken for granted today, at least among those people who have been generally educated or widely read. Large groups of people throughout the world interact pragmatically. If they have not despaired of the notion of a universal truth, they have ceased to expect that all will share much more than some sentimental principles and values. Even these will take on particular local color. The dynamism of crosscultural communication looks more like pragmatic negotiation than an effort at agreement in a shared internalized truth.

Pluralist consciousness may be scarcely different from historical consciousness. But it carries a distinct quality that may be new: people on a large scale are beginning not only to expect difference but to appraise it positively. The transcendent dimensions of ultimate reality, in the face of an undreamed of explosion of scientific knowledge, have grown more and more opaque, so that different perspectives on it are welcome as enriching our appreciation of absolute mystery.

Against the background of these developments and these ideas, the term "missionary" has become tinged with imperialism. It is associated with an earlier stage of Christian presence in the world, especially its connection with the colonialism of Western nations. And when one shifts the field of reference to the relationship of the church to society and civil rule, one finds a resistance to church influence analogous to reaction against earlier forms of clericalism. Just as cultures and religions are distinct and autonomous, so too are the spheres of society and government, so that the church is denied right of entry by reason of lack of expertise. In other words, in contrast to the missionary impulse of the church that is constitutive of its very nature, late modernity or global postmodern culture seems to insist that the church become self-contained within a narrow privatized religious sphere and thus marginalized from "the world."[8]

The resistance to mission can be analyzed at each of the three levels of the world that have been represented in the first part of the chapter. Relative to society, modernity has witnessed an increased division of labor. By virtue of expanded experience, complexification, analysis, and technology, the differentiations between spheres of expertise have become harder and stronger. Secularization has pushed institutional religion outside the mechanisms of social control. And pluralism in urban environments prevents a single religion or church having a dominant role in civic life.

Correspondingly, in the West the separation of church and state has become a kind of standard arrangement, even though it is rarely absolute and takes different forms in different nations. The corollary of this separation is frequently an extension of the right to exist to different or to all religions and their equal protection under law. These provisions at once recognize religious pluralism and disenfranchise a particular religion from having a determining role in the running of state affairs in a pluralistic situation.

On the international level, one might expect that the development of an international recognition of human rights, including the right of religious freedom, would open the way to an acceptance of missionaries from outside particular nations. But for many areas of the world the Christian church is associated with the massive power of Western nations and culture, and missionary activity implicitly connotes a desire for conversion. It thus appears as inherently subversive activity to increasingly self-conscious non-Christian identities. Added

---

8. It is remarkable how many conservative churches seem to be willing to espouse this late modern or postmodern settlement and thereby seriously curtail the relevance of the gospel.

to this is the development among Christians of various Christian theologies of religions that view other religions more positively than in the past. This, too, undermines to some extent the absoluteness of the missionary mandate.

To conclude this particular analysis, no one can fail to notice that the practice and the very concept of missionary activity have come under considerable pressure during the course of the twentieth century. The problems have their source for the most part in changes that are worldwide and historical; a new world-situation has given rise to new questions about the mission of the church.

The Question

The problems that have been discussed here do not undermine the universal relevance of the Christian message nor the desire to communicate it to others. The foundational impulse to communicate the Christian message is constitutive of the Christian church. But an understanding of missionary strategy, of the practical relationships that are to govern the church's relationship to the world, has to adjust to the world in which the church actually exists. That being said, it is still the case that the area of missionary activity remains one in which the churches are quite divided, where implicit differences become explicit. The questions then are these: Can the missionary activity of the church be preserved in a way that all churches can appropriate it? Can the active relationship of the church to the world be formulated in a way that allows mutual understanding and appreciation among the churches?

DIALOGUE WITH THE WORLD

The notion and strategy of dialogue are playing an increasingly important role in Christian theology and more broadly in world politics. Dialogue provides a way of taking the pluralistic character of the present situation with utmost seriousness while at the same time not surrendering commitment to a common truth that makes claims on all. But dialogue is not a simple concept. It contains an implicit ethic, a set of rules that governs its authenticity. For example, dialogue presupposes a mutual respect of each participant for the freedom and integrity of the other party. Without conscious attention to some of these conventions, dialogue can easily slip into attempts at manipulation.

The proposal advanced here is that human freedom and dialogue constitute a field and imply a set of premises for understanding the relationship of the church to the world in our current historical situation. The discussion that follows roots these ideas in Christian sources and then draws out in large terms for common acceptance how the relation of the church to the world might be conceived today.

Human Freedom and Dialogue

The conception of the relation of the church to the world proposed in this chapter places considerable weight on the metaphor of dialogue. Some brief reflection on the premises behind this term will situate the construction in a larger anthropological and theological framework.

The place of human freedom in Christian revelation. Human existence in any analysis is an intricate phenomenon, and any attempt to reduce it to a universally appreciable essence will meet resistance. At the same time, most conceptions of humanity revolve around some center of gravity that operates as a kind of holistic clearinghouse that organizes data and releases meaning in many different directions. Human freedom can play this role in a comprehensive anthropology.

In many respects freedom names the characteristic capacity distinguishing the human from other creatures. One could also organize a conception of the distinctively human around the ability of human beings to know, or, more specifically, to know reflectively so that they self-consciously know they know in the act of knowing. But the complex of mind, intellect, reason, and certainty functions within the dynamics of human existing or living, so that knowledge works in conjunction with valuing, appreciating, willing, and deciding, and these in turn lead to action and sometimes long-term commitment. This existentialist context of human living allows freedom to assume a central position in a conception of the human. The human spirit's being consciously present to itself is its freedom. In such a view, human knowing itself appears distinctively human because of the thematic of freedom. At this level freedom refers to the measure of transcendence over pure mechanism and material determinism that qualifies the human spirit and that appears when the human is compared with other animal life. Human freedom at this elemental level is being-present-to-itself in a conscious way. But the point is not to defend an anthropology centered in human freedom against its competitors, but to lay out the otherwise hidden premises of the discussion which follows.

An anthropology that finds its center in a deep and pervasive concept of freedom correlates with Jewish and Christian biblical revelation. The very concept of revelation presupposes a human freedom that can perceive it and respond to it. The Bible from beginning to end implicitly affirms and addresses human freedom, even when it conceives that freedom existing in some internalized bondage of egoism or external control by the power of the sin of the world. Various conceptions of the many forms of internal constraint and external containment provide the background for the antithetical contrast experience that gives meaning to the idea of salvation. Scripture consistently depicts salvation as some form of liberation or release, so that human existence can finally be free the way it is intended to be. The freedom that constitutes salvation has a depth, a breadth, and a height that are as variegated as the kinds of bondage that restrain human freedom: blindness, slavery, underdevelopment, frustration, guilt, sickness, death.

An overview of Christian thought across history reveals two distinct but inseparable levels in which the effects of salvation can be experienced within human freedom, the one personal and the other social. Each individual is most aware of sin within his or her own human freedom. Salvation relative to personal freedom is not measured in terms of the simple power to choose. The choices of the aesthete, who merely moves from pleasure to pleasure, rank so low on the scale of human freedom that they can sometimes become confused with a kind of compulsion. Distinctively human freedom begins with constancy and commitment to stable values. The highest level of self-disposition transcends logic and adheres to a lofty reality that fills the human person with transcendent value of that to which it clings. Both Paul and Augustine point out what human experience confirms: an inner bondage of the human spirit within itself blocks self-transcendence and requires a power from beyond the self, grace, in order for it to open up in generous self-gift. Paul describes the divided self. Augustine wonders why human freedom that can move the body cannot move itself to transcend the self in a gift of self outside the self in love of the other. Salvation is a release of human freedom from within to be fully itself in self-transcendence.

The operation of sin on a social level, as distinct from necessity or fate, has not always been as clearly manifest. Surely the church has always been concerned about the material dimension of human lives on a personal and social level. But it took the historical and social consciousness of thinkers such as Karl Marx to establish the connection between human freedom and social structures. The social gospel movements and liberation theologies that emerged in the nineteenth century and flourished in the twentieth have established the connection between social oppression and human responsibility. Much human social degradation is sinful, and few if any can escape social guilt. Salvation includes emancipation from external bondage, but participation in this salvation as a relationship with God occurs when one joins in the movement for the liberation of others.

From the perspective of an anthropology centered in human freedom, reflection on the binary of sin and salvation can be understood in terms of the bondage and release of freedom. The ideal of the truly human takes the form of being free at all levels in one's relationships to the self, God, the world, and other people individually and socially. Salvation by grace occurs precisely within these many forms of the liberation of human freedom from bondage. In this context, by contrast, every form of coercion on the part of the church compromises its essential revelation of the freeing character of the power of salvation from God. The relationship of the human person to God has to be free in order to be authentic. Forcing an authentic religious response upon or against freedom is not only simply wrong; it is impossible. A genuinely religious response can only consist in free self-affirmation and self-disposition.

The centrality of human freedom in any conception of the human, of God's creation of and dealing with the human for salvation, and of the elementary structure of the human religious response to God serves as a premise for an understanding of the church's relationship to the world. The Christian conception of salvation is rooted in a historical narrative of God's entering into dialogue with human freedom. If the church is to represent this initiative of God to the world as it has been revealed in Jesus Christ, it must do this in a way that has the deepest respect for human freedom.

Dialogue: being open to the world. We are looking for a fundamental attitude toward the world. Is there a root metaphor that contains a generative outlook upon the world that in turn will respect the freedom of the world to be itself? The notion of dialogue as an activity provides a metaphor for such an attitude. The analysis that follows remains on a foundational and conceptual level that incorporates into itself several more or less distinct theological conversations such as the relation of the church to the world, mission theology, interreligious dialogue, and the theology of religions. The point of remaining on this elementary level is to lay down premises that enjoy the largest consensus.

The prime analogate for the idea of dialogue is the conversation between two persons about a subject matter. Each one has a view; each listens while the other speaks. What unites them is not necessarily possessed by each, at least not in the same way, but the subject matter facing each as a third thing. Sometimes the partners themselves may be the subject matter in an exchange that seeks mutual understanding. Then each one assumes a stance of openness toward the other, acted out by listening and hearing the self-disclosure of the dialogue partner. But even in this case mediating objects or themes bridge the communication. Ordinarily the two points of view and experiences of dialogue partners are not isomorphic, but different in varying degrees. The differences make the dialogue go forward by point and counterpoint, or by serve and volley, adding, subtracting, accumulating, comparing, qualifying, changing one's mind, and concluding. The conversation respects the freedom of the dialogue partner and the autonomy of his or her testimony.

But this generic description of dialogue remains analogous because, in terms of actual practice, it conceals a multitude of different kinds or types of interchange. The differences depend principally upon the motives and goals of the participants. For example, a dialogue might be a debate in which the goal is to change the mind of the other and win it by conversion to one's own position. The dialogue could be a negotiation whose goal is compromise in a statement that can be agreed upon by both parties. An interchange may be motivated by the desire to learn from the other so that each one enriches his or her own understanding of reality. Dialogue can be a joint project of mutual discovery of something new for each party and affirmed together from different perspectives.[9] On the level of a practical activity, therefore, to affirm that two parties are in dialogue still leaves many questions unanswered. It defines in general terms a relationship that allows for significant differences.

One area in which these differences may be sharply defined lies in a fundamental attitude assumed by a church in relation to the secular or civic sphere. Earlier I referred to the distinct types of stances to the world that H. Richard Niebuhr outlined in his work *Christ and Culture.* David Lochhead also develops a typology of comprehensive reactions to the world that would color the dialogue.[10]

When the metaphor of dialogue is used to describe the fundamental relationship of the church to the world it transcends these other possible relationships but does not negate them. The church in dialogue with the world means a church that is open to and encounters the world as it is. The church is impelled to be open to the world. "When we speak in terms of the dialogical imperative, however, we are talking of attitude and relationship rather than activity. What is universally binding is not a life of going from one 'dialogue' to the next 'dialogue' but entering into relationships marked by openness, honesty, and the search for understanding."[11] This attitude finds grounding most fundamentally in a theology of creation. It would be difficult to justify a church rejecting a priori the world created by God. But at the same time, this fundamental attitude does not negate the thematics of other possible reactions to various aspects

---

9. I have appropriated this analysis from David Lochhead, *The Dialogical Imperative: A Christian Reflection on Interfaith Encounter* (Maryknoll, N.Y.: Orbis Books, 1988), 54–76.

10. Ibid., 5–30.

11. Ibid., 85.

of the world. The symbol "sin" points to the many areas of human life that have been corrupted by human egoism. An honest and open attitude to the world is a comprehensive a priori that seeks to learn about the world as it is. This openness, however, does not forbid but engenders a prophetic reaction to the sin of the world wherever it is encountered.

In sum, dialogue is a root metaphor that describes the fundamental attitude of the church to the world. This relationship has its mooring in God's dialogue with the world as that is depicted in the economy of salvation. The chief characteristics of this relationship are openness to the world and respect for the freedom and autonomy of the world.[12] This foundational attitude and relationship, however, leaves room for different particular relationships to various aspects of the world. With these presuppositions in place, the discussion turns to the relation of the church to society, state, and culture.

Church and Society

Beginning with the character of the relation of the church to society, two general rules have already been described. The first states that because the church exists in a twofold relationship to God and to the world, both of which influence each other, the distinctive way the church relates to society is governed by its relation to God. That relationship to God is revealed in the person and message of Jesus Christ; it is made continuously actual in the world by the power of God as Spirit; this presence is conscious and explicit in the Christian community. But to discern the direction of the Spirit in the church at any given time, the church turns back to the person of Jesus as he is preserved in the New Testament as the church's historical foundation and constant inspiration. The Faith and Order Commission expresses this general norm for the church's relation to the social world in this way:

---

12. Metaphysically, in a Christian view of things, this autonomy could be looked upon as the semiautonomous character of the systems of the world. This autonomy is established in and by God's creative action. Autonomy is seen as a gift that paradoxically includes the God-given ability of human freedom to sin, to react against the values of God. Some Christian theologians, such as Dietrich Bonhoeffer and Johann Baptist Metz, ground the autonomy of the world in Christ and specifically the incarnation.

Christian discipleship is based on the life and teaching of Jesus
of Nazareth testified to in scripture. Christians are called to discipleship in response to the living Word of God by obeying God
rather than human beings, repenting of sinful actions, forgiving
others, and living sacrificial lives of service. The source of their
passion for the transformation of the world lies in their communion with God in Jesus Christ. They believe that God, who
is absolute love, mercy and justice, is working through them by
the Holy Spirit. The Christian community always lives within
the sphere of divine forgiveness and peace.[13]

The Christian church is charged with the mission of being engaged
with the world after the pattern of Jesus' revelatory ministry.

The second general rule governing the relationship of the church to
society was outlined in the preceding section of this chapter under the
broad relationship of dialogue. The church is called upon to be open
to the world. This means that prior to more specific reactions to the
world, the church approaches the world positively. This is reflected in
the stipulation of Faith and Order that generally speaking the church
is sent to the world and hence is for the world: "One of the convictions which governs our reflections in this text is that the church
was intended by God, not for its own sake, but as an instrument,
in God's hands, for the transformation of the world. Thus service
(diakonia) belongs to the very being of the church" (NMC, 109).

A third general principle for understanding the church's relation
to society can be formulated negatively: no general prescription can
apply universally to the way the church should react to all societies.
Rather, the church should react differently to different societies precisely on the basis of the particularity and distinctiveness of each
one. Historical ecclesiology provides no more forceful single lesson
than the different requirements that are called forth from the church
in different social historical situations. This principle of recognizing
the particularity of every social situation follows as another consequence of the twofold relation of the church to God and to the world.
The church is called to address the society in which it finds itself and

---

13. NPC, #113.

doing so will constitute new needs and imperatives that will in turn generate new responses and ministries.

The historical principle that the church's relationship to society will vary according to historical circumstance does not prevent certain reflections of a strictly formal nature. The history of the church and ecclesiology show that the church under certain precise conditions has legitimately related to society in at least three ways: as critic, as leaven, and as partner.

When and in the measure to which the church finds itself in a society marked by flagrant injustice, oppression of particular groups, and other systemic degradations of human life, the church, reflecting the ministry of Jesus, must become a critic of society. The church as a corporate entity is committed to love of neighbor, and one of the examples Jesus proffered for this love was the parable of the Good Samaritan. But today social consciousness makes us distinctly aware that the oppressive structures of society are not due simply to fate or blind socioeconomic laws but in some measure are controllable by the human beings who make up society. Therefore, true love of neighbor in situations of social injustice and oppression, as distinct from sentimental feeling, must include active concern for the causes of human suffering and an impulse to change the dehumanizing structures. The church has always been socially concerned with the poor and the marginalized throughout the course of its history. But in the modern period this spontaneous Christian reaction has been deepened by critical historical and social consciousness.[14] Faith and Order, reflecting this critical consciousness, describes the churches' reaction to the world with these words: "There are occasions when ethical issues challenge the integrity of the Christian community itself and make it necessary to take a common stance to preserve its authenticity and credibility" (NMC, 116). The phrase "make it necessary" means that sometimes the situation impels a corporate decision. But it also suggests a more radical condition in which churches literally

---

14. As I indicated earlier in passing, this new consciousness is reflected in the rise of a social interpretation of the exigencies of Christian faith in the changing situations of society during the nineteenth century. The Social Gospel movement and, more recently, the movement of liberation theologies reflect these spontaneous reactions of the church to various forms of social human oppression and diminishment.

cannot escape taking a position. Many situations are such that failure to take an explicit stand on a social crisis or in the face of social policies is itself support of the status quo.

The church also assumes a relationship that may be metaphorically expressed as a leaven of society. The church cannot only denounce injustice; it also has to announce the values and promises of the kingdom of God. The gospel calls upon the church to participate, in a manner fitting its being church, in building structures of justice. The Good Samaritan today will not only bind up the victim's wounds but also participate in making the road to Jericho safe. This role in large measure takes the form of challenging the awareness of members of the church who participate in society and can influence its structures. "The integrity of the mission of the church . . . is at stake in witness through proclamation and in concrete actions for justice, peace and [the] integrity of creation. The latter will often be undertaken with those outside the community of faith" (NPC, 112).

In some instances, the church may also become engaged in society as a partner with other social agencies. As soon as the church became a recognized institution within the Roman Empire, its reflex of concern for those who needed assistance was quickly transformed into institutional forms of engagement in society. In bureaucratically underdeveloped societies one can expect that the church, when it is able, will create social agencies to address social problems where these are lacking. It is quite normal for the church to sponsor hospitals, schools, and a variety of agencies of social engagement and thereby to participate in the common social task of addressing the needs of the poor and other victims of society. Frequently, this informal cooperation with other civil social agencies becomes a partnership when the networks of the churches, which reach all the way to individuals in society, are used as channels for the distribution of assistance.

All churches feel a need to be an agent of material assistance to groups of people who are in need. The churches mobilize their members according to their size and resources; all are impelled by the gospel to reach out beyond their constituency to the common good.

Church and State

From its very beginnings the Christian movement was concerned about its relation to political authority. Thus Paul wrote to the Christians in Rome: "Let every person be subject to the governing authorities. For there is no authority except from God, and those that exist have been instituted by God" (Rom 13:1). Despite divine authorization on both sides, people could always distinguish between the lines of authority in the church and in civil rule. At various times each authority overreached what today are considered clear boundaries. Gradually, the modern secularization of civil government that accompanied the development of nation states ruled by human law allowed the appearance of various conceptions of a separation of church and state. For example, the First Amendment of the Constitution of the United States affirms that "Congress shall make no law respecting an establishment of religion, or prohibiting the free exercise thereof." This straightforward proposition guarantees the exercise of religion in freedom, not only without interference from government, but with protection by government. Different forms of this provision are being recognized as salutary in religiously pluralistic societies.

Most churches conceive of civil government in positive terms. Theologians propose a certain harmony between the authorities of church and state in the ideal realm. But as was said of society, no two governments are alike, and the historical situations in which they exist are always changing. Concretely one must expect tension between two institutions that claim authority, on different grounds and for different goals, with regard to the basic patterns of human life. As in the relationship between the church and society, it is impossible to formulate specific prescriptions that can apply universally to such a variety of different churches within such a variety of different governmental systems. But one can posit formal principles that offer guidelines relative to specific cases.

The church and the state enjoy a freedom and autonomous authority within their distinct spheres. The authority of the state is independent of and not rooted in religion or more particularly the church. And the authority of the church is specifically religious, that is, it stems from the actual, ongoing relation of the church to God recognized by its constituents. Religious authority appeals to freedom and is only authoritative religiously insofar as it mediates transcendent meaning and value that make an appeal to human conscience.[15] These two spheres of authority, therefore, are quite distinct because different relationships are engaged in their prescriptions. But they can and frequently do overlap in a given prescription. Early on Christians were commanded by civil authority to perform an act of recognition of what they perceived as an idolatrous object of civil religion. They were thus faced with a dilemma of obeying one or the other of two authorities whose commands contradicted each other. This dilemma is perennial; Christians of all times and places are continually being placed in this same dilemma in one form or another.

Given the overlapping of these two authorities within the consciences of Christians, one has to conceive of an active relationship and interchange between church and state. In other words, there will always be a constant battle between these two authorities and an active constructive interchange. As in the case of society, the church, along with other religions, may be a critic of the values that are operative in government and of the effects of the policies of the state from the religious perspective of its vision of humanity. One would expect that the church would be the corporate advocate of the poor and otherwise voiceless in society in virtue of the Christian perception of the absolute value of the human person. Different churches, because of their different sizes, will have considerably different leverage and resources to exert influence on government. But all churches are constantly reacting to government in one way or another.

What is said negatively with reference to prophetic criticism of governmental inaction or partisan bias and injustice can be stated positively when the relationship appears to be more cooperative and constructive. The churches and the religions can be thought

---

15. I distinguish this religious authority of the church from its organizational and disciplinary authority. The church as an organization possesses a bureaucratic authority by which it regulates the community. This has religious roots and theological grounding, and its exercise is theologically motivated. But it carries religious authority to individuals successfully only in the degree to which it mediates a dimension of transcendence, that is, an experience that one's transcendent relation to God is at stake in any particular prescription.

of as the social agencies that preserve deep humanitarian values which should in turn motivate governmental policies. In this light, churches should be willing to articulate publicly and to interpret constructively the values of the kingdom of God that Jesus preached as they apply to the policies of the state. As Faith and Order explains:

> Not only must Christians seek to promote the values of the kingdom of God by working together with adherents of other religions and even with those of no religious belief, but it is also incumbent upon them to witness to the kingdom in the realms of politics and economics. In particular, despite dangers and distortions the relation between church and state has been, over the centuries, an arena for Christian advocacy for the transformation of society along the lines which Jesus sketched out in the gospel. Many historical, cultural and demographic factors condition the relation between church and state, or between church and society. One expression of the diversity or catholicity of the church is the variety of models that these relations to societal structures can take. In each case, the explicit call of Jesus that his disciples be "salt of the earth" and "light of the world" (cf. Mt 5:13–16), and that they preach the kingdom (the role of which in society is comparable to that of leaven which makes the whole dough rise [cf. Mt 13:33]), invites Christians to collaborate with political and economic authorities to promote the values of God's kingdom, and to oppose policies and initiatives which contradict them. In this way Christians may stand in the tradition of the prophets who proclaimed God's judgment on all injustice. (NMC, 115)[16]

---

16. "One feature of the contemporary ecumenical situation is the frequency with which moral stances have become potentially church-dividing, both within and between churches. An increasing range of issues, including those of human sexuality, have polarized Christian communities and risk damaging or destroying the bonds of *koinonia* already existing. The closer churches come to an agreement on ecclesiology, the more they are challenged to address the tolerable limits of moral diversity compatible with *koinonia*. Continual ecumenical dialogue, discernment, accountability and Christian charity are required to that end" (NPC, 117, box). This statement has to be taken as a prayerful lament. It points to a disgraceful failure of the churches to recognize the fundamental difference between the sacrality of what holds the church together and disagreement in moral practices. If Christians cannot remain together in the task of moral discernment on the basis of what they share in common, how can these same

Church and Culture

Two major problems have their roots in the complex and dynamic relationship between the church and culture. The one is the question of the inculturation of the church in the lives of different groups of people. This issue is thoroughly debated in the discipline of missiology and remains an ongoing global problem. The other lies in the christological question of the relationship between Jesus Christ and other religions, but overflows into the question of the church's strategy in the pursuit of its mission to the nations in the face of other religions. This issue has generated a flood of theological literature in recent decades. The symbol of dialogue offers a resource for understanding both of these issues and opens up practical ways of moving forward.

Inculturation. Inculturation refers to the incarnation of Christianity in the thought-forms and mentality of a group of people in such a way that it becomes indigenous to their ways of thinking, valuing, and acting. By inculturation Christianity passes from being an "outside" influence or alien system relative to a nation or society to being appropriated in a way that makes the church an internalized part of its identity. Such a process takes time. The results are often a matter of degree, and success can be measured by its depth. The outcome of a process of inculturation is roughly related to the goal of missionary activity, but in fact missionaries cannot accomplish inculturation. As a corporate task, it falls upon the responsibility of the people who share a given culture.

The transition of the Jesus movement from a Jewish Semitic background to a church that flourished in Greco-Roman culture in the patristic period offers a prime example of inculturation in the history of Christianity. The term "hellenization" often connotes negativity if patristic forms are considered antievangelical, that is, changes that distorted the Christian message. But many believe that the thought-forms and practices of the Greek and Roman churches were necessary and in fact preserved the meaning of Christianity from extinction within a new culture. Thus the process may also be read as a massive process of the communication of Christianity to the gentile peoples

---

churches expect pluralistic societies to engage in civil conversation and seek mutual understanding?

within the Roman Empire. In any case, the dialogue between the leaders of the Western churches, with their particular intellectual languages, and the scriptural texts never ceased. The patristic church teaches forceful lessons in a debate between the right and the left on inculturation: that the church can change quite radically, and that such changes can lift up perennial and classical doctrines.

Whether or not the patristic church be judged a successful example, inculturation defines a necessary ideal and goal. Without some measure of inculturation the Christian gospel cannot be communicated, appropriated, or authentically practiced. One cannot deeply understand something that is proposed in an alien language. One cannot deeply make one's own something that remains unintelligible and foreign. One cannot spontaneously express deep spiritual experiences in alien ritual practices. The inculturation of Christianity, practically speaking, is synonymous with a Christianity that is rendered accessible in one's own language, appropriated, and authentically lived.

The problems connected with inculturation have been present to the church from the beginning. For example, just as patristic theology represented an extended exercise of inculturation, so too other developments in theology in the course of the history of Christian thought can be so interpreted. But especially since cultures have become self-consciously aware of their difference from various Western cultures with which Christianity has been associated, this particular appreciation of the problem of evangelization has come to the fore. Some of the issues currently at stake have been stated bluntly by the Faith and Order Commission. "There are a number of problems concerning the relation between gospel and culture: when one culture seeks to capture the gospel and claims to be the one and only authentic way of celebrating the gospel; when one culture seeks to impose its expression of the gospel on others as the only authentic expression of the gospel; when the gospel is held captive within a particular cultural expression; when one culture finds it impossible to recognize the gospel being faithfully proclaimed in another culture" (NPC, 64, box).[17] This particular view of the problem reflects

---

17. This list of problems is developed further in NMC, 63 box.

the perspective of non-Western cultures that are actively seeking to reinterpret Christian truth, value, and practice into the indigenous forms of their own cultural experience.

The perspective of the Western churches on the same problem yields a slightly different formulation. How is the Christian message to survive when it becomes fragmented into so many different languages and symbol systems? Inculturation entails change. Inculturation does not consist in transliteration of the gospel but in interpretation in new cultural forms. How do the whole church and any particular church in it guarantee that a particular interpretation of the gospel is faithful to the original and originating revelation in the person of Jesus Christ? Here the bias leans toward scriptural origins as norms and traditions guaranteeing fidelity to the gospel. The historicity and particularity of the revelation in Jesus Christ includes this conservative instinct.

There are no neat resolutions to these problems. The only solution lies in dealing with the issues with a historical strategy. And one such strategy consists in a commitment to dialogue, or to multiple dialogues, or to a large conversation across cultural and denominational lines. History provides no noncultural or supracultural standard to measure the authenticity of any cultural expression of Christian faith. Rather, the whole church exhibits an existential criterion of relating to Jesus as the bringer of God's salvation. The criterion of faith and worship together offer a common ground upon which to build.[18] The efforts at inculturation in various cultures go forward on that basis. On that premise, too, a strategy for addressing the problems that arise as the process of inculturation goes forward may be found in a willingness to enter into conversation with other churches on the basis of a communion in faith. Gradually, the positions of one's own church and other churches will become better understood by comparative interaction.

Dialogue with other religions. During the last third of the twentieth century, Christian theology of religions emerged as a major topic of discussion. Theologians of different ecclesial traditions engaged

---

18. The criterion of existential faith is inseparable but distinct from the propositional formulas of belief; the criterion of existential worship is inseparable but distinct from specific ceremonies.

the issues, and the World Council of Churches produced a report.[19] These reflections come to a focus in the question of the status of Jesus Christ in God's economy of salvation that embraces the whole human race. This conversation has direct bearing upon the missionary activity of the church because of the way the church's mission was carried forward in the past. I have already described the imperialistic tendencies of this missionary activity. More particularly criticism has taken aim at the explicit goal of Christian mission when it is formulated as the conversion of other people to the Christian church from religions that are deeply rooted in a specific culture and sometimes are part of a national identity. This can generate a hostile reaction that may lead to political suppression of the mission by the nations receiving missionaries. It may also lead to suppression of the Christian church within a given nation.

A practical way of approaching this problem, if not a solution in itself, may be found once again in dialogue. From the earliest period the goal of missionary activity was understood as the spread of Christian revelation among the nations. Implicitly, this seemed to entail conversion to the Christian church. Conversion means that the dialogue partners move away from the religions of their birth to the religion of the other. But many Christians have entered into dialogue with people of other faiths without any desire of seeking the conversion of the dialogue partners to the Christian church. This raises the question whether, more generally, the goal of Christian mission might be reinterpreted in such a way that it too does not explicitly aim at conversion.[20] Pragmatically, the goal of conversion seems to be socially unrealistic relative to whole nations or cultures. More modest goals of dialogue were suggested earlier; they aim at mutual understanding, deepening of the understanding of one's own faith,

---

19. "Religious Plurality: Theological Perspectives and Affirmations, 1990," *The Ecumenical Movement: An Anthology of Key Texts and Voices,* ed. Michael Kinnamon and Brian E. Cope (Geneva: WCC Publications; Grand Rapids: William B. Eerdmans, 1997), 417–20. The document affirms that the influence of God as Father and creator, the saving mystery of Christ, and the action of the Holy Spirit can be found at work in other religions so that Christians can learn about God in dialogue with them.

20. The point here is not to rule out the possibility of conversion in the encounters among religions. The point is rather to prevent programmatic strategies that urge conversion as distinct from absolute care in respecting religious freedom.

sharing new experiences of and insights into the nature of human existence and ultimate reality. The goal of mission when this unfolds within the context of other religions is so to enter into dialogue with the other culture and religion that one communicates to the other who Jesus Christ is according to Christian faith at the same time that one learns about the faith and belief of the religion of the other culture.

The Christian church does not have to alter its self-conception or its understanding of the place of Jesus Christ in relation to other religious mediators in order to enter into dialogue at this practical but no less profound level. Such a self-restriction on the part of the Christian churches should not be depicted as endangering the mission project itself. This would be an alarmist reaction. The real danger is one that threatens a breakdown of interreligious relationships. Rarely in the history of the human race has there been such a crucial need for mutual understanding between peoples of different religions than there is today.

This strategy seems to be possible for both conservative and progressive Christian churches. One can enter into dialogue with other religions on a practical level with the explicit goal of mutual understanding without necessarily having to posit a status to the religions of the world that would be unacceptable to conservative Christians.[21] There is much more to be said on this question in terms of fundamental theology and the logic of the affirmation of ultimate truth. But this is better taken up in the discipline of christology where these problems have their source and find the rationales for their resolution. The issue far transcends this ecclesial discussion, which can very readily remain on the practical level. This also entails accepting the situation of religious pluralism as at least a temporary and foreseeable historical inevitability as distinct from an eschatological future.

---

21. The pragmatic character of this strategy is not the last word on this problem. The debate within Christianity and the Christian theology of religions goes on. But this practical ecclesiological strategy should be acceptable to both conservative Christians and the members of the various world religions. Missionaries would have to be explicit and honest in their disavowal of conversion to Christianity as the primary goal of missionary activity. Those countries that possess a more or less established religious culture would have to be explicit and honest about a policy of religious freedom.

To conclude: how can one characterize the relationship of the Christian church to the world? The response proposed at this broad level of a transdenominational ecclesiology can be described as an engagement with the world through critical dialogue. The term "dialogue" in this construction represents a mode of human interaction filled with subtleties. It respects freedom on all sides and supposes the value of the human person as the beloved of God. This makes the church critical of all worldly arrangements that diminish individuals or groups and supportive of movements that enhance human life. In this policy the church acts in the name of the values of the kingdom of God announced by Jesus.

ECCLESIAL EXISTENCE

The slogan that "the world sets the agenda for the church" does not mean that the world dictates the nature of the church. Rather, the many different worlds the church addresses summon forth its inner divine resources so that this relationship reveals these potentialities. Ecclesial existence under this formality refers to the inner disposition of church members to respond to the world around them. Beneath the different relations to a multifaceted world, one can draw out many apostolic features of the mission of the church that ground a shared ecclesial existence. This represents something common to all churches because it is essential to being a Christian. I highlight features of this aspect of ecclesial existence in two steps. In the first I recall the source of a mission spirituality in Jesus Christ. In the second I show how ecclesial mission to the world shapes ecclesial existence in several ways that all churches might identify with.

The Primal Experience of Mission to the World

The feeling, experience, and idea of "being sent" or having a commission to do something, or to act, seems to have accompanied the Easter experience of the disciples of Jesus. The stories of the appearances of the risen Jesus to his followers frequently carry the co-theme of mission. "Go forth to every part of the world" (Mk 16:15; Mt 28:19); "you are the witnesses" (Lk 24:48); "As the Father sent me, so I send you" (John 20:21). The experience of Jesus' "being raised" and of

their own "being sent" as his witnessing representatives to the world
was the event that constituted the Christian movement that became
the church.

Luke's two-volume work more than any other gives a sense of
the continuity between Jesus' ministry and the formation of a Jesus
movement. God as Spirit in many ways is the major actor that spans
the whole Lukan story. This literary witness in turn points to an experience of a divine movement in history in which the disciples and
the people who joined them were caught up. That mission comes
from God and in missiological literature is called the mission of
God. God addresses the world in Jesus Christ. In Luke's design the
church carries forward the mission of God in history that is the person of Jesus by continuing to represent or actualize his ministry in
the world.

To be a member of an organization entails internalizing its mission. Ecclesial existence consists in participating in the mission of the
church, thinking with the church, doing what the church is meant
to do. Mission spirituality corresponding to this dimension of the
church describes the commitment of all members to the mission
of the church and in some degree a responsibility for shouldering
it. The mission of the church is not carried by the leaders of the
church alone. It is not left solely to clergy and church institutions.
The whole community's embrace of its mission becomes in some
measure a constituent of ecclesial existence itself.

The Missionary Dimension of Ecclesial Existence

This chapter has addressed various aspects of the world to which
the church relates: society, state, culture, religions. Reversing the
perspective, what dimensions of the Christian life do the various
relationships of the church to the world reveal and propose to the
members for their internalization?

First of all, one can characterize ecclesial existence as a positive
openness to the world. I call two sixteenth-century witnesses to this
profoundly positive attitude to human existence and life in the world:
Ignatius of Loyola and John Calvin. Basing himself on a doctrine of
creation, Ignatius believed the Christian should be able to find God
in all things. He echoed the Psalmist on this point: "Whither shall I

go from your Spirit? Or whither shall I flee from your presence?" (Ps 139:7) Ignatius calls upon the Christian to consider how God dwells in all creatures, including oneself, making us God's temple. He counsels people to look and see how God "labors and works" for us in the creatures of the world.[22] Several of Calvin's principles for a Christian life move in a complementary direction. The creatures of this world should not be avoided but used according to their inner, created teleology. Human beings are stewards of the world; the world has been entrusted to our care. Calvin's sense of providence and calling mean that human beings grow closer to God by participating in the secular roles of life that are constructive of community and society.[23]

Another aspect of the world that usually dominates the discussion of the church-world relationship is society. Because social life is so complex, and because societies have such distinctive and diverse characters, one cannot be specific about ecclesial attitudes toward society. But a relatively new social awareness has sent a new message to the missionary dimension of ecclesial existence and altered the quality of Christian concern for social existence. Members of the church cannot be indifferent or stoic in the face of social injustice. Social injustice has become something for which we feel more responsible than in the past simply because social conditions are more consciously held in place by a social will. The responsibility for the world reflected in Calvin's sense of stewardship has been expanded and deepened. We have a sense of responsibility for history in a way Christians never had prior to the nineteenth century. And this has expanded a sense of sin to include public and social conditions that can only be combated by social grace working through social virtues and social action. The social liberation theologies of the nineteenth and twentieth centuries are natural outgrowths of a Christian spirituality that appreciates sin in society and urges a human response that will help protect human life on a social level. If the church and more generally the religions do not actively support the poor, the marginalized, the powerless, and the many victims of society, they will not

---

22. Ignatius of Loyola, *Spiritual Exercises*, nos. 235–36 in *Ignatius of Loyola: Spiritual Exercises and Selected Works*, The Classics of Western Spirituality, ed. George E. Ganns et al. (New York, Mahwah, N.J.: Paulist Press, 1991), 176–77.

23. CCH, II, 120–21.

have an audible voice. This deep existential concern for those who suffer socially runs prior to and does not in itself prejudge strategies and tactics for social amelioration. Rather, this ecclesial spirituality should allow Christians of different social outlooks to strategize with each other out of this shared concern that is learned from Jesus Christ.

The relation of the church to government or state has undergone a change in the modern West that is as radical as was the shift in the Constantinian period, but in an opposite direction. Historians, sociologists of religion, and theologians all chart the shifts in the church and ecclesial existence that accompanied the imperial legitimization of the church. The shift from national churches to interior and privatized religion and faith in the modern period has had equally thoroughgoing effects. Against this privatization and individualism typical of Western societies, the mission of the church forbids churches from disengaging ecclesial existence from public policy. If the message of the church has a bearing on the whole of human existence, it cannot promote apolitical attitudes. It is clear that Christians as Christians possess no political formula for political life. But in the pattern of Jesus of Nazareth ecclesial existence spontaneously reacts against regimes that devalue or suppress individuals or groups who lack the power to defend themselves. Ecclesial existence is critical of oppressive government and looks after the fortunes of the victims of society.

Because churches must communicate with the culture in which they exist, ecclesial existence should become part of the local culture. Even when churches resist certain cultural norms, by that very fact they engage culture. A vital missionary ecclesial existence, wherever the church exists, should feel and participate in this tension because the process of inculturation goes forward willy nilly. In fact, the church spontaneously adjusts to the culture of each world in which it exists. Ecclesial existence, therefore, should self-consciously look not only for sin but also for signs of the vitality of God's Spirit at work everywhere in the world. Wherever there is sin, according to God's promise in Jesus Christ, one will also find the resistance of God's Spirit to that sin. Ecclesial existence should have a sense for the various movements of the Spirit in other churches and in other religions. One way in which this missionary openness manifests itself is simply through casual or vital relationships with people of other religions or religious beliefs. One of the strongest ecumenical agencies in our world today is friendship.

A hard question. The hard question that arises when one considers the relation of the church to the world is single and profound, but it takes many forms. The question presupposes that the church is always in dialogue with the world and that inculturation is a positive and necessary historical development of the church. But this interchange consistently and in various ways raises the question of whether a particular adaptation to the world is compatible with ecclesial existence. In matters of doctrinal formulation, moral conduct, cooperation with society or government, dialogue and learning from other religions, when does or should an inculturation of one church put it at odds with other churches? When is a partnership with the world in one part of the world a compromise of Christian faith generally? The challenge of this hard question practically speaking addresses the love, patience, and communitarian solidarity that faith in Jesus Christ provides. Churches should be very slow to abandon communion with other churches because of their relationship with the world because the Spirit of God as represented by Jesus reaches across differences as a power of reconciliation.

Chapter 8

Ecclesial Existence
and Partial Communion

In this final chapter of the book and of this three-volume ecclesiology from below, I propose the following simple thesis: ecclesial existence provides the grounds for partial communion among the churches. The burden of this chapter consists in exploring and explaining what this proposition means and entails. Its implications are far more complex than the proposal itself; it remains embryonic and at the same time programmatic. Despite its challenges, I believe that the majority of Christians, at least in the West, are ready for this movement forward.

I will develop the thesis in an argument with three logical steps. The first section of the chapter speaks of ecclesial existence as a spirituality. The comparative ecclesiology of this volume discursively sketched an objective account of the apostolic church as it appears across the various church traditions that make up the Christian ecumene today. This objective analysis of a transdenominational ecclesiology implicitly contains an existential ecclesial existence that constitutes a rudimentary spirituality shared by all Christians.

This existence common among all the churches provides in turn the grounding for the partial communion that I will introduce in the second section of the chapter. What does the idea of partial communion stand for? It appears best in contrast to the ecumenical concept of "full communion," and I will represent it against that foil. It is a simple and yet tensive and dynamic concept.

In the third section I invite readers to consider whether the ecclesial existence that spans the two millennia of the church's journey through history and that I have tried to characterize from a current perspective in chapters 3 to 7 can serve as a grounding for a general

Christian ecclesiological policy of seeking partial communion among the churches.

ECCLESIAL EXISTENCE AS ECCLESIAL SPIRITUALITY

Ecclesial existence as I intend the phrase has two inseparable dimensions: it refers to a mode of human existence in the community of the church and also to a more objective thematic understanding of this existence. To bring out these two dimensions I characterize ecclesial existence as an ecclesial spirituality because the existential character of spirituality has a wider recognition.

"Spirituality" on an Existential and a Notional Level

The term "spirituality" has been released from the writings of solitary mystics and the cloistered precincts of monasteries and convents. One can now pick up books on spirituality in the kiosks of airports and train terminals. They deal with anything from formulas for self-improvement, to psychological self-examination, to Eastern practices of concentration and meditation. Spirituality remains as well a subdiscipline of theology, but it covers a range from schools of praying and relating to God to techniques of accompanying people in their religious lives. This eclectic expansion of the sphere of spirituality has the merit of relating it to everyday secular life. But it requires of anyone using the term to be clear about a particular usage and meaning.

I use the term "spirituality" to refer to the encompassing logic of how people live their lives with implicit or explicit reference to ultimate reality. People's spirituality is the way they live their lives. This usage capitalizes on the democratization and secularization of the term: everyone has a spirituality. Spirituality is not the stale stuff of a faded religion; it is the positive élan that drives each person's life. The notion goes far deeper than "lifestyle" and thus should not be equated merely with what transpires on the surface of time and place, the ad hoc of doing this or that. Spirituality, by recalling the human spirit, calls up the depth of the intentional direction of particular human lives, singly or in groups, toward some implicit or explicit goal. Thus spirituality includes the entire range of human activities, but its formal or defining mark lies in its reference to ultimate reality. In Christianity that ultimate reality is God. Spirituality thus refers to the quality of one's whole life as it stands before God. Spirituality opens up the entire range of the "Christian life" as this is directed toward and is measured by God as God is revealed in Jesus Christ.

Spirituality so understood always carries two dimensions. The one may be called existential and consists in the actual decisions and actions that make up the daily course of life. The other consists in the understanding, rationale, or reflective analysis that both governs and is contained in the existential living. This second dimension may be embedded within a person's behavior and not reflectively examined; or it may be a quite explicit theorizing about the character and quality of Christian life. Spirituality in this second sense, when it is formally objectivized, constitutes the discipline analyzed in books and studied in courses. But the real point of this distinction between existential and formal spirituality is not to separate these inseparable dimensions of spiritual life but to insist that the two should always be held together in any understanding of the term "spirituality." The theoretical reflection always refers back to life on the ground; seemingly mindless routine behaviors act out latent motivations, implicit goals, or reasoned teleologies. Transferring these reflections to ecclesial existence highlights the deep existential level at which all Christians are bound together.

Ecclesial Existence as Synonymous with Ecclesial Spirituality

Reflection on the idea of ecclesial existence as it has been described in this book shows that at bottom it is the equivalent of a spirituality, more specifically a personal and a corporate ecclesial spirituality. This can be shown logically by a simple comparison of the meaning of these terms. Ecclesial existence refers to the apostolic faith in Jesus Christ as that is organized in the many churches that constitute the Christian movement. This ecclesial existence at its base is a way of life lived within the Christian community or by the community itself. But this is just the understanding of spirituality offered here: a form of life, lived in this case in community, with reference to the ultimate reality of God. Considering ecclesial existence in terms of spirituality brings out the existential or living substance underlying community structures and the objective understanding that accompanies them. Even the theoretical formulae for expressing ecclesial existence, the theologies of the church, of baptism, of ministerial office, for example, ultimately have to be referred back to life lived in community in order to verify their meaning, their accuracy, and their truth.

But there is another way of understanding and explaining the convergence of ecclesial existence and ecclesial spirituality that deepens the semantic analysis. A brief reflection on the dynamics operative within the historical formation of the church brings out the existential logic of ecclesial existence as a spirituality. I summarize this interpretation of the development of the church in three propositions.[1]

1. Christianity began as a spirituality of following Jesus of Nazareth. Even though there is little evidence for the view that Jesus intended to found what later became the Christian church, it is clear that the church developed from the teaching, ministry, and person of Jesus of Nazareth. The disciples who followed Jesus in his lifetime became, after his death and resurrection, the movement which gradually grew into an autonomous Christian church. The characterization of this attachment to and following of Jesus as a spirituality seems to be most appropriate: it brings out both the visceral or existential depth of the commitment and the lively theoretical activity in the first decades that formulated interpretations of both Jesus and the newly forming community itself.

2. This movement of spirituality became a church. During the course of the first century, in a complex development, the Jesus movement evolved into the Christian church. A sociologist would describe the process as a gradual objectification of certain patterns of behavior that characterized the various communities of Christians. Sometimes these practices diverged from the synagogues, but they also retained deep continuities because of the attachment to Jesus shaped in the nascent community. The community itself also

---

1. A more extensive analysis of this same subject matter is contained in CCH, I, 69–139.

bore witness to the dynamism of God as Spirit working within the movement and urging it to become church.

3. Thereafter, the church became the medium of Christian spirituality. The development of churches was chronologically uneven, but by the second generation in each case the church as a more or less objective community began actively to form the ecclesial spirituality of the new members. What began as an objectification of the life in the Spirit of Jesus within shifted to become the objective medium initiating new members into an ecclesial-Jesus spirituality. The convergence of ecclesial existence and ecclesial spirituality became complete: the two were identical in reality and function. Ecclesial spirituality and ecclesial existence are together both the product of existential spirituality and the media for its dissemination to the members of the community.

Comparative Ecclesiology and a Common Ecclesial Existence

The comparative ecclesiology of this volume is an effort to uncover and put into words the common apostolic dimensions of the church that are shared by all Christian churches. Behind it and serving as its point of reference lies the history of ecclesiology of the first two volumes of *Christian Community in History*. This history, as schematic as it is, expands the horizon of reflections on the church beyond a local or denominational field. While the story of the church over these centuries readily displays change and diversity, it also more forcefully shows how the church retained a common apostolic identity under the plurality of institutional forms. This common apostolic identity does not always lie on the surface, and judgment is too often misled by phenomenal appearances. Constructive comparative ecclesiology aims at going below the surface of the different individual forms of the churches to find the existential commitments they share.

The comparison between ecclesial existence and spirituality, and the judgment that ecclesial existence is a spirituality, open up a way of conceiving its inner character as an existential reality. It also clarifies the conditions of the possibility of apostolicity. Ecclesial existence most fundamentally consists in a way of life fashioned around fundamental commitments and a few constitutional elements. This way of life has a communitarian structure: people are socialized into it. But that into which Christians are socialized cannot be captured by, in the sense of reduced to, a set of doctrines, or the particular institutional forms, or the routinized pattern of the community's behavior. Rather the existential way of life exceeds and overflows these structures. Nor is ecclesial existence identical with the patterns of worship and ethics that are articulated by the particular churches. All of these are constituent ingredients of particular forms of the lives lived in community, but they are changeable. They have substance only in the measure in which they express the inner corporate subjectivity that gave rise to them and that they in turn objectify. This distinction between the existential lived reality and its objective forms or vehicles of expression, without any intent of separation between them, allows the possibility of there being a continuity between the apostolicity of the primitive Jesus movement and the church of the twenty-first century. This continuity lives within, but is not identical with, its external forms. If this were not the case, there could be no continuity with apostolic times because linear history entails change of the objective forms of the church. As was seen in the history of ecclesiology, they change most when they are kept rigidly the same across different historical contexts.

To sum up this first stage of the analysis, the aim of constructive comparative ecclesiology is to uncover the latent apostolic church that subsists in the church today across the denominations. But beneath the language that tries to formulate that common Christian ecclesiology lies ecclesial existence, the existential reality of being a Christian that is actualized in a wide variety of church forms and institutions. Recognition that the vast majority of Christians participate in this ecclesial existence will open up the imagination of churches, and especially church leaders, to the salutary idea and strategy of partial communion.

THE CONCEPT OF PARTIAL COMMUNION

One has to make the case for the usefulness of constructive comparative ecclesiology because it appears somewhat theoretical when compared with denominational ecclesiology, which articulates for the members of a given church an understanding of their particular ecclesial existence. This usefulness generally finds its rationale within the ecumenical movement and the quest for unity in a world church that should not be divided even though differences will always prevail. In other words, like all comparative theologies, it is dealing with pluralism. I believe that the usefulness of constructive comparative ecclesiology appears best in a comparison between the ecumenical ideas of "full communion" and what may be called "partial communion." I begin then with a characterization of full communion.

Full Communion

Communion among churches by definition means unity amid differences; it presupposes a distinction of churches and names a unity between two or more distinct churches. Full communion roughly means mutual recognition of one another by two or more churches in every essential aspect of what it means to be church despite differences that do not make a substantial difference. The Assembly of the World Council of Churches in Canberra, Australia addressed the issue.[2] From the perspective of Canberra the following four characteristics or marks would add up to full communion: a common confession of the apostolic faith, a common sacramental life revolving around baptism and the eucharist, a set of ministries in the churches that was mutually recognized, and a common mission to evangelize the world.[3] By these criteria the churches recognize in the others a possession of all the elements of what it means to be church according to apostolic standards. To this Canberra added: "The goal of the search for full communion is realized when all the churches are able to recognize in one another the one, holy, catholic, and apostolic church in its fullness. This full communion will be expressed

2. O. C. Edwards Jr. describes the results of an extensive study of the meaning of the phrase "full communion" among many typical church traditions in the wake of Canberra. He finds a large range of different meanings or expectations or conditions for it to occur. There are also many churches for which the concept bears little meaning at all. See "Meanings of Full Communion: The Essence of Life in the Body," in *Speaking of Unity* 1 (2005): 9–35. *Speaking of Unity* is an electronic journal published by the Faith and Order Commission of the National Council of the Churches of Christ in the U.S.A. Its address is *www.ncccusa.org/speakingofunity/*.

3. Ibid., 10.

on the local and the universal levels through conciliar forms of life and action. In such communion churches are bound in all aspects of their life together at all levels in confessing the one faith, sharing sacramental life, and engaging in common witness, sustained by recognized and reconciled ministry."[4] The idea of full communion thus sets a high ideal that requires considerable work even when the churches are somewhat congruous with each other.

In the light of study, however, the meaning of full communion as it is actually understood by the churches turned out to be in some cases rather far from the ideal set out by Canberra. Some churches could operate within this fourfold framework or with a set of criteria analogous to it. Several churches already have set out mutual agreements for full communion with other churches. But in the case of other churches differences were so great that the criteria did not even fit. Some churches, moreover, are in fact not interested in full communion with other churches. Others are willing only to speak of covenant relationships or various degrees of fellowship. Despite the fact that many churches have entered into full communion with each other, the idea of "full" communion proposes a standard that seems unattainable for many churches relative to others. In some cases the idea of full communion with other churches is something to be avoided because it means compromise of their own identity.

Partial Communion

In contrast to full communion, partial communion among churches means mutual recognition despite substantial or significant differences or disagreements. One object or goal of transdenominational ecclesiology using a constructive comparative method is to create the conditions that may allow for partial communion among churches. Transdenominational ecclesiology proposes to churches positive reasons for entering into a relationship of communion with another church which may be seriously different from themselves. Notice that the idea of partial communion is itself a fluid historical concept that admits of many degrees. Negatively, it is not possible to

---

4. Ibid., 11.

determine the limits of partial communion, that is, what can prevent it. No standard exists to measure unbridgeable differences. The constant shifting of history excludes an a priori determination of the nature or degree of differences that would stand in the way of partial communion. Perhaps there are none at all. But three constructive aspects of a transdenominational ecclesiology positively open the way to possible partial communions among churches that seriously differ on important matters.

First, the goal of constructive comparative theology is to express as fully as possible the common apostolic ecclesial existence that all churches claim subsists in them or that they possess. This constructive comparative theology strives to express in abstract but existentially relevant language the ecclesial existence that is the equivalent in our time of apostolic ecclesial existence. In the measure it succeeds in constructing an account of the apostolic existence in which all claim to participate, in the same measure does it provide the basis for a communion that transcends all differences. If churches recognize ecclesial apostolicity in the results of this constructive effort, they should also recognize and have no reason not to recognize bases for a partial communion with other churches.[5]

Second, an elaborated transdenominational ecclesiology that succeeds in approaching a contemporary expression of apostolic ecclesial faith demonstrates the complex hybridity of ecclesial identity.[6] Ecclesial existence is not simple, either historically or theologically. A reading of the Faith and Order's study documents BEM and NMC, although they are brief and schematic, illustrate the amount of complex data that have been digested and carefully formulated. This

5. Ormond Rush expresses what is going on here in the context of a bilateral ecumenical discussion: "Instead of comparing and contrasting traditions, both parties attempt to interpret together the apostolic tradition. If each can recognize in the other's interpretation 'the apostolic faith,' then surprising agreement and common ground can be achieved." Ormond Rush, *Still Interpreting Vatican II: Some Hermeneutical Principles* (New York: Paulist Press, 2004), 67. This describes the intention of the convergence documents of Faith and Order: they aim to state in a commonly accepted language the common apostolic faith.

6. I take this line of argument from Jeannine Hill Fletcher, *Monopoly on Salvation? A Feminist Approach to Religious Pluralism* (New York: Continuum, 2005), 82–101. "Using the resources of feminist theory, we can challenge the logic of identity and rethink 'specific difference' to recognize that the categories of all religions are made up of diverse identities." Ibid., 88.

complexity shows Paul's seemingly simple formula, "one Lord, one faith, one baptism, and one Spirit," will not yield to a simple exegesis.[7] Each church's identity is a hybrid of multiple factors from history and theological interpretations that cannot be reduced to simple terms. But this complexity also implies that the bonds of relationship that join the churches are many. The churches that seem most distant from each other at the same time share an enormous legacy of common tradition that relates them to each other. The fallacy of specific difference proposes that an individual or a group can be captured in a single trait or a specific defining quality. For example, a church is "hierarchical," or a church is "congregational." The fallacy reduces complexity to a single focused element and thereby neglects the full historical reality of the person or group. Constructive comparative ecclesiology effectively breaks the hold that this common tendency has on the imagination. It shows the depth and complexity of ecclesial existence and the degree to which sometimes seemingly radically different ecclesial bodies share many common defining elements. These constitute the basis for partial communion.

The third condition for partial communion among churches lies less in objective data and more in the subjective will of the churches. The churches have to want to affirm the other churches. To do this a church must strive to transcend its own self-understanding in order to grasp the apostolic ecclesial existence in the other despite its otherness. Any church can resist communion because of difference from itself. It does so on the grounds of a rationale that implicitly sets up its own ecclesial form as the norm for apostolic ecclesial existence. On this basis, it says communion is not possible because we embody the integrity of the faith and others do not. We must protect authentic ecclesial existence against others who distort it. The integrity of faith cannot be compromised. Somehow, in a historicist and pluralist world, recognizing pluralism is taken as a threat to authentic ecclesial existence. This stance mistakenly takes a particular version of apostolic tradition to represent the whole. The impulse of the Spirit, according to Schleiermacher, always leans toward unity; the drag of

---

7. See supra, 13, n. 11.

sin, which exists in all the churches, militates against it. But as Ignatius of Loyola recognized, the angel of darkness always poses as the angel of light.

A Tensive Concept

"Partial communion" is a tensive concept because it combines in tension a positive and a negative value. "Communion" clearly communicates an ideal, some believe an eschatological ideal. At the same time many are convinced that the grounds for communion exist in the churches and are blocked by failure to acknowledge them. By God's grace communion can be achieved. But a "partial" communion carries negative connotations: a partial communion is precisely a failure at full communion, a full communion not achieved, or a communion only partially realized. In offering partial communion as an achievable goal, does the idea actually work against the eschatological pressure to strive for full communion? Should we go forward with phrases that are more positive? Would language like "initial communion" be more energizing? Would terms such as "covenant relationships" or "degrees of fellowship" between churches be more realistic and less pretentious?

I will not try to respond to these questions of terminology at this point. I simply move forward on the basis of what I consider the straightforward character of the term "partial communion." A limited value remains a value to which the church may cling. What this study holds out to the churches is a recommendation for working toward relationships that quite precisely result in partial communion among the churches. Such partial communions will by definition be in some degree deficient. By being explicit about that deficiency, the category becomes a constant reminder that the churches could do better.[8]

---

8. The communion achieved by the Church of England, the Federation of the Evangelical Churches in the German Democratic Republic, and the Evangelical Church in Germany in 1991 represents a good example of partial communion in the sense in which it is intended here. Called the Meissen Agreement, it has a written foundation in three documents. The first is the "Meissen Common Statement: On the Way to Visible Unity" that sets out in six short chapters the grounds of communion between these churches and significant remaining differences that prevent full

In sum, partial communion consists in a formal recognition between given churches that they share common bonds between them.
There exists at the present time a large amount of implicit recognition between members of different churches about how much they
share with other autonomous churches distinct from themselves.
The partial communion I am speaking of consists in the public affirmation of this commonality. It will take different forms among
different churches as they declare these mutual relationships.

ECCLESIAL EXISTENCE AS THE APOSTOLIC BASIS FOR PARTIAL COMMUNION

What are the grounds for promoting the idea of partial communion
among the churches? Several lines of objective consideration push
Christian consciousness toward an explicit strategy of entering into
formal pacts of partial communion with other churches. These three
volumes have considered the following analytical approaches: first, a
developmental account of the church and the churches in line with
historical consciousness has shown the constant emergence of new
forms of church. The pluralism of church organization in the New
Testament, the church's normative document, seems to urge mutual
church recognition. Second, the coherent claims of apostolicity made
by churches with different structures of authority and ministry de-
serve attention. Third, the health and vitality of different churches
within their historical contexts suggest the presence of God as Spirit
within them. On these bases this volume has followed the example
of the Faith and Order Commission and tried to outline an objective

mutual recognition of ministries. The second document bears the title "The Meissen Declaration." It consists in a brief mutual acknowledgement of the character of
both churches and then contracts or agrees in seven points to take practical steps
together that will solidify the communion. It declares: "We commit ourselves to
share a common life and mission. We will take all possible steps to closer fellowship
in as many areas of Christian life and witness as possible, so that all our members together may advance on the way to full, visible unity." A third document,
entitled "The Implementation Agreement," spells out in closer detail the measures
that will nurture and deepen the communion. It specifies further theological conversation, educational exchanges among ministers and students, conferences, agencies
for different forms of joint actions, and concrete projects to be undertaken conjointly.
www.cofe.anglican.org/info/ccu/europe/ecumbackground/meisseninfo.rtf.

description of the apostolic church that actually subsists in all the churches today.

But in one respect the "objective" history of the church has always been there; the data has not changed. The major stimulus for a new open attitude of the churches to one another finds its more immediate basis in the new experiences of the faithful within the churches. Following the lead of the dynamics of spirituality outlined in the first section of this chapter, I suggest that the real ground and impulse for partial communion among the churches comes from the experience of ordinary Christians in the churches. I thus turn to the five aspects of the structure of the church considered in chapters 3 through 7 and characterize the experience of a large number of Christians today in existential terms corresponding to these objective aspects of the church.

The Experience of Common Ecclesial Existence

On the nature of the church, the definitions of the church learned by the members of different churches may differ slightly, but most members experience their church as the religious community in which they assemble in order to worship and pray to God. This God is mediated to them in and through Jesus Christ. The primary home of these church members is the congregation, the parish, the community with whom they gather and the place in which they meet. They assemble to express their Christian faith in God. Most would know and perhaps be moved by the New Testament characterizations of the Church as the people of God, the body of Christ, the temple of the Holy Spirit. Most would no longer conceive of themselves as competing with other churches; few would think that other Christians are not doing the same as they when they gather, even when the objective forms are quite different. In other words, they have a deep sense that there is one faith, one Lord, one baptism of membership, and life in one Spirit of God.

Is this really the case? Do not different sets of belief, different christologies, different conceptions of baptism, and different conceptions of what the Spirit of God is up to really divide Christians and therefore the churches? I will return to this issue further on where leaders explicitly affirm these divisions on the criterion of their own possession of the truth. But the attitude of many Christians today has transcended these sectarian feelings. Since God is transcendent, no particular church has an exclusive claim. More and more Christians have become realistic about unity, holiness, apostolicity, and catholicity: these marks admit of diversity, sin, plurality, and contextualization, but they still refer to a substance that the churches together share: one faith, one Lord, one baptism, and one Spirit.

On the organization of the church's authority and ministry, few Christians would be unaware of the differences among the churches. Most Christians who grow up in one church tradition are probably not fully aware of how pervasive this difference in structure affects basic Christian attitudes and expectations. But modernity and more forcefully postmodernity have introduced into Christian consciousness a new ingredient that has deeply affected Christian attitudes to other churches, namely, a sense of pluralism. By pluralism I do not mean the scandalous disorientation of sheer plurality, but a sense that history and context and social location generate different interests and perceptions and that this is expected and valuable. Once again, on the level of ideals, a competitive spirit has yielded to a spirit of mutual understanding and cooperation at least in principle. A pluralism of churches is not anomalous today but anticipated, not necessarily divisive but potentially generative and positive. This sense of pluralism allows Christians in the different churches to recognize other churches and yet not think that the different polities of other churches undermine the polity of my church.

The consciousness of being a member of the church today, in taking on some of the distinctiveness of our time, also assumes several of its tensions. Each one is a member of a particular church and at the same time associates in various degrees with people of different churches and different religions. The democratic spirit of modernity has influenced the perception of clericalism and authoritarianism within the church and lowered the tolerance for both. Most Christians will recognize that a certain measure of pluralism of beliefs may exist in their own church, so that they expect other churches to have different beliefs. They also expect or perceive that these differences subsist within a core of solid central Christian convictions and loyalties. A tension already alluded to consists in feeling completely at home in one's own church and yet recognizing that other churches are equally authentic in their differences. This background conviction makes re-baptism offensive to many as distinct from baptism of believers which as a practice is theologically justified. Re-baptism implicitly denies the validity of the baptism, ministry, and polity of the original baptizing church. It is potentially exclusionary and sectarian and as such strikes against a general Christian ecclesial sensibility.

Shifting to liturgical ministry and practice, if the ordinary church-goer were to study the history of liturgy, he or she would probably be surprised at the developmental character of the beginnings of worship, the wide variety of styles and forms this activity has taken, and the different forms of worship that mark the Christian churches today. Yet this form of activity like no other shapes the consciousness and thus the identity of each member. This is one reason why forms of worship frequently have divided churches. Yet serious reflection on the worship of Christians across the differences among the churches can also reveal a substantial sameness in what they are doing. It can also show how the differences need not always be taken as essential or church dividing. Practically speaking, with only some exceptions, all Christians gather in community to hear and listen to commentary on the word of God. They share in the meal of discipleship of Jesus. They experience the Spirit, the real presence of God, within the gathered community. Modern Christians by and large do not recognize a substantial difference between the minister whose ordination is considered somehow "ontologically" real and the minister whose ordination is considered functional, as if the actual ministry and God's action through it were less than real. Many of the classic reasons for the divisions between the churches on these matters of worship are simply not appreciated by the members of the church. In fact they tend to dismiss them as arcane theological niceties on the stronger palpable grounds of the bonds that hold Christians together.

The other activities that members of the church participate in, more secular in character, also contribute significantly to the formation of a consciousness of solidarity and community in a given church. The differences in quality and style of community are endless: every community is unique. But the stronger the sense that the church is a caring community, the stronger the feeling of belonging.

Finally, the way members of the church as such experience their relationship to society varies as widely as the worlds in which the church exists. I made this point earlier: a simple contrast between being a member of the only Christian church in a town in India or China today and being a church member in Western Europe during the Middle Ages immediately communicates the differences in ecclesial existence mediated by the world. Overall, the fundamental message of Jesus Christ calls for a positive attitude toward that world despite the sin that affects all. Christians should be able to find God in all things, identify and reject sin in society, favor the victims of society, criticize public policy when it flouts the values of the kingdom of God, promote the inculturation of the church in society, and look for the Spirit of God at work in other religions. Across the different patterns of relating to the world, therefore, Christians participate in the common mission of the church and share a responsibility for it. One of the factors that urge partial communion is the realization that division effectively neutralizes the mission of the church in crucial issues. As the dangers facing humankind in a globalized world increase, so too does the need for a positive reconciling effectiveness of the church in the world.

The Apostolicity of Ecclesial Existence and Partial Communion

The apostolic character of common ecclesial existence provides the grounds for partial communion. The following considerations lead to this conclusion: first of all, the project of this book has been to show that an inner core of human response that is apostolic in nature subsists in all the churches. The description of ecclesial existence just offered attempts to represent, however inadequately, in a few paragraphs, the potential experience of Christians in all the churches. Moreover, this common ecclesial experience is apostolic in character. This means, second, that it can be called analogously the same, if I may use such a paradoxical phrase, as what was experienced by the first-century disciples of Jesus. Third, as a common apostolic dimension in all the churches, this ecclesial existence contains the possibility to serve as a basis for partial communion among the churches. Indeed, it urges such communion and even demands it. These three points are straightforward enough, but some commentary may further clarify what they intend.

Ecclesial existence is common to all the churches. One frequently hears the ecumenical caution against ignoring differences among the churches. There seems to be little danger of that. The churches are used to noting differences; theologians make a living by making distinctions; we seem wedded to the logic of specific differences that separate; churches insist on their identities and the boundaries that distinguish them; ecclesiology seems decidedly competitive;[9] church leaders tell their churches that they are number one; each church occupies a little center of the universe. By contrast, the ability to recognize sameness amid difference, or elementary analogies, often depends on the horizon of perception. The recognition of the commonality of ecclesial existence requires stepping beyond the sphere of Christian churches staring at each other in a self-absorbed way. Common life today unfolds in a pluralistic world of different human cultures and different vital religions. In this horizon the commonalities of the Christian churches appear more clearly; one can distinguish between centers and peripheries, essentials and incidentals; what really counts in this church also really counts in the others. The world is pluralistic and this means unities or sets of commonalities amid differences. Where the drift seems decidedly tilted toward fragmentation, churches should begin to stress what we share in common. The differences seem to be able to take care of themselves.

The commonality that is shared by all the churches can best be appreciated at the level of a core spirituality, which can in turn be characterized as a transcendental Christian response to Jesus Christ in community. It is also apostolic; it possesses a structure and a content that are analogously the same as the response of Christians in the apostolic period as that period is represented in the New Testament. To assert such a sameness across history seems counterintuitive because the essence of history is linear change, however gradual, into novelty. I call it analogously the same to preserve the

---

9. I have consistently characterized it pejoratively as "tribal" in this regard.

tensive and problematic character of this sameness while not surrendering the sameness itself. It is a sameness amid differences. Two explanations for such a sameness arose in the development of doctrine debate in modern Roman Catholicism. The one measures the sameness in the existential human response to God through Jesus, a response that is constant and continuous even though it assumes different expressive forms in words and actions in the course of history. Beneath these symbols one can always find the "same" faith response to the God revealed or mediated through Jesus.[10] The other is postmodern and relies on hermeneutical theory that continually reinterprets a constant past preserved in originating documents in new forms in new situations. Each analysis allows for newness and difference but saves a constancy, continuity, sameness, and thus unity within the differences.[11] Ultimately that sameness cannot be captured in propositions that line up in a one-to-one correspondence between the apostolic period and the present. It remains a project of interpretation and admits of considerable pluralism.

Insofar as churches admit the possibility of apostolicity in the first place, which most do in their own regard, and then extend the possibility to churches other than themselves, there immediately arises the grounds for and the possibility of partial communion between those churches. Partial communion does not mean full communion. The differences that remain among churches may prevent full communion, and this may not be something to be regretted. Genuine pluralism, as something valuable, may require a diversity of churches that cannot and should not reach full institutional agreement. But partial communion does negate no communion at all. Schleiermacher expressed this ecclesiological principle in a most explicit way: no Christian church should fall out of communion with another

---

10. The word "same" is placed in quotation marks to highlight the tensive character of an analogous sameness: it is a sameness with differences. It therefore both is and is not literally the same.

11. These two theories can be found respectively in Edward Schillebeeckx, *Church: The Human Story of God* (New York: Crossroad, 1990), 40–45, and John E. Thiel, *Senses of Tradition: Continuity and Development in Catholic Faith* (Oxford: University Press, 2000), 56–99. Thiel develops his own postmodern theory of development in contrast to nineteenth- and twentieth-century organic models whose programmed "organicity" does not allow real novelty. Schillebeeckx's theory is not "organic" in this sense but historical.

Christian church; the Spirit of God always urges communion.[12] This means that the movement toward communion is a measure of the degree of the acceptance of the Spirit by a given church.

Responding to the Imperative of Partial Communion

Few ignore the impulse of the Spirit toward unity among the churches. All churches feel the imperative to open up attitudes toward other churches and to lessen the distance between them. Frequently, however, the size of the problems involved kills enthusiasm, and the perceptions of impasse prevent ambitious work at solidarity. I bring this work to a close with a procedural reflection on how leaders of the churches could help the process move forward and how they should not proceed. Perhaps it is best to put on the table again one of the most serious of ecumenical divisions, one already mentioned, the radical difference between hierarchical and congregational churches.

Among the variety of different ecclesiologies the two most antithetical conceptions of the church appear as the large hierarchical institution and the congregational free church. The differences are foundational because they exert their influence on every major area of ecclesiology. The one ecclesiology conceives the church as a large hierarchically structured community with an order that is claimed to relate back to Jesus Christ; the other conceives the church as a relatively small community or large congregation of shared faith, also relating back to Jesus Christ, and possessing within itself the authority of Christ and the Spirit, which it in turn delegates to its ministers. Both of these views can be subjected to a typological elaboration that shows the deep and distinctive character of these grounding visions and experiences of church and how far their corresponding conceptions reach.[13] Hierarchal orders are antithetical to the church in one view; a human and infinitely variable polity eviscerates the

---

12. CCH, II, 334–35.

13. See CCH, II, 276–88. Note that both of these "types" of church and ecclesiology are represented positively as apostolically valid. One can, of course, construct or find actual ecclesiologies that coherently synthesize themes and values from these two seemingly antithetical types. But that would constitute a third type or model. The problem consists precisely in the antithetical character of these two different types which will always be actualized in some churches because of their correspondence with certain fundamental kinds of experience.

divine grounding of the church for the other. One set of churches places the demands of communion so high that they are practically speaking unreachable; another set of churches is not convinced a regulated communion among congregations is desirable at all. Can a constructive comparative approach mediate between these seemingly irreconcilable differences? I respond to this question by first holding up an example of an approach that leads to stalemate.

To illustrate by contrast the way attention to a common ecclesial existence and spirituality can open up positive attitudes toward other churches, I hold up first a certain church's negative appreciation of the ambiguity it found in BEM.[14] Ambiguity can be construed and appreciated in a positive or a negative way. Deliberate ambiguity may be positive when it provides a formula which different parties can agree on precisely because it allows for different interpretations. Or ambiguity can be considered negative for the same reason on the supposition that only one reading is correct. A document geared toward rapprochement among the churches will contain many such ambiguous statements. To such ambiguity this church responded:

> [W]e are dismayed by a great deal of ambiguity in the BEM document.... Terms are used in the document to indicate unity of belief when actually they are sources of division. For example, "real presence" bears a very different meaning among Roman, Lutheran, Reformed and Zwinglian exponents.... It is impossible to know whether we agree or disagree with them since their meaning is shrouded in obscurity. Wide divergences between differing positions and views are greatly minimized by use of a "both/and" rather than an "either/or" approach. The questions constantly in our minds are: how far can such wide divergences in faith and practice be accommodated without compromising authentic convergence?[15]

This statement does not reject conversation among the churches, but it displays a narrow appreciation of what a common document

---

14. This reaction to BEM is not representative of the majority of the responses; they were overwhelmingly positive. But the logic displayed here is repeated by several churches; it is therefore representative of a common attitude among some churches.

15. BEMresponses, II, 153.

may truthfully say. The "correct statement" is judged from the perspective of the particular church. The limits for acceptance of a
common statement are possessed by the church in question. On the
one hand, BEM is welcomed as an expression of emerging common
ground. It is a starting point and basis for dialogue and mutual exchange. On the other hand, BEM does not express the faith of this
particular church. BEM is not "a statement which we can unequivocally accept as expressing adequately the basic elements of our faith
and understanding. It is not a statement which can be viewed by our
church as being in any way definitive since it is not sufficiently Reformed in ethos or orientation."[16] It then adds a hope for a document
that is more acceptable from a Reformed perspective. In other words,
it is expected that dialogue will bring the consensus statement closer
to the perspective of this particular church.

But if ambiguity and a certain degree of vagueness obtained through
abstraction are deliberate and viewed positively, everything changes.
The underlying suppositions are not that differences should be con-
cealed, covered over, and harbored in silence, but remain matters for
further conversation. It is supposed that in matters of the transcendent object of faith, no formula exhausts understanding of faith so
that more than one construal of a given statement may be encouraged. It is not wrong to try to be clear about possible understandings
of transcendent realities, but it seems arrogant to decide that all attempts to understand the object of faith and all arrangements of the
order of the church will never exceed what is already possessed by a
particular church.

The idea and strategy of partial communion to some extent dissolve this problem by not resolving it. First of all, constructive
comparative ecclesiology does not describe a common polity that
unites the two types of churches posited at the outset. It is a theological discipline and not a formula for communion. The product
of its reflection, a transdenominational ecclesiology, displays bonds
for communion that transcend the differences between churches but
does not necessarily alter them. This ecclesiology aims at generating

---

16. Ibid., 158.

insight into what they share in common despite the most fundamental differences. Through a consideration of the data of the origins of the church, the different forms the church has taken through history, and the variety among the churches today, it finds that all churches have some polity, that no standardized polity is reflected in the canonical literature, that church polities developed historically, and that they are always understood to be subject to the influence of the Holy Spirit at any given time. The historical data and the theological witness to the church thus suggest that both these organizational types are coherent, valid theologically, and inspired by the Spirit in continuity with the apostolic church.

Constructive comparative ecclesiology thus suggests that both kinds of churches could accept, not the other church's order for itself, but the *apostolicity* of its order. How are churches able to recognize the apostolicity of a structure of the church that they do not share and thus remain in partial communion with the other? Two basic insights are the condition for the possibility. The first recognizes a depth and complexity of the apostolic tradition that allows for pluralism. No single tradition can exhaust the historical possibilities of the apostolic tradition. History seems to prove this, and the pluralism produced across cultures and societies at any given time structurally replicates the pluralism produced by history across time. No particular historical part can exhaustively contain the whole. The second insight consists in a recognition of the values represented in other traditions. Every form of church structure mediates values that are not as fully represented in other structural forms. Positive assessments of pluralism require recognition that different orders of ministry can be inspired by and bear the Spirit of God. What was true in the normative apostolic period is true today.

Constructive comparative ecclesiology also leads to the conviction that, on the basis of a host of other aspects of a complex church identity that are shared in common, two churches with such different church orders could enter into a formal relationship of partial communion. It would be hard to see how they could enter into full communion because of the major differences that these two fundamental views of the church actualize. But a constructive comparative method in ecclesiology so refocuses the imagination on the size and depth of what binds churches together that this positive connection allows even major differences to become more like subjects of an internal conversation between partners than a debate between aliens. Beneath the many beliefs and practices these churches hold in common, that which binds them most closely together, despite differences, is an ecclesial spirituality that has its roots in what Paul called the very basis of Christian unity: one faith, one Lord, one baptism, and life in one Spirit.

To conclude: because the human race is entering into significantly new conditions for its life together in the world, so too is the Christian church facing some new challenges. These must be met with new attitudes and new theological initiatives. Comparative ecclesiology in its many forms accepts our historical and pluralistic condition as a given, finds the Spirit of God at work in it, and seeks new ecclesial initiatives that will follow where the Spirit leads. This essay in constructive comparative ecclesiology aims at opening up an ecclesiological imagination that will begin to take these exigencies seriously and reckon the ways in which God as Spirit in the church is inviting the churches to move closer together in solidarity. The *missio Dei* and the world to which the church is sent require more of the churches. Partial communion proposes ideals that are truly ideals relative to the status quo and yet also practicable.

This ecclesiology from below, in line with the high christology of *Jesus Symbol of God* which was also developed from below, plays out the conception and method of theology presented in *Dynamics of Theology*. Together they represent an effort to remain faithful to the apostolic faith by entering into dialogue with our world today.

Index